Y0-EIK-152

Language and Literature in the African American Imagination

**Recent Titles in
Contributions in Afro-American and African Studies**

Black Journalists in Paradox: Historical Perspectives and Current Dilemmas
Clint C. Wilson II

Dream and Reality: The Modern Black Struggle for Freedom and Equality
Jeannine Swift, editor

An Unillustrious Alliance: The African American and Jewish American Communities
William M. Phillips, Jr.

From Exclusion to Inclusion: The Long Struggle for African American Political Power
Ralph C. Gomes and Linda Faye Williams, editors

Mental and Social Disorder in Sub-Saharan Africa: The Case of Sierra Leone, 1787-1900
Leland V. Bell

The Racial Problem in the Works of Richard Wright and James Baldwin
Jean-François Gounard; Joseph J. Rodgers, Jr., translator

Renaissance Man from Louisiana: A Biography of Arna Wendell Bontemps
Kirkland C. Jones

A Struggle Worthy of Note: The Engineering and Technological Education of Black Americans
David E. Wharton

African American Soldiers in the National Guard: Recruitment and Deployment During Peacetime and War
Charles Johnson, Jr.

Religion and Suicide in the African-American Community
Kevin E. Early

State Against Development: The Experience of Post-1965 Zaire
Mondonga M. Mokoli

Dusky Maidens: The Odyssey of the Early Black Dramatic Actress
Jo A. Tanner

Language and Literature in the African American Imagination

Edited by
Carol Aisha Blackshire-Belay

Contributions in Afro-American and African Studies,
Number 154

Greenwood Press
Westport, Connecticut • London

Library of Congress Cataloging-in-Publication Data

Language and literature in the African American imagination / edited by Carol Aisha Blackshire-Belay.
    p. cm.—(Contributions in Afro-American and African studies, ISSN 0069-9624 ; no. 154)
  Includes index.
  ISBN 0-313-27826-1 (alk. paper)
    1. American literature—Afro-American authors—History and criticism—Theory, etc. 2. American literature—Afro-American authors—History and criticism. 3. English language—United States—Foreign elements—African. 4. American literature—African influences. 5. Afro-Americans—Intellectual life. 6. Afro-Americans in literature. 7. Afro-American aesthetics. 8. Afro-Americans—Language. 9. Africa in literature.   I. Blackshire-Belay, Carol. II. Series.
PS153.N5L36   1992
810.9'896073—dc20   92-12509

British Library Cataloguing in Publication Data is available.

Copyright © 1992 by Carol Aisha Blackshire-Belay

All rights reserved. No portion of this book may be reproduced, by any process or technique, without the express written consent of the publisher.

Library of Congress Catalog Card Number: 92-12509
ISBN: 0-313-27826-1
ISSN: 0069-9624

First published in 1992

Greenwood Press, 88 Post Road West, Westport, CT 06881
An imprint of Greenwood Publishing Group, Inc.

Printed in the United States of America

The paper used in this book complies with the Permanent Paper Standard issued by the National Information Standards Organization (Z39.48-1984).

10 9 8 7 6 5 4 3 2 1

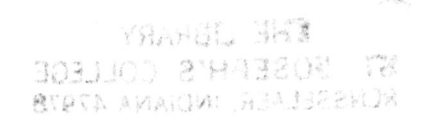

Copyright Acknowledgments

The author and publisher are grateful to the following sources for granting permission to reprint material:

Extracts from *Under a Soprano Sky* (Trenton, NJ: Africa World Press, Inc., 1987), *Homegirls and Handgrenades* (New York: Thunder's Mouth Press, 1984), and *Love Poems* (New York: The Third Press, Inc., Joseph Opaku Publishing Co.), by Sonia Sanchez. Used by permission of the author.

Copyright © 1987 by J. California Cooper. From the book *Some Soul to Keep* and reprinted with permission from St. Martin's Press, Inc., New York, NY.

Copyright © 1986 by J. California Cooper. From the book *Homemade Love* and reprinted with permission from St. Martin's Press, Inc., New York, NY.

"The House Slave" reprinted from *Ten Poems* by Rita Dove, published by Penembra Press. Copyright © 1977 by Rita Dove. Reprinted by permission of the author.

Excerpts from *Copacetic* (1984), *I Apologize for the Eyes in My Head* (1986), *Magic City* (1992), *Dien Cai Dau* (1988), by Yusef Komunyakaa (Middletown, Conn.: Wesleyan University Press) by permission of University Press of New England.

Excerpts reprinted with permission of Macmillan Publishing Company and Methuen from *For Colored Girls Who Have Considered Suicide/When the Rainbow is Enuf* by Ntozake Shange. Copyright © 1975, 1976, 1977 by Ntozake Shange.

Copyright © 1985 by Ntozake Shange. From the book *Betsey Brown* and reprinted with permission from St. Martin's Press, Inc., New York, NY.

Copyright © 1982 by Ntozake Shange. From the book *sassafrass, cypress, and indigo* and reprinted with permission from St. Martin's Press, Inc., New York, NY, and Octopus Publishing Group Library.

Extracts from *The Weary Blues* by Langston Hughes (New York: Harold Ober Associates, 1927).

Selections reprinted from *Cane* by Jean Toomer, by permission of Liveright Publishing Corporation. Copyright 1923 by Boni and Liveright. Copyright renewed 1951 by Jean Toomer.

Dedicated to the ancestors,
those whose lives were texts and
whose movement was rhythm.

Contents

I. THE AFROCENTRIC IMAGINATION: THEORY AND ANALYSIS

1. Afrocentricity and Literary Theory: The Maturing Imagination
   Carol Aisha Blackshire-Belay   3
2. Locating a Text: Implications of Afrocentric Theory
   Molefi Kete Asante   9
3. Refusing to Be Boxed In: Sonia Sanchez's Transformation of the Haiku Form
   Frenzella Elaine De Lancey   21
4. Reassessing African American Literature through an Afrocentric Paradigm: Zora N. Hurston and James Baldwin
   Carolyn L. Holmes   37

II. LANGUAGE REALITIES: STUDIES IN MODERN SOCIETIES

5. Cultural and Linguistic Transitions: The Comparative Case of African Americans and Ethnic Minorities in Germany
   Carol Aisha Blackshire-Belay   55
6. African Languages in the African American Experience
   Alamin Mazrui   75
7. Kitchen Table Talk: J. California Cooper's Use of Nommo—Female Bonding and Transcendence
   Barbara J. Marshall   91

III. LITERARY ANALYSIS: STYLE AND SUBSTANCE

8. Dilemma of the Dutiful Servant: The Poetry of
   Jupiter Hammon
   Lonnell E. Johnson   105

9. The Blue/Black Poetics of Sonia Sanchez
   Regina B. Jennings   119

10. Afrocentric Aesthetics in Selected Harlem Renaissance Poetry
    Abu Shardow Abarry   133

IV. REFLECTIVE DESIGNS IN LITERARY WORKS

11. Folk Idiom in the Literary Expression of Two African
    American Authors: Rita Dove and Yusef Komunyakaa
    Kirkland C. Jones   149

12. From Nice Colored Girl to Womanist: An Exploration of
    Development in Ntozake Shange's Writings
    Geta LeSeur   167

13. De Jure Maurorum in Europa (On the Rights of Blacks in
    Europe): A Black Civil Rights Activist in Europe in the
    Eighteenth Century
    Reginald Bess   181

V. AFTERWORD

14. The African American Imagination in Language and Literature:
    An Afterword
    Carol Aisha Blackshire-Belay   197

Index   203

About the Contributors   209

I

The Afrocentric Imagination: Theory and Analysis

1

Afrocentricity and Literary Theory: The Maturing Imagination

Carol Aisha Blackshire-Belay

The aim of this volume is to advance the theoretical aspects of African American language and literature. In the last few years there has been a growing appreciation of the critical tradition in African American studies. The current criticism shows a variety of theoretical interests: Afrocentrism, deconstruction, womanism, feminism, Africana womanism, and Marxism. Scholars have explored the dimensions of song, dance, railroads, spirituals, and akimbos in African American literature.

In addition, the research into the nature of social and economic factors on speech, language, and literature suggests certain fundamental categories that might be comparable between African Americans and other ethnic groups. An exploration of the numerous aspects, for example, of the migration experience on the language and culture of African Americans may be profitable related to such developments in German society. The pursuit of the African American imagination in the patterns of migration is just as valid as the pursuit of that imagination in stable domiciles. Language and literature are two aspects of the communication genre that might be seen to reflect the social, economic, and cultural orientation and condition of people.

Language is a regularized symbolic code that connects its users in a symbiosis of substance. We are produced and produce through language. Language is, in essence, a fascinating phenomenon. Because of its unique role in capturing the breadth of human thought and endeavor, we utilize it as a vehicle of communication on many different levels. Thereby we are capable of expressing a multiplicity of worldviews, literature, and lifestyles. As we look back at the thoughts of our ancestors we find that we can only see as far as language (both written and oral) allow us to see. We look forward into time only to realize that we can propose, plan, and organize our dreams and our aspirations through language. We look outward into the cosmic sphere and send symbols of communication (be they either signs, icons, or a combination of both to allow the astronaut to communicate with the man on the moon. Thus it is through language that we produce and develop meaning.

Literature in its most profound sense, is the most complex use of language to create meaning. African American language and literature are the twin generators of a productive cultural thrust into American literature. Language is the means by which we understand ourselves and the societies in which we play a part. Language is also pertinent to resolving some of the problems and tensions that arise from human interaction. Linguistic problems rarely admit simple solutions, however, and it is this very elementary observation that has led to the present volume.

The African American has had an abundant linguistic, communication, and literary history. As the inheritors of this bounty we have often sought to understand it in the context of our own lives. From the old shouts and hollers of the South to the new rap and rappers of the North, our word magicians, babalowos, jales, and singers of a new sun have made our situation much more bearable than it would have been otherwise. The complexity of the language of the Gullah, that is, the so-called Geechee language of the coastal regions of Georgia and South Carolina, is tied to the historical experiences of our people. We are not disconnected or detached from those who have lived before or who have spoken and written this language before us. Paul Laurence Dunbar is as real today in Detroit, Los Angeles, and Dayton as he has ever been. Only when we see with the eyes of our centered selves can we truly appreciate the depth of our literary being. That is precisely where the critic and the theorist come into the picture. They are interpreters and guides to our culture. Of course, the critics and theorists must operate from the same universe of information as the writers. In the process of criticism new ideas are refined and sharpened and the artistic functions are clarified, both for the writers and the critics.

No aspect of African American writing is out of bounds to the critic schooled in the nuances of language, style, and behavior of African Americans. Already such women writers as Eleanor Traylor, Barbara Christian, Deborah McDowell, Nell Painter, Paula Giddings, Joyce Ann Joyce, and Nancy Fitch among others have explored the meaning of culture in the writings of black women. They have given attention to gender, class, and Eurocentrism in their analyses. In *Black Literature and*

1. Afrocentricity and Literary Theory: The Maturing Imagination 5

Literacy Theory, Henry Louis Gates, Jr., and others introduced the discussion of African American literature within the context of modern European literary theory. Earlier Paul Carter Harrison, Larry Neal, and Houston Baker, Jr. had written on Afrocentric aspects of black literature. Harrison attempted to explain African American theater and literature from the point of view of African cultural developments. Harrison saw the concept of *Nommo*, the productive force of the spoken word, as a fundamental modality of African American literature. Larry Neal, the intellectual pilot of the Black Arts Movement, sought a theory and criticism with roots in the nature of the African American community. All criticism had to respond to the political, social, and cultural milieu of the people. Attached to the historical project of liberation, the Black Arts Movement heightened the interest in black literature.

Women writers such as Alice Walker, Toni Morrison, Gloria Naylor, Toni Cade Bambara, and Paula Marshall wrote novels and short stories depicting areas of African American life that had gone untouched by many male African American writers. While the tradition of novelists John A. Williams, Richard Wright, James Baldwin, and Ralph Ellison became the standard by which critics evaluated African American letters prior to the 1970s, strong women writers emerged to demonstrate the broad scope of black literature. The rediscovery of Zora Neale Hurston by literary critics underscored the maturity of the new awakening in African American literature. The formation of a critical literary canon continued with the publication of Susan Willis's *Specifying: Black Women Writing the American Experience*.

The African American person, critic, theorist, or writer operates in a context of opposition to oppressive situations. Black women are transformed by their appeal to humanity. Black men are transformed by their openness to change. Both are opposed to enslavement, either physical or psychological.

Jupiter Hammon and Phillis Wheatley represent the beginning of the African American literary tradition, although Wheatley in some respects might be considered an African writer. Both had been thoroughly conditioned by their servitude to accept the ideas of white privilege. In fact, Hammon suggests that the whites may have done a favor for Africans by enslavement. His reasoning was based on the belief that Christianity was a valuable tool for African civilization. African American literary figures have gone through numerous transmutations over the past 372 years. From Wheatley and Hammon to Morrison and Baldwin the task of the writer has been to present the most mature image of the African at the time.

In presenting the image of the African, the writers have demonstrated the immensity of our experiences. They have explored every aspect of Africans' lives in the United States. Committed to the proposition that our lives and histories are integral to an understanding of the American society, many writers have attempted to show how the African American experience is the principal marker by which America itself should be judged. Thus, James Baldwin, though never given the top prizes in literature in his own country, received those awards in the hearts of the African American people. Understanding the writers means that the literary critics and theorists must listen to similar drums and dance to the same type of music.

Susan Willis's "specifying," Henry Gates's "signifyin'," and Houston Baker's "vernacular theory of African American literature" all bend toward what Molefi Asante refers to as "analyses which are Afrocentric," that is, conform to the centrality of the subject in the literature. The authors of the following essays possess Afrocentric tendencies though they do not necessarily declare themselves in that school of thought.

Specifically what is the nature of the maturing imagination? First and foremost, the writer uses language that reflects the culture. Second, the writer understands the universality of African peoples' experience, that is, the emotion and attitudes are universal to the African audience. Third, the writer transcends the local or fixed boundary of imagination in style, imagery, and form. Lastly, the writer shows a quest for justice, harmony, and peace.

My aim was to provide a volume with a broad range of critical ideas, excavating the subtleties of African American language and literature in a fresh manner. To this end as a linguist I have included essays that treat the syntax of themes, geothematics, and locational aspects of literature. One of the tasks we face as scholars is aligning our discourse in theory and criticism with the actual practice of language and literature. Therefore, how we approach the works of a Zora Neale Hurston, J. California Cooper, Sonia Sanchez, or Langston Hughes is a study in confrontation. In other words, we face and interface with a myriad of possibilities bequeathed to us by social circumstances and historical realities.

The African American person, whether critic, theorist, or writer, operates within a rhetorical context placed in opposition to oppressive

1. Afrocentricity and Literary Theory: The Maturing Imagination

situations. This is the unique character of the literature produced by African American women and men in this country, indeed, throughout the entire Americas. We are transformed by openness to change, by proactive creation by the new, the novel, the useful. By our admission of freedom, we oppose enslavement, physical or psychological. But of course it is true that we have not always been successful in the positions we have taken. However, on the whole, from the earliest in the history of our literature until the present we have been on a journey for truth and righteousness. In effect, this literary process has been a prominent part of our quest for liberation in the sense that clarifying our roles in the larger flow of humanity introduces us to the world in essential and necessary use of language.

In some instances we are alerted to utopian aspirations in some of the literature and in other works we see the sobered experiences of a people who face disease, danger, and death every day. We are definitely undefined as theorists and critics by any one school though we are more mature, confident, and assured of our aesthetic location. Clearly, part of the reason why we are just now developing a robust criticism in African American literature resides in the ambiguous nature or rather complexity of our being under domination. In the past, our writers have presented us with too many examples of this ambiguity for any coalescing theory to emerge. Thus, we questioned whether the voices of Hurston and Ellison and Wright were meant for us or for white audiences. Were we only a sideshow in their discourse? Was the object to explain us to whites? Were we the aesthetic material for a larger social point than the narrative discourse? Of course, we knew, as I know now that no one person could adequately answer those questions for the complex American audience. Even more so the ability to articulate the links between African Americans and the social-political context and the visions of union was demanding and perhaps futile given the encapsulating artistic environment. Could Zora Neale Hurston ever write to and for black people as her primary audience? I shall leave that question rhetorical in order to allow the reader to assess how the authors in this volume have sought to redefine the dialogue around language and literature.

2

Locating a Text: Implications of Afrocentric Theory
Molefi Kete Asante

We have finally arrived at a cultural junction where several critical avenues present themselves to the serious textual reader. Any fair estimate of the road that got us to this point must conclude that it has been a difficult one, filled with intellectual potholes and myopic cultural roadblocks, but at last there is an Afrocentric viewpoint on texts. In recent years this view has been developed on the basis of works by scholars such as Houston Baker, Jr. Abu Abarry, Carol Aisha Blackshire, Henry Louis Gates, Jr., and Trudier Harris. There seems to be a growing number of writers who have abandoned or are attempting to abandon the staid domains of an encapsulated theory.

Afrocentric theory as advanced in numerous works, including my own, establishes two fundamental realities in situating a text: "location" and "dislocation." The serious textual reader is able to locate a text by certain symbolic boundaries and iconic signposts offered from within the text itself. However, much like any traveler the reader's location is also important in order to determine the exact location of the text.

An inordinate number of African American scholars have become lost souls trying to negotiate the Eurocentric pathways of mono-culturalism and mono-historicalism. An equal number of non-African scholars have floated around ethereally when it came to locating an African American text. Both sets of readers have been victims of a breach in good highway manners. They have ignored all of the signs of Afrocentric literacy in favor of blind alleys based in a mono-cultural reality. What I hope to demonstrate is that multi-cultural literacy can lead to a critical transformation in the way we approach any discourse.

However, multi-cultural literacy does not exist apart from the substantive knowledge of specific cultural communities. There is no multi-cultural literacy apart from cultural bases. It is the ability to use and integrate these cultural bases that allows us to speak of multi-cultural literacy. An examination of an African American writer such as Henry Dumas provides an example of the range and vision of Afrocentric theory.

AN ORIENTATION TO MOTIF

Charles Fuller, a colleague in my department who won the Pulitzer Prize for drama in 1982 for his work *A Soldier's Play*, claims that many of the dramatic characters for his plays come from people he knew on Broad Street in North Philadelphia. Not knowing what Fuller knows and not seeing what he sees in the faces of people on Broad Street might create difficulty in understanding the nuances of his drama. While there are certain readily understandable guideposts in good literature, accessible to the least literate of us, to truly capture the setting of Charles Fuller's drama one must have more than a passing appreciation of African American culture. Indeed the good critic and serious reader of African American literature should have been exposed to a variety of cultural information, for example, the Dozens, folk tales, Ebonics, barber shops or beauty parlors, Baptist churches, Hoodoo and Root rituals, *Ebony Magazine*, *Jet*, and numerous authors and musicians. All of this information may not be useful on every trip through the literary territory in the African American world, but it is surely advantageous on most occasions for the critic and reader. This means that critics must take courses in African American culture and history as they take courses in Euro-American history and culture. In fact, they must search the ancient foundations of the African's cultural response to reality and environment much as one looks to Greece or Rome for analogues in the Euro-American writers and authors. The only reason, it seems to me, that this is not done in the first place is the abiding bias against African culture that continues to disorient most critics.[1]

---

[1] The controversy over the "Great Books" that ensued in 1990 is a case in point. The fact that Mortimer Adler and others who organized and published the works considered "great" did not include one book by a writer of African descent demonstrates the point made by numerous authors that mono-

2. Locating a Text: Implications of Afrocentric Theory

An explosion of interest in multi-cultural issues, diversity in the classroom, and centered visions in curricula has contributed to a critical transformation in literature. Like Tuthmosis IV, who in the third year of his reign asked his scribes to take a retrospective of all that had gone before, we must take a critical look at what has happened in the last few years in multi-cultural literacy. The king's intentions were to re-establish the foundations of the kingdom, to examine the preparations for the future, and to re-assert the unity of the Two Lands. Our aim in a retrospective is simply to be able to navigate the cultural highways of a multi-cultural society.

A NEW HISTORIOGRAPHY AS THE BASIS OF LOCATION

The critical spirit that has served to temper the received position on certain texts is the result of a multi-cultural consciousness brought about by a new historiography. Based on the idea that ancient Kemet and Nubia are to the rest of Africa as Greece and Rome are to the rest of Europe, this new historiography has insinuated itself into contemporary thinking in education, anthropology, sociology, history, and literature.[2] Pioneered by African and African American scholars such as George James, Chancellor Williams, Leo Hansberry, Cheikh Anta Diop, and Theophile Obenga, this critical historiography influences the most elementary discussions of text by bringing the gift of new information. Unfortunately, as Martin Bernal has said in his monumental re-assessment of the European classical tradition, *Black Athena*, most white scholars have ignored the writings of these scholars (434-437). Bernal believes that in the last five centuries racism has been the source of the mono-ethnic and mono-cultural portrayal of the production and acquisition of knowledge.

---

culturalism remains the dominant ideology of the literary establishment in the West.

[2] Among the works in this vein are Molefi Asante, *The Afrocentric Idea* (Philadelphia: Temple University Press, 1987); Molefi Asante, *Kemet, Afrocentricity, and Knowledge* (Trenton, N.J.: Africa World Press, 1990); Cheikh Anta Diop, *The African Origin of Civilization*. (New York: Lawrence Hill, 1974); Martin Bernal, *Black Athena* (New Brunswick, N.J.: Rutgers University Press, 1987).

In his book *The African Origin of Civilization: Myth or Reality?*, Cheikh Anta Diop laid a revolutionary foundation for the new pathways of critical knowledge in the field of human creativity. He argued a position that was radical only because for five hundred years the Western world had denied Africa's role in human history. Diop contended that western scholars had tried to take ancient Egypt out of Africa and Africans out of Egypt. The context for this attack on Africa was the rise and promotion of the European slave trade. So massive was this vulgar trade in human beings that it colored every relationship in the European and African worlds. Nothing was untouched by the anti-African attitudes developed in the fifteenth century. Art, literature, dance, music, theology, and philosophy were adjusted to deal with the Great Enslavement and domination of Africans. Defamation of Africans and African intellectual gifts was sanctioned at the highest levels of western literature and goverment; subjugation of Africa was confirmed ultimately in the way writers wrote about the encounter between the two peoples.

In the *Mismeasure of Man*, Stephen Jay Gould reports that some of the key leaders of the West recorded their anti-African attitudes in clear and straightforward terms. For example, Thomas Jefferson wrote, "I advance it, therefore, as a suspicion only, that the blacks, whether originally a distinct race or made distinct by time and circumstance, are inferior to the whites in the endowments of both body and mind" (32). Indeed Gould demonstrates that the British philosopher David Hume held negative attitudes about the contributions of Africans to human society. David Hume asserted "I am apt to suspect the Negroes and in general all the other species of men to be naturally inferior to the whites. There never was a civilized nation of any other complexion than white, or even any individual eminent either in action or speculation, no ingenious manufacturers among them, no art, no sciences" (41). Indeed Louis Agassiz wrote of Africa, "there has never been a regulated society of black men developed on the continent" (47). Arnold Toynbee, one of the Western world's leading historians said, "When we classify mankind by color, the only one of the primary races, given by this classification, which has not made a creative contribution to any of our twenty-one civilizations is the black race" (41). The famous German philosopher Georg Wilhelm Friedrich Hegel wrote of Africa, "This is the land where men are children, a land lying beyond the daylight of self conscious history, and enveloped in the black color of night. At this point, let us forget Africa not to mention it again. Africa is no historical part of the world..." (Davidson, 1984:64). These attitudes often find a place in the most contemporary views of western thinkers. The publication of the *Great Books of the Western World* in 1990 under the editorship of Mortimer J. Adler continues the Eurocentric idea that Africans have made no contribution to the West. A typical collection of white male writers (there are only four white women writers out of the total of 130 writers) the *Great Books of the Western World* serves as an instrument to block the road to multi-culturalism. With no African Americans and only four women included in the list of writers, the collection is certain to be without much enduring credibility. Any group of "Great Books" that does not include writings from Frederick Douglass, W. E. B. DuBois, Edward Blyden, Richard Wright, Martin Luther King, Jr., Zora Neale Hurston, Langston Hughes, James Baldwin, Ralph Ellison, Alice Walker, or Toni Morrison is surely a pretense to inclusiveness.

LOCATING A TEXT

There are several elements that help to locate an African American text or any text: *language, attitude,* and *direction.* These elements might be used alone or in combination. I shall examine each of these elements as they relate to African American writers and critics. However, a word should be written about the nature of the creative production derived from authors engaged in the communicative process with readers. Writers are fundamentally committed to the principle of expression; one cannot express one's self without leaving some insignia. From the writer's own textual expression the Afrocentric critic is able to ascertain the cultural and intellectual address of the author.

THE PLACE

Among the complications in the location process for critics of African American texts is the devastating extent to which African American authors have been removed from general cultural terms. There are two types of texts produced by individuals who have been removed or have removed themselves from terms of blackness: the *decapitated text* and the *lynched text.* A text that is decapitated exists without cultural presence in the historical experiences of the creator; a lynched text is one that has been strung up with the tropes and figures of the dominating culture. African American authors who have tried to "shed their race" have been known to produce both types of texts.

The decapitated text is the contribution of the author who writes with no discernible African cultural element, whose aim appears to be to distance herself or himself from the African cultural self. Among the best practitioners of this genre is the author Frank Yerby. His contributions to literature have been made as a part of the European and white experience in the West. Although he responded to criticism long enough to write the *Dahomeans*, he remained fundamentally committed to a style of writing that placed him outside of his own historical experiences. Thus his African voice remains essentially silent. Yerby is the kind of author one reads and says, "If you do not know that, this must be a white writer." Even my white students are surprised to discover that the author of some of the finest Southern plantation novels is an African American. While he became relatively successful in a commercial sense in this vein of writing, Frank Yerby has no clear literary tradition and adds to no new school of aesthetics. He produces decapitated texts with no guiding heads and no sense of soul.

The lynched text is more easily produced by African American authors who have literary skills but little cultural or historical knowledge. Images tend to be thoroughly Eurocentric, producing lines such as "the warlike natives" in a historical novel or "the Valhallian quest of the black hero" in poetry. An African writer who uses such language may be rewarded by the Eurocentric establishment for demonstrating a mastery over or expertise in handling European themes, but it does not mean that the writer is placed in his or her own center. Since the literary establishment often reinforces Africans the more removed we are from our cultural terms, there is social pressure on the writer to "write what whites write." One can perhaps see why James Baldwin, Richard Wright, Toni Morrison, John A. Killens, and John Edgar Wideman are not given greater prominence in the literary curricula of this nation. Neither attempted to shed blackness; in fact, some tried to re-accumulate what they had lost through education.

ELEMENTS OF LOCATION

Language

Normally we say that language is a regularized code that has been agreed upon by a community of users. There is nothing particularly wrong with this general definition of language. However, language can be said to involve grammatical rules, nuances, words, and deep structures. In that case, if we concentrate on one aspect of language, words, for instance, we can obtain a fairly good assessment of where a writer is located.

Words have function, meaning, and etymology; my concern in this discussion is primarily with meaning. An African American author or any author, for that matter, who writes of "Hottentots," "bushmen," and "pygmies" has already told the Afrocentric critic something about where she or he is located. Of course, the same observation can be made by any critic of any author. Location is determined by the signposts. In any situation where the author is trapped in the language of a racist society that provides pejorative terms, the critic is seeking to see how the particular writer handles the situation. What turn of phrases, what lacunae and nuances, what unique rendering make this particular writer succeed. Language is the most important element because it is the most easily manifest in the text. One sees words on paper. If one sees a reference to Africans as primitives or to Native Americans as "a bunch of wild Indians" or Latinos as "greasy," then one knows the cultural address of the author. While it is true that authors might use irony, sarcasm, and other techniques of language to deliver a certain point or perspective, the Afrocentric critic is sensitive to the persistent and uniform use of pejoratives as demonstrating the author's location. When an author uses pejoratives unknowingly to refer to Africans, the critic often is being confronted with an unconscious writer, one who is oblivious to the social and cultural milieu.

Attitude

Attitude refers to a predisposition to respond in a characteristic manner to some situation, value, idea, object, person, or group of persons. The writer signals his or her location by attitude toward certain ideas, persons, or objects. Thus, the critic in pursuit of the precise location of the author can determine from the writer's characteristic or persistent response to certain things where the writer is located. The attitude is not the motive; attitudes are more numerous and varied than motives. Consequently, the attempt to locate a writer by referring to "motivating attitudes" may be useful in some situations. The common adage, "I cannot hear what you say because what you are shouts so loudly in my ear" is a remarkable example of how our attitudes influence our appraisal of those around us. This is the same for writers. Once a critic has read certain portions of a text to "get the drift" of what it is the writer is getting at, he or she can usually locate the author.

Direction

The line along which the author's sentiments, themes, and interests lie with reference to the point at which they are aimed I refer to as direction. It is the tendency or inclination present in the literary work with regard to the author's objective. One is able to identify this tendency by the symbols that occur in the text. For example, a writer who uses Ebonics, African American language, in his or her works demonstrates a tendency along the lines of Afrocentric space. The reader is capable of digesting some of the arguments, the poetic allusions, and situations because of the tendency identified in the writing.

Therefore, a text must be seen in the light of language, attitude, and direction when the serious reader wants to locate it. Each text carries its own signature, a stamp, if you will, of the place to which it belongs or to where it is going. In any case, the reader will be able to adequately locate the text in order to make judgments about the author's creative abilities as well as the author's philosophical underpinning. Ultimately a text must fit within a multiplicity of places, each one defined by the dynamic interplay of culture and purpose.

AN EXAMPLE FROM HISTORY

One of the greatest (in my judgment) African American writers was born on July 29, 1924 and killed in New York on May 23, 1968. His name was Henry Dumas and his death at the age of thirty four cut short the brilliant career of a poet and short story writer who gave meaning to the Afrocentric term, *located*.

Henry Dumas's work, *Ark of Bones and Other Stories* and *Poetry for My People*, was published posthumously. However, he had been engaged in teaching at the Experiment in Higher Education at Southern Illinois University and served as a member of the editorial staff of the

2. Locating a Text: Implications of Afrocentric Theory 17

Hiram *Poetry Review* and through these activities had made many friends and acquaintances who knew his creative power. Hale Chatfield and Eugene Redmond ably brought Henry Dumas to life again in the editing of his works. Few African American writers have been so successful as Henry Dumas in demonstrating the opposite perspective of the race shedders. Dumas was pre-eminently an Afrocentric writer in every aspect of the term.

For the reader seeking to possess the literacy necessary to understand the stories or the poetry of Dumas, it suffices to say that one must pay attention to every nuance of the African American culture. That is to say, one must understand the "bop" and the "do." Furthermore, the reader must be able to see how nicknames locate a person in the text as well as the author's ability to write culturally, that is, out of the culture. For example, Henry Dumas gives his characters names like Blue, Fish, Tate, and Grease. These are important names in the context of Dumas's stories. Actually, each of the names carries definite meanings. Blue, for example, relates to a person's being so black he looks blue. Fish is the nickname for a a person who swims very well. Tate is the nickname for a person whose head is shaped like a potato. Grease is the name of a smooth-talking individual. There are several reasons why these names are significant in Dumas's cultural understanding and our appreciation of his art. In the first place, nicknames are means for placement, location, identity. They are often more descriptive and defining than the European names given to African American children. Since many people did not have access to African names, the practice of nicknaming became a major avenue for the maintenance of African culture and expression. Names could still mean something, much like names had meant among the Yoruba, Ibo, Fanti, Asante, and Congo. Dumas understands the relevance of the nickname and appropriates its use to the functions of his art. Another reason Dumas's use of these names is important comes from the creation of atmosphere in his works. He seeks always to expand the boundaries, to move against the tide, and to raise the difficult questions. There is no better way to create atmosphere than to allow the traditions to blossom, particularly in reference to what people call things, that is, the words given to identify persons and objects.

The richness of Dumas's language, the clarity of his symbolic attitude, and the rhythm of his trajectory cannot be over-estimated. He impressed himself as well as others with the tremendously accurate portrayal of the African American language. Indeed, Eugene Redmond wrote in his introduction to *Ark of Bones and Other Stones*, "Dumas--a brilliant, creative linguist--contracts and expands English, Black Language and various African tribal [*sic*] sounds to come up with what is perhaps a 'found' utterance" (xiv). Redmond's introduction to the stories of Henry Dumas is a penetrating look at the style of the artist. What Redmond observes in the language of Dumas is what places him squarely within an Afrocentric location. When Redmond says "Dumas is also the first among young black writers to re-acculturate," he is speaking to Dumas' love of his language (xv). There is no caricature of the African in his use of African language; no self-conscious concentration on loss exists in the mind of Henry Dumas. He finds the African American language richly endowed, as he found the people.

In the powerful story "Ark of Bones," Dumas brings together all of the experiences of his young life to produce a text richly contoured with cultural artifacts of language. Headeye, one of the characters, had a *mojo bone* in his hand. But we learn that "Headeye, he ain't got no *devil* in him." His only problem was that he had "this *notion* in his head about me *hoggin* the luck." Dumas knows the close community language as well as the religious allusions, but his knowledge of this language is a gift of his sensitivity to the voices he has heard. The reader knows precisely where Dumas is at all times, even though as you read him you know that he is aware of everything he is doing in the text. There is no stream of words here floating endlessly on with no point; this is a master writer whose point is made in every sentence. "Headeye acted like he was *iggin* me" is about as precise as you can get with language. To understand *iggin* is to be right in the center of the culture; however, it is an understanding that comes from experience or from study. One of the most insidious forms of critical hierarchy is the criticism of Afrocentric writers by those who have neither studied nor lived the culture. The assumption that one can simply make critical judgment and commentary about the text, perhaps *locate* the writer, without serious study of the culture is an arrogant and false assumption. As one who does not know white American culture cannot truly understand it without some background, neither can Afrocentric writers be understood without some background. Normally, the student of American literature gains the knowledge of the nuances of white American literature and can adequately place the writers. But Afrocentric literature is much like Old English literature in the sense that it must be studied seriously or else the reader will usually miss the point. I am not just speaking about knowing the meaning of

2. Locating a Text: Implications of Afrocentric Theory

words or understanding the structure of Ebonics--that is a starting point. More fundamentally, the reader must know from what *center* of experience the writer writes. An African American writing from an Eurocentric basis will produce text that may have some references to the cultural materials of the African American people but will remain essentially a white writer with a black skin. Such a writer is not much different from a white writer who writes knowledgeably about certain cultural icons of the African American community. But to really come from an African centered perspective in literature, the writer must immerse herself or himself in the culture of the people. The value of this immersion is that one becomes more authenthically a voice of the culture, speaking much like Henry Dumas the language of the African American heritage with all of its universal implications in similar experiences of other people. To deny Afrocentric writers this possibility, either through criticism or creation, is to assume that the special language of the African American is somehow different from other languages, such as Spanish, Yoruba, Gikuyu, or Polish.

Dumas understood the nobility of the culture from which he had come and so when he wrote that Headeye's daddy "hauled off and smacked him side the head," he recognized that the perfection of action could only be told with two verbs. Rather than say, as might be said in English, that his daddy "smacked him side the head," Dumas goes into the culture and brings to bear the full meaning of this action. To truly complete the act the daddy had to have "hauled off and smacked him." This construction is like the one I often heard in Georgia as a child when someone had become a member of the local church. People would say, "Child, she got converted and joined the church." Another such construction of language is the command "Turn loose and jump down from there" to a child who is climbing a tree (Asante, 1990:233-252).

In his stories as in his poetry Dumas gives his readers all of the signposts of his location. He is not a writer without a place in his own culture; he is firmly planted in the midst of ancestors, ghosts, haints, and spirits of the past as well as the generative power of the present condition of African Americans. Among the expressions and terms that he employs are Glory Boat, Afro-horn, Aba, Heyboy, Sippi, catcher-clouds, and Saa saa aba saa saa. While his corpus is limited because of his early death, he remains one of the most centered of African American authors. Language, attitude, and direction are clearly demarcated in his works. When we read Dumas we are reading a profoundly honest writer who tells his and his people's special truth to the world. Contained in the language, the attitude, and the direction of his work is the symbolism of strength, mystery, energy, dynamism, intelligence, wisdom, and trust. A compact exists between Dumas and the characters of his stories that allows him to use their language to tell the truth. He "ain't give on to what he know," but the reader knows that Dumas found the center of his cultural being intact and never left it. Why should he have left? What other writers would be required to leave? How silly of a writer to think that he or she must leave the source of power in order to be universal; true universalism in literature adheres in the ability of a writer to capture the special story or stories of his or her own culture in ways that make those stories impact on others, regardless of the first language. In the end, the serious reader of writers must work to re-affirm the centrality of cultural experience as the place to begin to create a dynamic multi-cultural literacy because without rootedness in our own cultural territory, we have no authentic story to tell.

REFERENCES

Asante, Molefi Kete. (1990) "The African Essence in African American Language." In M. K. Asante and K. W. Asante, *African Culture: The Rhythms of Unity*, pp. 233-252, Trenton, N.J.: Africa World Press.

Bernal, Martin. (1987) *Black Athena*. New Brunswick, N.J.: Ruters University Press.

Davidson, Basil. (1984) *The Lost Cities of Africa*. New York: Little, Brown and Company.

Diop, Cheikh Anta. (1974) *The African Origin of Civilization: Myth or Reality*? New York: Lawrence Hill.

Dumas, Henry. (1970) *Ark of Bones and Other Stories* In Hale Chatfield and Eugene Redmond, eds., *Ark of Bones and Other Stories*, Carbondale: Southern Illinois University Press.

Gould, Stephen Jay. (1981) *The Mismeasure of Man*. New York: W. W. Norton.

Redmond, Eugene. (1970) "Introduction." In Hale Chatfield and Eugene Redmond, eds., *Ark of Bones and Other Stories*, pp. 1-15, Carbondale: Southern Illinois University Press.

3

Refusing to Be Boxed In: Sonia Sanchez's Transformation of the Haiku Form
Frenzella Elaine De Lancey

> It isn't after all, whether a black poet uses traditional Western poetic devices or not. The essential question is how does he do it? How does he make them his own, make them work for him in the same sense that black people generally, writers especially, have made an oppression language--English--work for them. Ultimately, the history of the black liberation in America may be equated with the progress of linguistic manumission.
>
> Alvin Aubert, Review: Sonia Sanchez
> *Black Academy Review* (Winter 1970)

One of the few titled haiku written by Sonia Sanchez, "Walking in the rain in Guyana" is an excellent example of both the poet's artistic vision and artistry:

> watusi like trees
> holding the day like green um/
> brella catching rain.
>
> (46)

Elements consistent with definitions of classical Japanese haiku as a lyric verse form in three unrhymed lines, with a 5-7-5 syllable count are evident, so, too, is the requisite emphasis on external nature. The clarifying title tells us that this haiku derives from a walk in the rain in Guyana and announces the poet's intention to "localize" the haiku in a particular manner. Sanchez uses Afrocentric motifs to textualize the haiku, making it not some universal statement about rain and tree but a particular experience, filtered through the poet's consciousness. Though Guyana is located in South America, African people are among its inhabitants; the watusi trees evoke images of the Burundi Watusi, again, images associated with Africa. Sanchez localizes this image by inserting "like" in the first line, forcing it into service as she forges an adjective-phrase, "watusi like" to describe the trees. Such techniques signal reader: this is haiku with a difference.

We recognize, however, that Sanchez's "Walking in the rain in Guyana" conforms to a basic concept of haiku to what haiku master Basho (1644-1694) describes as simply what is happening at this place at this moment. Equally evident is how much Sanchez's Afrocentric content textualizes the form. Forging function with ethos, she observes rules while breaking them. Sanchez's poetic practice is informed by a philosophy that utilizes function and ethos as two important distinctions in poetry. She sees poetry as form that accommodates political and personal ideas.[1] Imamu Amiri Baraka offers a useful definition of form and content that can be applied to Sanchez's transformation of the haiku form. According to Baraka, form is "simply how a thing exists (or what a thing exists as)." Content, on the other hand, "is why a thing exists" (380).

In her transformation of haiku Sanchez often forces the reader to ask "why." She notes that writing for her has been a "long tense road of saying what I wanted and needed to say" (Leibowitz, 1985:365). In "Walking in the rain in Guyana," the poet fuses an unspecific, unbounded image from external nature to a particular, specific moment,

---

[1] In my article, "Cracking the Skull and Mending the Soul: Sonia Sanchez's Role as Poet/Teacher/Healer" presented at the Twenty-Second Annual African Heritage Conference at City College in New York, on April 7, 1990, I connect Sanchez's theory of poetry with her Afrocentric praxis. Further in a now completed manuscript in circulation, I argue that Sanchez has developed a metatheory that forges her poetic praxis with her Afrocentric womanist philosophy. For my interest in Sanchez's use of the haiku form, I must thank Professor Kariamu Welsh at Temple University, who raised the question at the same conference and was the catalyst for my study of this aspect of Sanchez's poetry. For my re-examination of Sanchez's work, I must thank Carolyn Karcher who insisted that Sanchez's work was both "deep" and "wide." Professor Karcher also introduced me to Regina Jennings for whom Sonia Sanchez was mentor. Jennings has kept me close to the pulse of the African American poetry community, which is deeply influenced by Sanchez's work.

3. Sonia Sanchez's Transformation of the Haiku Form

filtered through her consciousness. More than a personal poetic construction, this haiku is also an example of Sonia Sanchez's conscious decision to imbue haiku form with Afrocentric motifs, and ultimately move beyond the form as prescribed to a fusion of traditional haiku form with her own structure. In other words, Sanchez is making the haiku say what she wants it to say.

Sanchez's transformation of the form is more radical than mere structural alteration, although she sometimes changes the structure of the haiku by using simile, conjunction, and metaphor. Her use of these structural markers can always be identified as functional; they are used to make the haiku speak her words, reveal her vision. In fact, Sanchez's use of the haiku form is a revolutionary textualization of both structure and form. Sometimes working within the structural strictures of classical Japanese haiku form, other times altering the form to fit her needs, and always textualizing it, Sanchez forces the form to accommodate her vision. By imbuing the haiku form with Afrocentric motifs, Sanchez textualizes the form in a specific manner, and in the instances where she must abrogate universally observed strictures, she does so to force the haiku to conform to her needs and her vision. In her haiku, then, the effect is a movement through the uneven strictures imposed by dicta reintroduced for the English haiku. Referring specifically to her book *I'VE BEEN A WOMAN*, Sanchez discusses her use of haiku and tanka, and her conscious use of African themes. In *I'VE BEEN A WOMAN*, she points out, "I have haiku, tankas, and again, the movement towards what I call 'African' ideas and feelings and also the movement toward a black ethic and a feminine one too" (quoted in Melhem, 1990:168).

The fifth section of *I'VE BEEN A WOMAN* is entitled "Haikus/Tankas & Other Love Syllables" and in it Sanchez offers haiku which focus on a number of subjects. Some are interesting fusions of nature and human elements:

> i have looked into
> my father's eyes and seen an
> african sunset.
>
> (67)

Often these fusions of external nature and humanity emphasize one over the other. At other times, humanity and elements signifying nature are perfectly balanced in metaphorical phrases. Thus, function and form are important in the transformation Sanchez effects. For example, her use of simile and conjunction is also functional. Though she only alters the haiku 5-7-5 infrequently, her use of simile, metaphor, and other structural devices usually alert readers to important structural changes and, of course, with these changes, an unusual textualization of form. In another haiku dedicated to Gwendolyn Brooks, Sanchez signals Brooks's importance by using images from external nature to create an image of Brooks's essence as sacred:

>   woman. whose color
>   of life is like the sun, whose
>   laughter is prayer.

(68)

We note Sanchez's use of metaphor and simile showcases Brooks. Such showcasing transforms this haiku into a compressed praise song for Gwendolyn Brooks, and external nature serves as handmaiden to Sanchez's vision. Suggesting that Brooks's vision is an exemplar, a sacred model, Sanchez clusters images for associative value within the permitted 5-7-5 syllable count and with the forbidden simile and metaphor. After establishing Brooks through metaphor, Sanchez equates Brooks's laughter with "prayer." In this final vehicle, this final image of a woman who is a sacred model, is effective in this haiku. Again, Sanchez fuses human and natural elements through clustered images and structural transformation, a woman whose essence rivals the sun becomes a sacred figure.

In the same section of *I'VE BEEN A WOMAN*, there are other haiku in which nature takes on the coloring of the human actors in the poetic structure. And although most of the haiku offered below do not have discernible Afrocentric motifs, they are examples of the poet's willingness to abrogate haiku strictures to accommodate her vision:

>   shedding my years
>   earthbound now. midnite trees are
>   more to my liking.

(77)

Nature becomes the clarifying element as the image of rooted trees suggests the experience of being earthbound. Sanchez converts this feeling into a transformative moment consonant with the speaker's perspective

3. Sonia Sanchez's Transformation of the Haiku Form

by playing against our most commonly held conception of trees. Viewed at midnight, rather than in the sharply clarifying light of day, the trees as image are subject to greater imaginative possibilities. Earthbound, the speaker continues to retain the right to see things in her own way.

With the same ease that she subordinates external nature to humans in some haiku, Sanchez also imbues her haiku with highly personal moments, ignoring the stricture against the personal in haiku.

> the rain tastes lovely
> like yo/sweat draping my body
> after lovemaking.

(83)

Traditional haiku conventions of nature, taste, feeling, and present time all interact in a rather unconventional manner here. Most noticeable, of course, is "rain" representing nature in the first line perfectly balanced against "lovemaking" in the last. Between the first and the last line, water as in rain has been transformed into the perspiration produced by the efforts of the two lovers. The haiku's argument suggests nature as human and other, and its structure effectively forges the two. But this is also a haiku imbued with the personal and is, therefore, a transgression of conventional practice. In another transgression, Sanchez dares to be intensely introspective in her haiku:

> what is it about
> me that i claim all the wrong
> lives, the same endings?

(80)

Signaling metaphysical crisis, the speaker questions past practices and centers herself in the haiku. In this profoundly personal and introspective moment of crisis, the speaker questions the patterns of her life, and to do so, she moves from present to past. Her mistakes are tallied in words like "all" and the plural "lives" and "endings." Ignoring the censure demanding external nature, Sanchez transforms the haiku form in incisive and startling linguistic turns:

> you have pierced me so
> deeply i cannot turn a
> round without bleeding.

(86)

> missing you is like
> spring standing still on a hill
> amid winter snow.

(86)

Introspective moments rarely produce epiphanies; at most, they are moments of fragmented insight. The haiku form complements Sanchez's poetic renderings of such moments and is thus particularly appropriate; yet, this is a revolutionary move. In their quiet intensity, each haiku represents the poet's vision. While not obviously Afrocentric in terms of motifs, these haiku represent the view of an African American woman. Specifically, they represent an artist aware of censure choosing to work against the imposed norm. Even in those haiku that are not decidedly Afrocentric, one finds Sanchez presenting her own vision in her own way and saying what she wants to say.

So far, I have advanced the notion of Sanchez's haiku as decidedly revolutionary, whether she is presenting introspective moments or making political statements. In changing the form by textualizing it, Sanchez demonstrates her own considerable skill as poet. But to truly understand the imperative that informs Sanchez's transformations, one must examine briefly the nature of certain strictures in haiku writing.

Claims about what constitutes haiku are curiously antithetical to general practices. For example, there seems to be general agreement that Japanese haiku is rimeless, its seventeen syllables usually arranged in three lines, often following a 5-7-5 pattern. However, in *The Art and Craft of Poetry: An Introduction*, Lawrence John Zillman writes that in haiku one is not concerned "with metrical feet, rime, or contrived stanzas." Rather the emphasis should be on the "two basic patterns" in which "everything is to be said in either thirty-one or seventeen syllables. The tanka, the longer structure, is made up of five lines, of tanka 5-7-5-7-7 syllables respectively" (94). In fact, writers of English haiku often ignore such patterns. Rime, then, appears to mark the important difference between Japanese and English haiku. This single adjustment seems to be the only acknowledged transition from the Japanese to the

3. Sonia Sanchez's Transformation of the Haiku Form

English haiku. But it is also evident that certain strictures are deeply ingrained. Still to be considered is the often cited constraint from Basho urging the restriction of content in haiku to what is happening in this place and this moment.

Editors and critics frequently ignore the flexibility of Basho's definition of haiku. Rather, they evoke the strongest strictures, insisting not only upon the "present moment" in haiku, but also that the subject matter of haiku focus on external nature--that the poet focus on what can be seen, heard, smelled, tasted, or touched. In her haiku, Sanchez most often observes one stricture while transforming another. While her observation of the 5-7-5 seventeen syllable stricture is most consistent, she takes the "present moment" and imbues it with any number of Afrocentric images or her unique, sometimes introspective vision. In the intensely personal haiku about lovemaking, she reinvests the stricture of taste, taking it from conventional dicta and turning it on its head.

According to X. J. Kennedy, "Haiku is an art of few words, many suggestions. A haiku starts us thinking and feeling" (75-76). Sonia Sanchez uses the haiku form in a manner that forces her readers to think, and she does it successfully because she alters the form. It would seem then that some flexibility must be offered to the poet who wants to textualize haiku; yet, a cursory examination of the *1990 Poet's Market* finds that many strictures continue to dominate in a rather monolithic manner: "Do not use metaphor/simile/" (138) and "Do not tell your emotions" (152).

Unlike Kennedy or Zillman, many editors are unyielding proponents of traditional strictures. They expect the content in haiku to focus on external nature; they expect haiku writers to reject simile and metaphor. And these editors exercise some control over poets by their ability to reject haiku that do not conform to strictures. This, in turn, influences the poetry community, wedding haiku writers who want to publish to traditional strictures. Apparently monolithic, this perspective seems to be based on false notions, and as in all arbitrary dicta, the contradictions serve as imperatives for poets who want to alter the form. One of the more clarifying statements about Japanese haiku is offered by Kennedy, but even his flexible comments present censures against Sanchez's transformation of the haiku form:

> Haiku poets look out upon a literal world, seldom looking inward to discuss their feelings. Japanese haiku tend to be sea-

sonal in subject, but because they are so highly compressed, they usually just imply a season: a blossom indicates spring; a crow on a branch, autumn; snow, winter. Not just pretty little sketches of nature (as some Westerners think), haiku assumes a view of the universe in which observer and nature are not separated. (76)

The obvious difference between the description offered by Kennedy and Sanchez's haiku is that she does not hesitate to look inward, producing introspective haiku. Yet Kennedy's statement confirms that there are still misconceptions among practitioners and editors about what constitutes haiku. Further, the obvious gap between these misconceptions and views such as Kennedy's, is a proving ground that Sanchez stakes out for herself as she redefines the haiku form. Thus, the contradictions become Sanchez's imperative for transforming haiku.

As Carolyn Rodgers, George Kent, and others point out, Sanchez has traditionally used new forms. In one of her articles "Black poetry-- where it's at," Rodgers offers a comprehensive typology of black expression in poetry. She identifies Sanchez's use of the "shouting" poem as an example of her utilization of new forms. George Kent offers a more extensive analysis of Sanchez's skill, not as a poet experimenting with new forms, but as a poet who has experimented with form and mastered it. Citing her mastery of mountain-top poetry, Kent refers specifically to Sanchez's *A Blues Book for Blue Black Magical Women* as "a culmination of spiritual and poetic powers" (197). He speaks of Sanchez's earlier experiments with language and spelling as "efforts to force the speaking voice to speak from the printed page." He applauds her "simplicity of diction" and her "careful but undistracting uses of natural and mechanically induced pauses" (198). In textualizing haiku, Sanchez produces exciting experimental forms and verifies earlier critical assessments of her work. Indeed, she reveals herself as a poet at the top of her craft. Just as she forces the stricture concerning nature in haiku to accommodate her vision of human nature and external nature, and the relationship they share, so, too, does she push the form and herself. This fusion of form finds Sanchez offering beautiful images of external nature in harmony with man:

3. Sonia Sanchez's Transformation of the Haiku Form

>   the trees are laughing
>   at us. positioning their
>   leaves in morning smiles.

(72)

Seemingly antithetical elements of nature are made to serve, through artistic skill, a different function:

>   We are sudden stars
>   you and i exploding in
>   our blue black skins.

(9)

In the forbidden use of metaphor Sanchez combines the external nature, represented by the "stars," with the human element, thereby creating a certain texture in the form: the "you and i" and the "blue black skins" are human elements fused with stars. One becomes the other. In another lyrical instance Sanchez combines disparate elements, including simile, to make external nature and humanity complement each other:

>   O this day like an
>   orange peeled against the sky
>   murmurs me and you.

(99)

Sanchez uses powerful elements from external nature perfectly equipoised against the human aspect. Furthermore, we have another instance of Sanchez using the forbidden simile and conjunction to establish the harmony important in human relationships and textualizing the poem in terms of several antithetical elements: structure and form; nature and man. The love for humanity comes through in this haiku precisely because Sanchez uses simile and conjunction. The effect of "like" between the orange and the sky balances them against the "me and you" of the haiku. Aspects of nature work for the humans in the poem, and there is harmony.

In another beautiful image of harmony, nature, and man, poet and haiku strictures merge to become a Sonia Sanchez construction wholly Afrocentric in technique, becoming what Carolyn Rodgers calls a "mindblowing" poem:

> morning snow falling
> astride this carousel called
> life. i am sailing.
>
> (75)

"Mindblowing" because it uses the haiku to demonstrate poetic skill as well as poetic vision, this haiku reveals a poet boxing her way out and away from prescriptive form. Her refusal to yield to form is a lesson in itself. The opening lines signal conventional haiku, but each line moves the haiku away from the conventional toward individual technique and vision. Internal punctuation in the last line suggests that the poet will simply settle for the injection of the word "life" to signal her experimentation with form. On this introspective note, she is, in fact, situated in the present, but as she muses about "carousel called life" we recognize this structure as both synchronic and diachronic in nature; it is, therefore, introspective. However, after the period, which makes it appear to be an afterthought, the phrase "i am sailing" alters our response to the haiku. One could argue that this is the most powerful line in the haiku. "Mindblower poems" according to Rodgers, "seek to expand our minds, to break the chains that strangle them, so that we can begin to image alternatives for black people" (339). The artist's technical finessing thrills the reader who expects the poem to move in one direction, but finds it moving in another. This haiku, like others, not only signals Sanchez's mastery of form, it also reveals her ability to forge her own technique with those aspects of haiku that she needs. Although she forces it to accommodate Afrocentric vision, Sanchez has healthy respect for haiku form. Keenly aware of the form's possibilities, she applauds its power to discipline novice poets. Thus, she is not attempting to destroy this existing form as a reactionary response to arbitrary dicta. In fact, an examination of her haiku convinces one that though her altering of structure is revolutionary, the extent to which Sanchez imbues the content and structure of haiku, filling it with an Afrocentric texture filtered through her unique womanist vision, is even more revolutionary. This tension between form as control and form as discipline informs Sanchez's most political haiku. Political vision in her work both disrupts the structure and offers future possibilities for form:

3. Sonia Sanchez's Transformation of the Haiku Form

> redlips open wide
> like a wound winding down on
> the city. clotting.
>
> (82)

A political poem that is indeed "mindblowing," this disturbing haiku offers a poetic argument. It incorporates the poet's sense of her role as vatic poet who serves the dual function of communicating with a particular community and the wider world. A powerful vignette, its vision is prophetic and moves the poet toward a new form that is Afrocentric in both structure and form. Sanchez breaks some rules while retaining others. As noted earlier, the insistence upon the present and external nature in haiku is important in conventional dicta. In this example, Sanchez turns this stricture on its head, inverting it so sharply that we sense an urgent note. The present tense Sanchez offers is not a soothing photograph of nature, but an intrusive and disturbing vignette, beginning an ominous chapter. Inherent in this haiku is the tension between present and future that the poet observes and advises. Thus, the texture, philosophy, and structure of this poem combine to render it wholly Afrocentric. As a poet, Sanchez observes and then tells what she sees, hinting at future implications. This is her strongest forte as a poet, and the haiku's compressed form works to her advantage. Forced to be brief, she must communicate her vision quickly. This rapid closure adds to the urgency of the moment.

As she forces this form to do much more than is expected, Sanchez also forces the reader to interact with the haiku, to go beyond the three lines to the implications of the vignette, to seek and know the future the poet thinks the circumstances augur. In effect, the reader is forced to inquire as to what is beyond its frame. Even if we did not have the dedication "for a blk/prostitute," we would recognize this as a political haiku. Sanchez's careful structuring also alerts us that we must become involved not only in analyzing her haiku, but in responding to the situation she describes. In effect, she is producing haiku that make us feel and respond in much the same way that X. J. Kennedy suggests. Sanchez goes beyond form, in this instance creating a personal situation between poet and community. Indeed, her technical skill moves this haiku beyond Afrocentric content to Afrocentric discourse as we recognize the required interaction between poem and reader as "call-and-response," an Afrocentric form of discourse.

From the beginning the images elicit associations bordering on the grotesque. The synecdochic image "redlips open wide" suggests the myriad functions the prostitute serves, but in the simile "like a wound" the grotesqueness is deepened with the comparison of the lips to a wound with infectious connotations. "Clotting" further suggests unnaturalness, but this impression is achieved by reversing our preconceived notion of clotting. We must shift from the impression of clotting as positive, stemming the loss of blood, to clotting as negative, cutting off the heart's circulation. As a clot, the prostitute places the entire community at risk. In the case of the African American community, she is a special risk, but because she is a member of the community, her pain becomes communal pain: "Winding down on the city" reinforces the image of veins, circumscribing blood's course through the body. This "black prostitute," then, is headed to the heart of our existence; as a clot, she presents mortal danger. Once we have the picture in focus, it becomes for us a vignette. Sanchez's message comes in her careful structuring of images. In addition to the alignment of images, she uses the end-stop powerfully. In fact, she is "bringing it on home" to the reader. "Redlips open wide" is a powerful, lingering image, etching in the mind's eye a picture of the prostitute walking down the street. But the whole of its impact is made by Sanchez's structural innovation. End-stop as used by Sanchez in this instance, provides the tension between present and future, between the poet's prescience and our own dawning awareness. The period after "city," and the final word "clotting" moves the reader from disinterested observer to worried inner-city dweller or African American member of the community.

Sanchez is perceived as a militant writer. Such a perception has as much to do with the themes she addresses in her poetry as the form she uses. Critics, however, tend to focus on her militant themes. Certainly it is understandable that critics focus on Sanchez's use of certain themes in her work, but her disruption of the haiku form is directly related to her fusion of function and ethos in poetry, and though she is consistently revolutionary, she is also a skilled artist. Ironically, because of the general perception of her as militant, Sanchez's use of the haiku puzzles some scholars who associate her militancy solely with free verse and rarely with haiku. In an interview with Herbert Leibowitz, Sanchez talks about the perception of her as militant and places her work in perspective:

3. Sonia Sanchez's Transformation of the Haiku Form

> My early poetry was introspective, poetry that probably denied or ignored I was black. I wrote about trees, and birds, and whatever, and that was hard, living in Harlem, since we didn't see too many trees, though I did draw on my residual memories of the South. People kept saying to me, if you write a political poem, it will be considered propaganda--an ineffective and poor poem--but I read Neruda and saw that he didn't deny the personal. In the early Sixties I became aware that the personal was the political. (Leibowitz, 365)

Sanchez's statement reveals her own philosophy of poetry: poetry can be both personal and political. Further, this statement accounts for her unique fusion of external elements, introspective elements, and highly personal elements in her haiku. For Sanchez, the use of nature in an artificial sense serves no useful purpose. Human concerns fuel her structures. She uses nature in a way that forces it to serve a function. As she points out, her journey from the point at which she struggled to write about trees and plants from residual memories to her own realization that she could write revolutionary poetry has been a "long, tense road."

Because of her tendency to focus on the human condition in her poetry, Sanchez is often associated with militancy. Two misconceptions account for this tendency: Sanchez's highly militant and often publicized free verse poetry, which employs tropes and themes associated with political struggle, and the conventional notion of haiku that influences both the poetry and critical community. Sanchez's insistence upon her own vision puzzles both critics and friends alike. Her account of a friend's reaction to her love poetry offers an example of how she is perceived:

> When I gave my book *Love Poems* to a friend, she said, "God, I didn't know you wrote love poems." But in every book of mine there's been a section of lyrical pieces. If you describe me, as some critics do, as a lyrical poet, I say yes I am, but I'm also a hard-hitting poet and a political poet because this is a lyrical world and a terrible world, too, and I have to talk about that. (Leibowitz, 1985:365)

Terrible lyricism informs and surprises in the haiku dedicated to John Brown:

> man of stained glass legs
> harvesting the blood of Nat
> in a hangman's noose.

(93)

A perfect 5-7-5 form, this praise poem for John Brown exemplifies the terrible lyricism to which Sanchez refers. This haiku does not focus on nature, but on the bravery of John Brown's stand, situating him in history with Nat Turner. But it also deconstructs history in a surprising manner. Though she concedes with the reference to "stained glass legs" that John Brown's stand deserves our respect, Sanchez is also making it clear that Nat Turner was the first to die. Ironically, John Brown, though branded as a maniac by Lincoln, receives recognition that makes him a hero in the fight for African American freedom from European slavery. Afrocentric texture is apparent in this haiku, but so is its "teaching" or "running it down" quality. Rodgers defines "teaching" or "running it down" poems as those attempting to give direction to African American people (42-49). And in this dedication to John Brown, as in the prostitute poem, Sanchez is teaching, "running it down" to those who suffer from historical amnesia.

What is most striking about this form is the reader's sense that Sanchez has almost overwhelmed the form with the weight of significance. Yet, her lyricism not only saves the haiku, but gives it a cutting edge: "stained glass legs" is an overwhelmingly beautiful image. The reader inclined toward facile sympathy for John Brown is prohibited by the clarifying images. The fragile, glass legs are placed in proper perspective by the images of Brown "harvesting" Nat Turner's blood. Nat Turner becomes the model for John Brown, as is made clear by the image of Nat in the "hangman's noose." This deliberate use of form is as shocking as the vignette of the prostitute moving down the street. In the prostitute haiku, Sanchez is poet predicting future consequences; in the haiku dedicated to John Brown, she is the poet correcting the past. In another haiku dedicated to Paul Robeson, Sanchez is the poet suggesting the importance of Afrocentric vision. Reading our figures through Afrocentric lenses moves us closer to our African roots.

3. Sonia Sanchez's Transformation of the Haiku Form

> your voice unwrapping
> itself from the Congo
> contagious as shrines.
>
> (86)

Interestingly, this haiku does not conform to the 5-7-5 haiku constraints (it is 5-6-5 in this case). In content and texture, it resembles the haiku dedicated to John Brown. Both poems were deliberately pressed into the service of the African American experience. Though both are Afrocentric in nature, in the latter example, we also see Sanchez's introduction of "African" motifs and forging connections with African as a homeland. In each case the dedication identifies the haiku as political. Most powerful is the poet's decision to connect a hero figure with the African homeland. Like the haiku that opens this essay, the haiku dedicated to John Brown and Paul Robeson are political, yet lyrical.

In *The Militant Black Writer in Africa and the United States* Stephen Henderson talks about the inevitable distortion which occurs when African Americans attempt to fit themselves into the disinterested categories America prescribes for them. Offering Phillis Wheatley as an example of an artist who experienced geometric death, Henderson maintains that Wheatley was boxed in by alien forms. He views Wheatley as a "privileged slave" or "black prodigy" unable "to come to grips honestly with her blackness." As a poet, she was "boxed in by the right angles of the heroic couplet, . . . an early emblem of geometric death" (84). Henderson sees Wheatley as a tragic African American poet subsumed by form. But even if we qualify this view by indicating the extenuating nature of Wheatley's circumstances, we must admit that African American authors frequently must renegotiate prescribed forms to offer their own vision of the world.[2]

In transforming haiku, Sonia Sanchez declares her own "linguistic manumission," refusing to be boxed in by its form. As she textualizes the

---

[2] For a more recent assessment of Phillis Wheatley, see June Jordan "The Difficult Miracle of Black Poetry in America," or "Something Like a Sonnet for Phillis Wheatley," in *Wild Women in the Whirlwind: Afro-American Culture and the Contemporary Literary Renaissance.* Joanne M. Braxton and Andree Nicola McLaughlin, eds. Trenton, N.J.: Rutgers University Press, 1990, 22-34.

form, forging her Afrocentric vision and Afrocentric structure within the discipline of the haiku form, she moves closer to a unique structure that carries her own signature.

REFERENCES

Aubert, Alvin. (1970) "Review: Sonia Sanchez." *Black Academy Review.*

Baraka, Imamu Amiri. (1973) "Hunting is Not Those Heads on the Wall." In *The Poetics of The New American Poetry*, pp. 378-82. New York: Gove Press.

Braxton, Joanne M. and Andree Nicola McLaughlin, eds. (1990) *Wild Women in the Whirlwind: Afro-American Culture and the Contemporary Literary Renaissance*. New Brunswick, N.J.: Rutgers University Press.

Henderson, Stephen. (1969) *The Militant Black Writer in Africa and the United States*. Madison and Milwaukee: University of Wisconsin Press.

Kennedy, X.J. (1982) *An Introduction to Poetry*. Boston: Little, Brown and Company.

Kent, George. (1975) "Notes on the 1974 Black Literary Scene." *Phylon* (June):197-198.

Leibowitz, Herbert. (1985) "Exploring Myths: An Interview with Sonia Sanchez." *Parnassus: Poetry in Review*. Lexington: University of Kentucky Press.

Melhem, D. H. (1990) *Heroism in the New Black Poetry* Lexington: University of Kentucky Press.

1990 Poet: Where and How to Publish Your Poetry. (1989) Cincinnati: F&W Publications.

Rodgers, Carolyn. (1972) *rappin' and stylin' out*. Edited by Thomas Kochman. Urbana: University of Illinois Press.

Sanchez, Sonia. (1978) *I'VE BEEN A WOMAN*. Sausalito: Black Scholar Press.

Zillman, Lawrence John. (1966) *The Art and Craft of Poetry*. New York: Macmillan.

4

Reassessing African American Literature through an Afrocentric Paradigm: Zora N. Hurston and James Baldwin

Carolyn L. Holmes

Nearly a quarter of a century ago the social and cultural fabric of the United States of America was shaken to the core of its European foundations by what has been termed a Black Revolution or Black Power Movement. The year 1966 witnessed the official beginning of this movement, when Stokely Carmichael, the new chairman of the Student Nonviolent Coordinating Committee (SNCC), announced his organization's redirection from its traditional methods of demonstrating and protesting for the civil rights denied to African Americans citizens, by laws and custom, for more than a century.

Carmichael challenged all "thinking" black folk to join SNCC in its quest for Black Power. The voice of Larry Neal, poet, critic, editor, and declared Black Nationalist, was soon heard responding to this call. Neal become the leading spirit and voice of the Black Arts Movement, which he referred to as the "aesthetic and spiritual sister of the Black Power concept. As such, it envisions an art that speaks directly to the needs and aspirations of Black America" (Neal, 1972:272).

A few years later he further explained the concept in an essay entitled "The Black Arts Movement" in *The Black Aesthetic*. The movement was described in its introduction

> as a corrective--a means of helping black people out of the polluted mainstream of Americanism and offering logical, reasoned arguments as to why African American writers should not desire to join the ranks of a Norman Mailer or a William Styron. To be an American writer is to be an American, and for black

people, there should no longer be honor attached to either position. (Gayle, Jr. 1971:xxiii)

Neal's essay reinforced the position outlined in the publication's introduction. He agreed that survival was at stake for black people--culturally, ethnically and spiritually.

As African Americans in Watts, Harlem, Detroit, Philadelphia, Hartford, and other cities across the nation responded with "fire" to the weight of oppression and white racism that had made their existence on this continent unbearable, the black artist was encouraged by Neal "to purify by fire" the old symbols, songs, myths, legends, and history that was the lost birthright of African peoples. Ethics, he explained, should not be divorced from aesthetics, and art must not be separate from black people and their own spiritual groundings.

The Black Power and Black Arts movements made a lasting impression on several men, women, and children who would later become leading voices in the African American's social and political struggles of the 1980s and 1990s. The challenge was and still is to "move the agenda" and guide the African American community--further away from Eurocentricism and toward Afrocentricism, self-determination, and ultimately, liberation.

Various educational leaders, including members of the National Alliance of Black School Educators (NABSE), with classical African civilizations such as Ancient Kemet (Egypt) as their model, expressed their determination "to save the African American child." They redefined the general concept of excellence in education as one that "prepares the African American student for *self-knowledge*, and to become a contributing problem solving member of his or her community, and in the wider world as well. No child can be ignorant of or lack respect for his or her own cultural group and meet others in the world on an equal footing, declared the members of this organisation" (NABSE, 1984).

The general purpose of this paper is to examine two African American literary geniuses, Zora Neale Hurston and James Baldwin, and two of their literary works created prior to the flowering of the Black Arts Movement, which was a precursor of the Afrocentric critical approach. This approach or method, according to Molefi Asante, "pursues a world voice distinctly African-centered in relationship to external phenomena ... the enterprise is framed by cosmological, epistemological, axiological, and aesthetic issues" (Asante, 1990:8).

4. African American Literature through an Afrocentric Paradigm

My overarching objective is to demonstrate an analytical method that utilizes an Afrocentric paradigm to reassess a literary legacy which will help to center African American youth by reconnecting them with their African and African American cultural heritage. In the 1990s, the survival of our youth has become the number one agenda issue, along with the cultural, spiritual, and ethical survival of African American families and communities within the larger society.

Hurston's masterpiece *Their Eyes Were Watching God*, and Baldwin's incendiary and polemical essay, "The Fire Next Time," will be analyzed; and each author will be "located" within the individual and collective African American historical and cultural aesthetic. An Afrocentric assessment of each's literary legacy will not only help today's youth and adults understand their own place on this cultural continuum, but also will help them identify some of the survival techniques that have been successful in the African American past and may be useful in the future.

To "locate" Hurston when she wrote *Their Eyes Were Watching God* in 1937 and was identified as one of the most prolific "flowers" of the Harlem Renaissance's literary explosion, one would have to go back to the turn of the century, to the rural South, and to Eatonville, Florida. It was there, in the all-black town in the heart of Dixie that Zora was born and began to form the cosmology, or worldview, that would later frame her creative expression.

While other African Americans living in the South were struggling for survival in the face of physical and mental repression and the loss of most of the rights obtained after the Civil War, Zora's childhood struggles had been very different and much more personal. She was one of eight children, a bright, high-spirited girl, the daughter of a sharecropper and "jack-leg" preacher. She struggled to find meaning in her life in the poor, rural, all-black village of her birth, where young ladies were supposed to be much less opinionated and less precocious than her own personality dictated.

Even though she lost the most important person in her life, her mother, at a very early age, she was determined to get an education and locate that "place in the sun" that her mother had convinced her she would one day find. Zora was certain that this was to be her destiny. It is quite possible that this drive to find her true self had come from somewhere deep within her African ancestral heritage, from a place and time when black women walked side by side with their men, ruled empires, and led armies into battle. This was part of her distant past that she never learned about in school or in her family's modest home, but somehow sensed anyway.

She grew up with loving memories of her people's religious fervor, their colorful stories, customs, music, and dramatic expression. When she left the South to follow her dreams, for an education and a new life, she took Eatonville with her, in heart and memory. She would eventually re-create the black world of her childhood in the unique pageantry of her folklore.

From an early age the few whites who directly touched her life were encouraging and supportive; she therefore refused to accept the greater reality of white oppression, racism, and brutality that so many of her people could not overlook in their daily existence in every region of the nation, including the South.

James Baldwin, although he was born a generation later than Hurston, in 1924, and reared in Harlem, New York, had no illusions about the racism, oppression, and discrimination that engulfed the masses of Harlem. Five years before he was born, the NAACP had led a mass demonstration of marchers through the streets of Harlem to protest the lynching and violence against African Americans that had become so common throughout the nation that the phrase "the Red Summer of 1919," had come into existence. As Baldwin grew up he was aware of this aspect of his country's history, and he was also aware of other cultural and social realities that made life in the nation's urban centers less than pleasant for members of his race. The "renaissance," that drew Zora to Harlem and to its world of optimism, intellectualism, and cultural elitism was occurring in the same city within a city that Baldwin viewed from cramped tenements, typified by crime, violence, and poverty (Huggins, 1971). By the time Baldwin celebrated his fifth birthday, the nation would have plunged into an economic depression that severely impacted the masses of African Americans that had already been struggling on the lowest rungs of the nation's economic ladder.

Like Hurston, Baldwin found refuge between the pages of the many books he read while helping his mother take care of his eight younger brothers and sisters. "He was often found with a child in one hand and a book in the other. The first book he read was *Uncle Tom's Cabin*, followed by numerous other works borrowed from the library on 135th Street, and devoured as if they were some type of soul food (Eckman, 1966:16)." Also like Hurston, Baldwin's stepfather was a minister, but a man so full of his own psychological problems that he could only alienate the stepson who wanted so desperately to love him.

The many years he spent in the Pentecostal Church led Baldwin into the pulpit at the tender age of fourteen years. For three years he preached in storefront churches and gained a reputation for his powerful delivery and great skill in spreading the gospel. These years allowed him to escape from the sins of the streets that he feared would claim him and destroy his life as it had done so many of his neighbors and friends. The drugs, alcohol, easy sex, and crime were ever-present antidotes for the harsh realities that life in the North's urban ghettos represented.

Instead of a strong love of the Lord and a personal need to be filled with the Holy Spirit, Baldwin's ministry was dominated by the love/hate relationship he shared with his stepfather and the young boy's need to compete with his tormentor on his own special turf--the church pulpit. Rather than buttressing the anger and resentment that was his constant childhood companion, his church experiences merely increased his bitterness.

Both Hurston's and Baldwin's early connections with the church were natural (or perhaps unnatural) outgrowths of their lost African ancestral heritage. In this hazy realm of what Larry Neal termed their "Epic Memory," when African peoples created "civilization," gave "light" to the world, and built temples and pyramids in the Nile Valley, their spirituality would have been the common denominator of their lives. As Hilliard, Carruthers, and Karenga have demonstrated through their efforts to restore the Ancient Kemetic sacred texts, Baldwin and Hurston's life objectives would have been to become "God-like" (Hilliard, 1984; Karenga, 1984; and Carruthers, 1984). In their off-centered worlds in the African diaspora, their spiritual educations still made a very powerful impact on their cosmological views, and this was reflected in their literary works.

While initial success in creative writing sent Hurston to Harlem's literary scene to develop her craft as she furthered her education, Baldwin was compelled to leave Harlem and the United States to grow in his chosen field: "It was November, 1948, Armistice Day. I left because I was a writer. I had discovered writing and I had a family to save. I had only one weapon to save them, my writing. And I couldn't write in the United States" (Gates, 1985).

By the time Hurston wrote *Their Eyes were Watching God*, she was well on the road that would reflect her prolific career as a leading voice in the twentieth-century African American literary scene:

> From 1925, when she first arrived in New York, "like a far-flung watermelon" to capture the illustrious *Opportunity Magazine* literary awards in the short story and play categories, to 1948, when she dropped a stitch and let slip her 4th novel. Zora produced over a dozen published stories, 2 original musicals, 1 libretto for a folk opera, several articles on voodoo, several on language and lore, 2 major collections of African American folklore (tales, raps, stories, songs, jokes, riddles, recipes, remedies, and other wisdoms), 4 novels and 1 autobiography. She'd traveled throughout the South, the Caribbean, Hollywood, Honduras, collected, lectured, won accolades, got talked about, was plagiarized, and went right on stepping. (Bambara, 1981)

In addition to her unique, controversial, and enlightening personal life, Hurston's fifth major publication, and what has been called her best novel, offers teachers of African American literature myriad instructional avenues for reaching teenage youth of the 1990s. The major themes of the book, feminism and black self-determinism, continue to be important issues impacting today's youth and adults alike. Undoubtedly, Hurston's development of the folkloric themes and motifs she had become familiar with during her childhood in Eatonville will provide the richest vehicles for reconnecting African Americans with their rich cultural heritage--a heritage that was rooted in African soil and flowered in spite of many oppressive forces in its new world reality.

Their Eyes Were Watching God is Janie Crawford's personal story and "journey to autonomy and spiritual liberation that is told to her friend Pheoby in the form of a reminiscence . . . Janie is the tale-teller and her story is a consciously artistic act, one in which she imposes order and meaning on the material of her life" (Crabtree, 1985). Hurston's use of a story within a story is at once a reflection of a major motif in the African aesthetic--circularity--and at the same time, a re-creation of the African and African American folk tradition of storytelling itself. Just as Zora began her own life's journey in a rural southern town, went out into the world to find herself and returned as a young anthropologist to study and collect the rich traditions of black southern life, Janie Crawford's life follows a similar circular developmental pattern.

4. African American Literature through an Afrocentric Paradigm

The very complex story that Janie unravels for Pheoby begins with the abrupt ending of Janie's childhood when the girl entered adolescence, and sexual curiosity and romantic musings became part of her life. Her grandmother's overwhelming fear that the girl would be misused by men, just as she had been misused by her master during slavery, and as Janie's own mother, her daughter, had been misused during the years immediately following Emancipation, directed the older woman to force Janie into a loveless sham of a marriage with Logan Killicks.

In the character of Janie's grandmother, Hurston was able to present the rich poetic imagery of the folk speech beside the misguided African American worldview that doomed the black female to an untenable Catch-22 reality:

> Honey, de white man is the ruler of everything as afar as ah been able tuh find out. Maybe it's some place way off in de ocean where de black man is in power, but we don't know nothin' but what we see. So de white man throw down de load and tell the nigger man tuh pick it up. He pick it up because he have to, but he don't tote it. He hand it to his women folks. De nigger woman is de mule uh de world so far as Ah can see. Ah been prayin' fuh it tah be different wid you. Lawd, Lawd. Lawd! (29)

Even though she refused to admit it for nearly a quarter of a century, Janie hated her grandmother who unwittingly had "taken the biggest thing God had made, the horizon--and pinched it into such a little bit of a thing that she could tie about her grand-daughter's neck tight enough to choke her" (29).

Refusing to become Logan Killicks's "mule," Janie jumped at the first opportunity to escape by running off with the handsome and ambitious Joe Starks. She felt certain that her second marriage to the man who was destined to become the first mayor of Eatonville, Florida, would bring her the love and happiness every young woman needed to fill her horizon.

She learned very quickly that Joe had his own ideas of where a woman's place should be, and this was as much on a shelf as her grandmother's vision would have placed her in a cage. To Joe Starks, who became the leading citizen in Eatonville, but with white inspired values, Janie was reduced to an attractive ornament to reflect his own accomplishments and sense of self-importance. Unhappily, Janie surrenders to this subservient role and spends the next twenty years on the outside looking into the highly colorful and dramatic folk life that Hurston depicts for the readers. The rich oral tradition reflected in African American folk life is revealed through the various townspeople who congregated on the front porch of the Stark's general store.

Through an Afrocentric analysis, teachers will be able to demonstrate the oral continuum in the rap songs, street poetry, and 1930s style "dozen playing" that continues to flourish in African American communities throughout the diaspora. The rhythm of such dialogue is a reflection of the African aesthetic synthesized and transformed in the diaspora.

Other aspects of this rich oral tradition are evident in the collective play-acting and "serious" speech-making occasions that are dramatized in the story. In one scene the structured improvisation element of the aesthetic was demonstrated when Tony attempted to give a speech to welcome the Starks to the Eatonville community. He was chastised by his friends for not including the "proper references" in his speech:

> "You can't welcome a man and his wife 'thout you make comparison to Isaac and Rebecca at the well, else it don't show de love between 'em if you don't."

> "Everybody agreed that that was right. It was sort of pitiful for Tony not to know he couldn't make a speech without saying that. Some tittered at his ignorance." (68)

Hurston wanted to make it clear that there was a special order and ethos to this unique African American community, one that embodied the collective spirit of its members. Janie was prevented from participating in this ethos because her husband decided that it was "too common" a reality for his wife. As an outsider, Janie was forced into a lonely existence in the midst of much joy and communal spirit. Houston Baker has stated that "Janie can be interpreted as a singer who (ontogenetically) recapitulates the blues experience of all black women treated as 'mules of the world.' She is, indeed, a member of a community of black women. And the expressiveness that she provides in her bleak situation in a racist South is equivalent to the song of sleepy John Estes" (Baker, 1984).

Not until Joe Starks dies from a dysfunctional kidney is Janie finally able to "let her hair down." She is no longer the young girl that ran off with Joe Starks so many years before, but she is a vibrant and

4. African American Literature through an Afrocentric Paradigm 45

handsome woman and when Vergible "Tea Cake" Woods saunters into her store one afternoon and captures Janie's long neglected heart and spirit, her life is changed forever. "Tea Cake expands Janie's horizons literally and figuratively by transplanting her to the Everglades to mingle with other itinerant workers, as well as by simply encouraging her to determine her own work and to take part in the 'play'--the music, dancing and gaming--of the workers in the 'muck' (Crabtree, 1985:57)."

In "Tea Cake," the handsome, black, fun-loving, and sexually liberated young man, ten years her junior, Janie at last has found the love of her life, as well as her own true self--the self that she has had to lock away for so many years: "Janie looked down on him and felt a self-crushing love. So her soul crawled out from its hiding place" (192).

Hurston's figurative and poetic language reached new heights when she wrote the dialogue shared between Tea Cake and Janie. High school students, with their appreciation for romance, will find these exchanges between this black man and woman particularly rewarding.

Down in the "muck" of the Everglades, where the newlyweds go to find work, several other folk experiences and folk characters are portrayed. The reader is shown how African Americans have been able to survive in spite of the most miserable poverty and repression. Hurston described the permanent transients who poured into the area to find work each picking season as "people ugly from ignorance and broken from being poor. All night long the jooks clanged and clamored. Pianos living, three lifetimes in one. Blues made and used right on the spot. Dancing, fighting, singing, crying, laughing, winning and losing every hour" (197). These people work hard and play hard. They know no other realities.

In the tragic flood scene that pits these mere mortals against the forces of nature, Hurston universalized her characters and their collective social experiences. At moments like these, when death seems to be imminent, only the Supreme Being can provide the answers. As Janie and Tea Cake huddled together with their friends, drawing comfort from one another as they waited out the storm, "they seemed to be staring at the dark, but *their eyes were watching God*" (236). This spiritual aspect of the African American folk experience is an ever-present element. Its roots can be traced to the African continent, where men and women were committed to living in harmony with nature and with God.

Tea Cake's tragic death sends Janie back to Eatonville. They have shared a year and a half that has meant more to Janie than the previous forty or so years of her life. As she sits on her back porch, telling her life story to her friend Pheoby, we know that her life has come full circle, and at last she is content, for she has found herself.

Hurston produced the bulk of her life's work when the Harlem Reniassance was ending due to the economic pressures of the Great Depression. She, in a sense, along with Langston Hughes and other stars of the period, was a link between this era and the next major period of American and African American history and literary development.

Richard Wright, who became the outstanding literary voice following the Renaissance period, reached out a hand and helped young James Baldwin to climb onto the literary stage. Baldwin became the major African American voice of the following era--the Civil Rights/Black Power era.

Although he left the United States in 1948, clutching his one-way ticket and vowing never to return to the land of his birth, Baldwin would in fact return again and again. His first return occurred four years after his first departure. He had completed his first novel, *Go Tell It on the Mountain*, and he came home to show it to his family and sell the work to a publisher. As soon as his goal was accomplished, Baldwin fled the country again.

In 1954, the year that Rosa Parks and young Rev. Martin Luther King, Jr.'s names would become household words, Baldwin was back again. This time his play *The Amen Corner* needed to be produced; and he had to find a publisher for his second novel, *Giovanni's Room*.

Throughout these years, writing for magazines, journals, and newspapers, with high periods and low periods, Baldwin continued to make a living from his writing and grew to become a major American literary voice. This voice, from the beginning to the end of his career, remained as angry, accusing, and unrelenting as Hurston's had been humorous and nonconfrontational. He was also very much like her, for the circular motif, reflective of the African aesthetic, would also typify the journey of his life.

In 1984 Baldwin had looked back over the sixty or so years of his life and reflected on these early years of his career: "I find it hard to re-create the journey. I was trying to discover myself--on the whole, . . . I was also trying to avoid myself--there was certainly, between that self and me, the accumulated rock of ages . . . a part of my inheritance. In order to claim my inheritance, it was necessary to challenge and claim the rock. Otherwise the rock claimed me" (Baldwin, 1984:xi).

4. African American Literature through an Afrocentric Paradigm

Throughout his career he reached back into his childhood years spent in the church to find images and inspiration for the burden he had chosen to lift. In accepting the inheritance--his birthright as an American of African descent--he was making it his personal job (or so it seemed at times) to "civilize" the white man who claimed to be the so-called civilizer of the world. He turned the tables and exposed the underside of the false myths and legends of absolute power and racial superiority that they continued to create as they tried to dehumanize the African. Instead, their brutality, inhumanity, and uncivility was exposed over and over again, so that they, along with the rest of the world, could not forget it.

In a similar manner Hurston had reminded her fellow Americans that African peoples, even those struggling to survive in the depths of this nation's "muck," had a voice of their own, a soul, a spirit, a mythology, a history, and a humanity that would not just die or be denied. She did this, in her own way, through the collective voice and folklore of her people. She did it for herself, but she also did it for the future generations of African peoples, off-center and disconnected, somewhere in their diasporan wasteland.

James Baldwin did the very same thing, but he did it his way. His way was to use his enemy's own language, his own mythology, aesthetic, and religion to force him/her to recognize the African's humanity. Many different words have been used by various critics to describe Baldwin's use of the white man's idiom--"forceful, clear, direct, accusatory, eloquent in its passion, logical, filled with fierce pride and dogged hope, clean, honest, logical, powerful, and angry"--to name only a few. Claude Lewis, an old friend of Baldwin, said it best when he paid tribute to him following his death: "He was an unusually gifted and authentic writer and thinker, a permanent performer that America had produced despite its poisonous attitude toward blacks. He was, as it turned out, a joke on racism"

Hurston wrote a feminist work (*Their Eyes*) long before the women's movement reached its peek in the 1960s. She was an innovator and pathfinder. Baldwin also refused to be caged within a mold designated for "a Negro writer." His second, and most controversial novel, *Giovanni's Room*, featured only white characters and championed homosexual rights. This was many years before homosexuals "opened closet doors" and stepped out for full public view, and unfortunately, public condemnation as well. His previous work, and his first collection of essays, *Notes of a Native Son*, had catapulted him into a reputation as "the most valuable literary property in the country." Baldwin was riding the crest of his national (and international) popularity when he published *The Fire Next Time*. He had been returning frequently to his home country to support its ever-growing Civil Rights Movement, in a sense becoming its official literary spokesperson. This collection of essays was viewed by many as another dimension of the African American struggle for equal rights and justice under the law. Frederick Douglass had told his people many years before that "nothing would be gained by Africans in this country without a struggle." Baldwin had merely added his own God-given gift of using his enemy's language as yet another weapon in his people's collective struggle.

As the nation and the world looked toward the violence, repression, and protest actions that unveiled the core of American racism, Baldwin's voice was heard reminding one and all that the North and its many urban ghettos were also extensions of this same disease. Yet Larry Neal and other youthful members of the Black Power and Black Nationalist movements criticized Baldwin and others they considered to be part of the "Negro establishment" for fighting for integration into the American mainstream:

> Baldwin's problem was that he was the conscience of a movement (civil rights) which has as its goal integration into a dying system, instead of the destruction of the white idea of the world. In *The Fire Next Time*, he begins to understand certain very basic things about black people in this society, the most important of which is that the only thing whites have that black people should want is power. (Neal, 1966:60-61)

Neal considered Baldwin a failure for focusing on morality as the central issue of the American race problem. He felt that Baldwin was in a sense a traitor to his people for not using "the traditional aspects of Afro-American culture" to speak directly to black people, not for them, but to their psychological and physical oppressor. It was not enough for this younger generation for Baldwin to remind whites that "fire" would destroy their world if they did not heed his warnings and make needed changes. They wanted him to go ahead and light the fire, not offer chances for redemption.

What Larry Neal and the others did not understand (and Afrocentricity teaches us this) was that Baldwin's emphasis on morality and his constant struggle to find truth and justice were very much a part of the African tradition. These features of Baldwin's cosmology had a deeper structure and possibly an Ancient Kemetic source. In *Kemet Afrocentricity and Knowledge*, Asante explains the concept of Ma'at, "a social, ethical, and rhetorical term that becomes a symbol of the search for existential peace and central notion in the questing life" (88-91). Rightness, righteousness, justice and truth (morality) were all features of Ma'at. Baldwin's search for his identity could very well have been the same search for unity that his ancient ancestors in the Nile Valley had struggled to attain thousands of years ago.

The Christian ethic that permeates his "Fire Next Time" essays also has a deeper structure. Karenga's and Carruther's translations of the ancient Kemetic sacred books reveal that all of the so-called great religions of the modern world, Christianity, Judaism, Muslim, for example, borrowed tenets from this primary source of spiritual inspiration.

Baldwin could not truly be called a traitor to his race when his words were written to elevate all of humanity, even when his focus seemed to be the white oppressor. C. Tsehloane Keto reminds us that the Afrocentric method offers a humanizing approach to social science: "It is a self-disciplining perspective; it creates, on the one hand, a self-affirming criterion of values and, it embodies, on the other hand, a practical concern for the positive welfare of Africans and all of humanity (Keto, 1989:31)."

Using a train metaphor to further develop this concept, Keto described African Americans as people on a station platform trying to convince the conductor of "Train America" that they are entitled to a seat on the approaching train. They become aware that the destination of that train is as important as a seat, especially if it is leading toward social disaster: "To be true to their fellow travellers, to themselves and to what they have learned from their own history, they have a duty to raise questions about the final destination of train America, in short, they must play the part of social critics who exhort America to live up to its best ideals (1-32)." James Baldwin had assumed this human/social responsibility for many years, and in spite of the bitterness and anger that threatened to overwhelm him, he never let that anger destroy his own humanity.

This is a very important lesson that needs to be taught to today's youth, who must individually and collectively make many important decisions about the path they will follow in life. For those who were not blessed with an articulate father or uncle who can help them make these decisions, Baldwin's first essay in *The Fire Next Time*, "My Dungeon Shook," written in the form of a loving and personal letter to his own nephew, will serve this purpose. Its powerful message is as needed today as it was when it was first written over a quarter of a century ago.

The letter can help African American youth understand that the various injustices that may be inflicted on them can only cause permanent damage if they accept them as just: "You can only be destroyed by believing that you really are what the white world calls a *nigger*." He goes on to explain that knowing their history will help them understand that there is really no limit to where they can go in life. This history also demonstrates that it has been our love for one another that has carried us through past storms. "And now you must survive because we love you, and for the sake of your children and your children's children."

Both Hurston and Baldwin have returned to the world of spirits, but their literary works remain as ancestral gifts that must be passed on as legacies for African American (and other) youth. The circle must not be broken and an Afrocentric paradigm may be used to spread the continuum into and beyond the twenty-first century.

To truly understand *The Fire Next Time* and *Their Eyes Were Watching God*, teachers must help students understand the African American man and woman who wrote them. To understand James Baldwin and Zora Neale Hurston it is necessary to "locate" them as individuals within the broader historical and cultural context of the entire black (African) experience. Asa Hilliard, Molefi Asante, and Maulana Karenga, Carol Aisha Blackshire, as well as as many other Afrocentric scholars, remind us that this experience is even longer than human civilization. If any aspect of this long and collective black experience will help today's youth find meaning in the complicated world of the 1990s, teachers should not hesitate to use it.

REFERENCES

Asante, Molefi Kete. (1990) *Kemet, Afrocentricity and Knowledge.* Trenton, N.J.: Africa World Press.

Baker, Houston A., Jr. (1984) *Ideology, and Afro-American Literature.* Chicago: The University of Chicago Press.

Baldwin, James. (1964) *The Fire Next Time.* New York: Dell Publishing Company.

Baldwin, James. (1984) *Notes of a Native Son.* New York: Beacon Press Books. (First published in 1955.)

Bambara, Toni Cade. (1981) "Some Forward Remarks" In *The Sanctified Church: The Folklore Writings of Zora Neale Hurston*, pp. 136-155. Berkeley, Calif.: Turtle Island Press.

Carruthers, Jacob. (1984) *Essays in Ancient Egyptian Studies*. Los Angeles: University of Sankore Press.

Crabtree, Claire. (1985) "The Confluence of Folklore, Feminism and black Self-Determination." In Zora Neale Hurston's *Their Eyes Were Watching God*. Southern Literary Journal 17, (2): 54-66.

Eckman, Tern Marja. (1966) *The Furious Passage of James Baldwin*. New York: M. Evans.

Gates, Henry Louis, Jr. (1985) "An Interview with Josephine Baker and James Baldwin." *The Southern Review* 21 (30).

Gayle, Addison, Jr., ed. (1971) *The Black Aesthetic*. New York: Doubleday and Company.

Hilliard Asa III. (1984) "Equity and Excellence in a Culturally Diverse Setting." *Eastern Pennsylvania Spring Regional Workshop--Equity and Excellence: A Response to a Nation at Risk*. Harrisburg, PA.

Huggins, Nathan Irvin. (1971) *Harlem Renaissance*. New York: Oxford University Press.

Hurston, Zora Neale. (1978) *Their Eyes Were Watching God*. Urbana: University of Illinois Press. (First published in 1937.)

Hurston, Zora Neale. (1981) *The Sanctified Church: The Folklore Writings Of Zora Neale Hurston*. Berkeley: Turtle Island Press.

Karenga, Maulana. (1984) *The Husia Sacred Wisdom of Ancient Egypt*. Los Angeles: University of Sankore Press.

Keto, C. Tsehloane. (1989) *The Africa Centered Perspective of History*. Blackwood, N.J.: K. A. Publications.

Lewis, Claude. (1987) "The Lessons Learned from James Baldwin." *Philadelphia Inquirer*, December 14, editorial page.

National Alliance of Black School Educators, Inc. (NABSE) (1984). "Saving the African American Child." Prepared by the *Task Force on Black Academic and Cultural Excellence*, November 1984.

Neal, Larry (1972). "The Black Arts Movement." In Addison Gayle, Jr. ed., *The Black Aesthetic*. New York: Doubleday and Company.

Neal, Larry. (1989) *Visions of a Liberated Future: Black Arts Movement Writings*. New York: Thunder's Mouth Press.

II

Language Realities:
Studies in Modern Societies

5

Cultural and Linguistic Transitions: The Comparative Case of African Americans and Ethnic Minorities in Germany
Carol Aisha Blackshire-Belay

The richly endowed linguistic and literary imagination of the African American community can be traced to a number of factors. Some of these factors have been debated since the works of E. Franklin Frazier, the sociologist, and Melvill Herskovits, the anthropologist. Frazier had held the position that African Americans retained almost no aspect of African culture, whereas Herskovits had written in his book *The Myth of the Negro Past* that African Americans retained a considerable legacy from Africa and that the enslavement did not eradicate all of the influences of Africa. Other factors exist, to be sure, in the development of the linguistic and literary imagination of the African American. These factors are not debatable in terms of their influence on the literary and linguistic imagination of the community. They include a unique community of speakers, similar cultural interference from outside the speech community, and religious language and symbolism. Of course there are profound social factors, such as the migration experience.

One could speak of the migration influence in terms of the forced migration from Africa to the Americas, the migration of many families in search of relatives immediately after the Civil War, or the more recent economic migration from the South to the North. It is this latter migration that holds an interest for this paper inasmuch as there are similarities between this Great Migration and others in the contemporary world. In effect, it was an economic migration with implications for the modification of culture, including particularly language and speech patterns.

Any discussion of cultural and linguistic transitions begins with the theme of rural-to-urban migration of population groups and the problems that arise as a result of this movement. This paper shall provide a preliminary study of the migration process and its impact on both language and culture of those who have migrated. It will be a unique comparison, one never before attempted: a comparative analysis between African Americans and ethnic minority groups in contemporary German society. I shall examine the migration of ethnic minorities from the most rural parts of Europe to the industrialized German cities in the western part of Germany with that of the migration of African Americans from the rural South to the urban cities of the North.

In a purely academic sense the cultural-linguistic examination of a given society is neither more nor less important than that of any other. Population groups, however, are rarely studied from a purely academic point of view. Russian and Chinese studies in the 1950s and 1960s, Black studies in the late 1960s, and German studies in the 1970s have provided knowledge and been used to establish social and political policy. But they have yet to be studied on a comparative basis. Such factors as housing, integration, segregation, assimilation, location, and types of jobs and services as they relate to the needs of people in society are dealt with in the countries in the world on an individual basis.

The cultural and linguistic transitions of Americans of African descent in the United States begin with the "forced migration" (enslavement) from the continent of Africa, the "economic migration" from the rural South to the urban North, to the problems facing us in our communities today. There is a growing need for African Americans to closely examine other ethnic minorities to discover how others cope with similar problems. This paper is an attempt to help meet these needs. I propose not only to present the general socio-cultural and linguistic situations affecting African Americans and ethnic minorities in Germany, but to bring the reader closer to some of the human beings who know the fear, experience the hope, and live the confusion that the process of human migration brings.

AFRICAN AMERICAN RURAL-URBAN MIGRATION PATTERNS

When we concern ourselves with the greatest change in the black population, it is not in numbers but in location, away from the South and the farms and into the cities of the North. While it is true that most of the early economic migrants went to cities in the Northeast, later the northcentral and western states gradually increased their share of black migrants. It was during the years 1860 to 1940 that the northeast and the northcentral regions received 90 percent of the black out-migration from the South. But in the years after 1940 the migration of blacks to the West increased, making up more than 20 percent of the total migration of southern blacks.[1]

Although the North has remained the major destination of blacks migrating from the South, the proportion of the migrants who head westward has increased. In 1970 the West was the destination of 22 percent of the blacks migrating from the South.[2]

Migration flows during this long period from 1860 to 1970 were not uniform. The small, steady migrations prior to 1910 were followed by the dramatic Great Migration of 1915. It was this migration that marked a significant change in the distribution of blacks in the United States. Most, if not all, of this increase in the northern, urban black population originated in the rural areas of the South. Attracted by better jobs in northern industries and more freedom, African Americans sought a better life in cities like Detroit, Cleveland, and St. Louis.

Until recently, the migration of blacks from the South to the North and West is considered to be the primary reason for the declining proportion of the black population in the South. In fact, migration to the North has often depopulated small black towns in the South. But it should be noted that prior to 1910 black migrants moved shorter distances and tended to stay within the South. It was only later that the movements were longer and to northern cities further away.

---

[1] Black population from 1790 to 1970 was taken from various Bureau of the Census reports.

[2] Recent studies indicate a migration wave back to the South once again for African Americans.

ETHNIC MINORITIES' EUROPEAN RURAL-URBAN MIGRATION PATTERNS

Max Frisch, a prominent Swiss author once said in reference to the recruitment of workers from other countries to Germany the following: "Man suchte Arbeitskräfte, aber da kamen Menschen." ["A foreign work force was sought, but human beings came instead."] This statement is extremely accurate in assessing the situation of ethnic minorities as workers recruited to industrialized Germany. It is to them that the German term *Gastarbeiter* (guest workers) applies, or to other workers in similiar situations. Germany has experienced two previous periods of foreign worker immigration (1871-1914 and 1939-1944) primarily from Eastern and Southern Europe (Herbert, 1986). The recent wave of *Gastarbeiter* immigration, which began in the late 1950s, is ethnically, linguistically, and culturally much more diverse. Foreign migration to the Federal Republic of Germany has had several remarkable features: its late beginning, its extremely rapid growth, and its character as highly organized labor migration.[3]

In 1945, West Germany and West Berlin had considerable unemployment, due to the wartime destruction and economic disorganization. In addition, eight million expellees from the lost eastern provinces added to the labor surplus. But economic recovery after the 1948 currency reform was so rapid that the unemployed and the expellees were soon absorbed into the labor force. A further source of labor was provided by the refugees from the German Democratic Republic who came to the Federal Republic throughout the fifties--there were about three million of them by 1961. This group too was rapidly integrated into the economy, and by the late fifties serious labor shortages were being felt (Castles and Kosack, 1985).

The German government concluded its first agreement on the recruitment and placement of foreign workers with Italy at the end of 1955. As labor needs grew, the German government concluded recruitment agreements with additional countries: Spain and Greece in 1960, Turkey in 1961, Portugal in 1964, and Yugoslavia in 1968. By the autumn of 1970 the foreign labor force totaled over two million. But

---

[3] The Federal Republic of Germany refers here to the western part of the country prior to unification of both the East and the West.

5. African Americans and Ethnic Minorities in Germany

because of the booming economy, Germans still considered the foreign population to be there on a temporary basis. One recalls all too vividly how on September 10, 1964 the German media announced to the public that the millionth guest worker from Portugal had been employed. He was greeted at the *Kölner Bahnhof* by a cheerful crowd, champagne was poured, and the worker received a moped from the German government as a gift. I have often wondered whatever happened to this particular worker. As one would say, this worker, like the majority of the so-called *Gastarbeiter*, "wore his welcome out." By 1973, the German government decided to put an end to this recruitment of foreign workers by initiating what was called the *Ausländer Anwerbestopp* (end of foreign recruitment).

Finally with the publication of Günter Wallraff's 1985 book entitled *Ganz Unten* (totally at the bottom), the German population was finally forced to address some of the major issues confronting the post-World War II recruited work force of foreign workers in its society. Günter Wallraff, a German journalist who was relatively active politically, had become known as someone who would go to any length to uncover wrongdoings within contemporary German society. In *Ganz Unten* Wallraff did it again! He disguised himself as a Turkish worker, sought employment in places where large numbers of foreigners were employed, and revealed in his best seller the trials and tribulations of this population group. There was great protest from the German community. He was accused of publishing falsehoods and exaggerating the facts. His life was threatened and ultimately Wallraff was forced to seek asylum in another country. In doing so he was able to experience firsthand the prejudice, discrimination, and injustice that ethnic minorities have to deal with every moment of their lives. Many readers have come to compare Wallraff's book with John Howard Griffin's *Black Like Me* (1961). It is the similarity in the content of these written texts that I seek to compare, discuss, and analyze in considering the dilemma of migrant workers and their families, both African Americans in the United States and ethnic minorities in the western part of Germany today.

In western Germany the post-war group of ethnic minorities is made up of those people who emigrated in the 1960s. During this period of economic growth, some industrialized countries started to recruit workers from the relatively poor Mediterranean countries. In Switzerland, Germany, the Netherlands, and Belgium many people from southern Italy, Turkey, and Morocco arrived in this way. Even after the official recruitment programs were discontinued because of growing unemployment problems in the wealthy countries, the immigration flow did not stop. In general, however, the guest workers did not see themselves as immigrants, they considered their stay a temporary one and planned to return to their native countries when circumstances would permit.

The children of these recruited workers, however, have grown up in Western European countries, speak the local language learned at school, and often do not intend to return to the country in which their parents were born. Thus some characteristics attributed to the first generation of workers are not prevalent among the second and third generations.

The situation described above is clearly different from that in the United States, for example. First, the native inhabitants of the United States constitute an ethnic minority today. Second, the people who are considered to belong to the ethnic majority in studies in the United States have only their (white) skin color in common, not their national or linguistic origin. These people are the descendants of European immigrants from such distinct countries as England, Germany, Poland, Ireland, the Netherlands, or France. Third, the largest minority group, African Americans, did not originally emigrate voluntarily, but was forcefully transported from Africa in the process of enslavement to serve as a labor force. Another difference between African Americans and ethnic minorities in Europe is that African Americans have been living in the United States for almost as many generations as white Americans; the minority-majority situation has existed for centuries.

The fact that the American ethnic situation differs from the European does not mean, however, that the social problems ethnic minorities encounter in Europe are very different from those in the United States. Ethnic stereotypes and racism have developed, and discrimination, both direct and indirect, does occur in Europe as well. In fact, new forms of discrimination are created as the majority population sees the ethnic minorities grow. Because the unification of East and West Germany has lead to increased violence against ethnic minorities, steps have been taken to safeguard them and their families.

MIGRANT SITUATIONS FOR COMPARISION

Although there are obvious differences between a migrant African American family and a migrant family from the southern part of Europe, there are characteristics shared by both. Allow me to cite a number of examples.

Place Names Synonymous with Migrant Groups

There has been the tendency of the majority society to identify American regions with place names, both specific and generic, that have become synonymous with black people. The Black Belt, Coontown, Buttermilk Bottom, Black Bottom, Negro Mountain, Harlem, Watts, Cotton Curtain, ghetto, and inner-city are examples.

The same can be observed among ethnic minorites in German society. "The Orient Express" refers to the subway line that travels to the area of West Berlin Kreuzberg, where a large percentage of the foreign workers live. "The Little Istanbul" or "The Little Ankara" refers to parts of a city where a large percentage of Turks and other minority groups live. And there are many other examples.

Types of Jobs

The primary factor singled out to be the major cause of the continued black migration to the North was the expanded economic opportunities and the hope for better jobs. As we know, there were two types of policies with regard to the hiring of blacks: one was to hire blacks in menial positions, the other was to employ no blacks at all. The majority of black men worked as porters, janitors, teamsters, chauffeurs, elevator operators, waiters, and in other service and general laborer jobs. Black women worked as domestics.

Such jobs were marginal and were replaced by machines or were abolished altogether. It is truly ironic that the intervention of the federal government to improve bad labor conditions in factories--those conditions under which most blacks worked--was a factor in increasing black unemployment.

The majority of migrants in Germany are employed as unskilled or semi-skilled manual workers. They are recruited for the types of work that are no longer taken by indigenous workers. Discriminatory regulations and practices tend to keep immigrants in such jobs. In addition, there are factors intrinsic in the situation of immigrant workers from underdeveloped regions that put them at a disadvantage in an achievement-oriented industrial society: they lack basic education and vocational training.

It is often asserted that migration to Western Europe gives migrants the opportunity to make up for these deficiencies. The employment of immigrant workers is hence seen an an important form of aid to underdeveloped countries, as a former president of the *Bundesanstalt für Arbeit* (German Federal Labour Office) has stated:

> By allowing foreign workers to enter, many people have been given work and a living. This is probably the most important development aid given by the Federal Republic so far. In this context, account must be taken not only of the wages transferred home by foreign workers, but also of the certainly more valuable contribution made by returning migrants. These foreign workers have gained vocational and specialist skills which, in the long run, are even more useful to their countries of origin (Sable, 166).

Whether the migrants and their home countries in fact gain in this way clearly depends on the opportunities for vocational training that are offered to immigrant workers in Western Europe.

Education

Lack of educational opportunities has been an additional factor in the low employment figures in the South and the desire to move North. Improved occupational mobility for blacks depends a great deal on better educational opportunities and manpower development. Vocational training that is available to blacks, for example, is limited to those types of jobs traditionally held by them. Blacks generally received training in courses such as cooking, cleaning, and some mechanics, while whites received training in machine shop, tool and die, and metal working. And the rate of illiteracy of blacks from the rural South to urban North was relatively high.

Illiteracy is a problem for ethnic minority groups in Europe as well. However, it is impossible to obtain figures on the number of illiterates, as no records on the education levels of immigrants are kept. The ability to read and write is of vital importance for everyday life in Western Europe. In addition, it is an essential precondition for vocational training and promotion. In Germany, Switzerland, and Britain, literacy and language teaching is almost entirely arranged by private associations or by individuals. I find the statement by Malcolm X most appropriate in reference to the issue of education for both groups: "The white man's brains that today explore space should have told the slavemaster that any slave, if he is educated, will no longer fear his master. History shows that an educated slave always begins to ask, and next demand, equality with his master" (Malcolm X, 1970:373-374).

The Speech of Migrants

Varieties of language can also signal ethnic identity. In fact, probably the most distinctive feature of ethnicity in (e)migrant groups is not their mother tongue (which may rarely be heard outside the home), but the foreign accent and dialect that characterizes their use of the majority language. In the course of time, many of these features have become established, resulting in new varieties of the majority language. One of the clearest examples of ethnic linguistic variety is provided by the contrast between the speech of African Americans and white Americans. The term *Black English* has been criticized because of its suggestion that all blacks use the same variety and has been replaced in academic study by *Black English vernacular*, (BEV), which refers to the non-standard English spoken by lower-class blacks in urban communities. Afrocentric scholars utilize the term *Ebonics* in reference to this same speech variety.

The foreign workers and the demands of their new life require a level of adaptation that transcends language frontiers, and these workers often do not make an issue of their linguistic identity. On the other hand, their communication skills are usually limited, and the social and educational problems of the receiving country are considerable. Meanwhile due to the need to communicate among themselves, the migrants have developed a form of communication among themselves, which I refer to as *Foreign Workers' German*.

The most obvious problem recurs in every respect of the immigrant's interaction with the receiving society. Once again, it must be remembered that the overwhelming majority of immigrant workers do not speak the language of the new country; nor do they learn it quickly for reasons connected both with their basic education and with their position in society. Ignorance of the language affects the position of the immigrant at work in various ways.

First, it keeps him/her out of more complex jobs, which require constant communication with relatively large numbers of people. Second, ignorance of the language cuts the immigrant off from his work mates. Third, methods used by employers to make possible the efficient utilization of immigrants who do not speak the language may further increase their segregation from other workers. The practice of putting immigrants into ethnic work groups appears to be common in all countries.

The social situation in which ethnic groups find themselves more often than ever lead to a development of a variety of speech identifiable with that group. Linguistically speaking, it is interesting to note similarities in the different linguistic systems, although evidence suggests no language contact of any sort between the different groups.

The Speech Patterns of African Americans: In the speech of many African Americans some of the following grammatical features are of note:[4]

1. No final "s" in the third-person singular present tense (e.g. "he walk" and "she come").

2. No use of forms of the verb "to be" in the present tense, when it is used as a copula, or "linking" verb, within a sentence (e.g. "they real fine" and "if you interested").

3. The use of the verb "to be" to mark habitual meaning, but without changing its grammatical form ("invariant be" (e.g. "sometime they be walking round here").

4. Use of "been" to express a meaning of past activity with current relevance (e.g. "I been know your name").

5. Use of "be done" in the sense of "will have" (e.g. "we be done washed all those cars soon").

6. Use of "it" to express "existential" meaning (cf. standard English "there") (e.g. "it's a boy in my class name Eugene").

7. Use of double negatives involving the auxiliary verb at the beginning of a sentence (e.g. "won't nobody do nothing about that").

The Speech Patterns of Ethnic Minorities: In the speech of ethnic minorities in Europe[5] some of the following features are considered characteristic of their speech:

---

[4] Most researchers are in agreement about the occurrence of these linguistic forms in the speech of many African Americans.

[5] For a more detailed reading on the linguistic behavior of foreign workers in

5. African Americans and Ethnic Minorities in Germany

1. The present indicative forms found in the superstrate are often unmarked for any inflectional categories.[6]

    Ve: dieses Frau rede so oder so oder so
                    3sg   speaks this way and that
          "this woman speaks this way and that way"

    Vst + du bringst du meine   Lotto   auch
                bring 2sg my   lottery numbers too
          "take my lottery numbers along with you"

    V(e)t eine Dusche funktioniert nur an Freitag
                3sg   function only on Friday
          "the shower could only be used on Fridays"

    Ven   nur wissen nix wie   heißt die Teil
          only know   not how   call   3sg
          "I didn't know what the name was for the item"

    V∅   weil   die Klima pass nix   meine Bruda
          because 3sg   agree not   my   brother
          "because the climate did not agree with my brother"

2. Passive-like constructions occur sporadically.

    wir sind so   arztlich untersucht   alle
    1pl are thus physically examined   all
    "we were all physically examined"

3. Discontinuous constituents occur almost always for the present perfect.

Germany, please consult: Carol Aisha Blackshire, *Language Contact: Verb Morphology in German of Foreign Workers*. (Tübingen: Gunter Narr Verlag, 1991).

[6] The following abbreviated forms may be interpreted as follows: 1sg = first-person singular; 2sg = second-person singular; 3sg = third-person singular; 1pl = first-person plural; 2pl = second-person plural; 3pl = third-person plural.

ich hab hier bei Siemens gelernen
1sg have here at Siemens learned
"I learned (my job) here at Siemens"

4. Admixtures and invented forms occur.

   1)Vst + du used for commands
      bringst du   mit   mir
      bring 2sg with   me
      "bring it to me"

   2)The past participle used for the past
      deutsche Leute meine Mutti gefragt
      German people   3sg   asked
      "my mother asked (some) Germans"

Cultural Ties and Traditions

African Americans, whether fully aware of it are not, are closely linked to their cultural ties and traditions from the continent of Africa, among them, the *wake* that takes place generally the evening before the funeral, the *ceremonial tradition* behind practically anything that deserves celebrating, *corn rows*, or *platting of the hair*, or *Egyptian hairstyling* which are indeed African in origin. It is only when the desire arises to identify with the majority society do black people refrain from the tradition. Assimilation is always an obstacle in a society of migrant workers. African Americans have been given this option, as have the ethnic minorities in Germany. In Germany it literally means the more German you become--that is in mannerism, language, and culture--the more likely you will succeed. That has been true in American society for blacks, as well as for other minorities.

In Germany the migrants usually come from societies that are very different from the receiving country. Their behavior is governed by norms, values, and customs that frequently differ widely from those of their fellow workers. Other problems relating to migrants' cultural background are specific to the various ethnic groups. Apart from the general rural background, the sending societies differ widely. Some immigrants come from completely different societies with quite distinct norms and values, often reflected in a different religious culture. Problems have arisen in connection with forms of dress, hygienic habits, eating habits, sexual behavior, manners, attitudes toward supervision, and so on. Such problems have on many occasions been the ostensible cause of efforts to prevent the employment of immigrants in certain workplaces. In other cases there have been calls for the segregation of toilet facilities and canteens.

The Segregated Work Situation

The factors described above frequently combine to cause a situation of relative segregation between immigrant and indigenous workers. It seems useful to distinguish between two basic variants of work situations for immigrants. First, there is the situation in which immigrants are employed in relatively small numbers and are intermingled with indigenous workers. This is usually only possible when the immigrant knows the language and has skills equal to those of the indigenous worker. Second, there is the situation in which large groups of immigrants are employed in certain jobs or departments. Such immigrant workers are usually unskilled and often ignorant of the language. Contact is extremely difficult because of the langauge problem, but matters are made worse by the tendency toward division of the labor force into homogeneous ethnic work groups.

These two situations may be regarded as ideal types. The employment situation of most immigrants lies somewhere between the two. But the majority of immigrants are certainly in work situations closer to the second type. In other words, the typical immigrant work situation is one of relative segregation from indigenous workers. This, of course, has been true of the situation of migrant workers from the rural South to the urban North as well.

A CASE STUDY OF AFRICAN AMERICAN MIGRATION

The following brief case study points out some of the many important problems and principles involved in the migration of African Americans from the rural south to the urban North and West.[7]

Charles was born in an agrarian era. During his youth he worked as a farm boy. Later in his lifetime Charles moved to Birmingham,

---

[7] Based on an interview with Charles, a male acquaintance in Detroit, Michigan, in 1986.

Alabama, where he worked in an iron foundry. Finally, Charles migrated to Detroit, Michigan where he participated in the most exciting and dynamic phase of the Industrial Revolution, the mass production of automobiles.

A friend of Charles took a trip to Detroit during one summer. This friend made the decision to make this city his home and thought he might convince others to follow. Ultimately he was successful in his arguments, and thus Charles prepared to make his trip to Detroit. His friend had promised that he would be able to find him a job because there were so many to go around. When Charles arrived he neither found a job, nor his friend. And the warm weather that his friend talked about was quite different from the climate that he had grown so accustomed to in the South.

Charles said that he discovered the weather to be the coldest and the hardest he had ever known. In fact, he jokingly said, "I didn't realize it could even get that cold." He finally found a place to live, but he never found his friend. He thus was meant to find his way in a "new" city and find a job for himself as well. He ultimately found a job with the Ford Motor Company and remained employed there until his retirement.

After the end of World War I, there was an industrial surge that brought the majority of African Americans into the industrial cities of the North, such as Chicago and Detroit. In Detroit, as in other areas, there were problems of housing. The pertinent question was precisely this: Where would these blacks live? As in most major cities of the time, many areas were totally unwilling to accept blacks. For factory workers at the Ford plant, the Ford family ultimately bought property in a small town called Inkster, where they rented, sublet, and sold to blacks. Charles still lives in Inkster today.

This short narrative points out three major patterns common to African American migration. First, black migration from the rural South to the urban North follows a hierarchy of movement, first to nearby small towns, then to larger cities within the South, and finally to the large cities of the North. Second, there is the tie to home and family that often keeps the migrants moving back to the South for brief periods. Finally, Charles's decision to move to Detroit was made easier by a friend who offered to "put him up" and help him find a job; but as often happens, these good intentions did not work out.

5. African Americans and Ethnic Minorities in Germany

A CASE STUDY OF YUGOSLAVIAN MIGRATION

The following brief case study points out some of the many important problems and principles involved in the migration of southern Europeans from the rural town to the industrialized cities in Europe.[8]

Vladimir was born in the agrarian part of Yugoslavia called Bosnia. He worked in the coal mines there for a number of years and then there was a cave in that killed the majority of workers. He was one of the lucky ones in terms of life, but not in terms of employment. Vladimir was suddenly out of a job. Then something happened. Vladimir, like many others had heard about a place called Germany where there was a lot of work, and his friend told him how money could be found on both the streets and sidewalks.

First he went to West Germany and worked in a shoe factory, but then he was told that if he went to West Berlin, he would earn more. Vladimir did just that, and shortly thereafter he sent for his wife and children. In Berlin he worked in the textile industry. It was a good time for all, and jobs were in abundance. Even though it was not planned for Vladimir's wife to work, she ultimately obtained a job in the same factory as her husband. Soon after Vladimir changed jobs and went to the steel industry, where at the time one could earn more. Today he regrets it because the earnings are much less. Presently his wife is out of work, and they can barely make ends meet. His wife will never find another job because she is illiterate in her native language, as well as in German, and it is simply impossible these days to find a job when you can neither read nor write. In essence this is their life, and they will never return to their own countries, but continue to remain as ethnic minorities in Germany.

PATTERNS OF ORGANIZATION AMONG ETHNIC MINORITIES

The German government's treatment of ethnic minority workers has greatly influenced the migrants' organizational possibilities. For example, these groups are entitled to very limited political participation. Voting in

---

[8] Based on an interview with Vladimir, a Yugoslavian male worker at his home in West Berlin, Germany, in 1990.

local or national elections is impossible.[9] What is even more surprising is that participation in welfare activities is hardly possible. The German charity organizations, called *Wohlfahrtsverbände*, monopolize the welfare and counseling activities of the groups, and have divided the ethnic groups up in the following manner. *Caritas* was assigned the Catholic groups: Italians, Spaniards, Portuguese, and part of the Yugoslavs; *Diakonishes Werk*, the Protestant organization took responsibility of the Greeks; and *Arbeiterwohlfahrt*, the Social Democratic organization, was assigned the Turks and the rest of the Yugoslavs. Thus most state and local authorities feel that they have fulfilled their responsibilities toward the ethnic groups through these assignments.

The development of migrants' organizations and other subcultural structures (Turkish press in Germany, a special video market, minority literature in Germany, ethnic supermarkets, etc.) has helped the migrants cope with their situation. A brief glimpse at such developments should be taken into consideration as a prerequisite for a comparative discussion of such migrant groups in other countries. The concept of "self-help" groups has taken a very strong position in the ethnic communities in Germany. Generally there are several throughout the city, normally each minority group is set aside from the others.[10] Such centers give the people a sense of self-worth and belonging that they generally do not find in the majority society. In addition, and most important, it gives them a place to go. For example, in various parts of many cities in Germany a Turkish woman, for example, has the option of going to *Baçim* (a cultural center for Turkish women) to sit, learn, and discuss topics with other Turkish women in similar situations. A Greek woman might choose to go to *To Spiti* (a cultural center for Greek women), and an Arab woman would likely go to *Al Dar* (a cultural center for Arab women). Men are also welcome at these centers, but there are also other options, such as the ethnic coffee houses or sport centers. In addition, other types of organ-

---

[9] It is interesting to note that in 1987 the new Hamburg coalition government of Social Democrats and Liberals committed itself to the enfranchisement of foreigners in city borough elections. Still today this issue remains highly controversial.

[10] With the rare exception of a center that I am aware of in Berlin that caters to both Yugoslavian and Turkish women.

izations have also been formed by the ethnic minorities, which I shall discuss in the following sections.

Turkish Workers

There are several Turkish organizations, but the strongest one in Germany is the Islamisches Kulturzentrum (IKZ). It is based in Cologne, and in 1982 it had two hundred and ten local centers throughout the country. It is part of the Süleymanli Movement[11] and it stood in opposition to Atatürk's reforms in Turkey. This organization is strongly opposed to the Christian and/or western influences on the lives of the Turks in Germany. Through the organization of Koran courses, IKZ has an important influence on many Turkish children. The organization is not truly political in nature, but it has definite links with other rightist organizations.

Spanish Workers

Spaniards represent the smallest ethnic minority worker group, but they also represent the most successful of the groups in the country. To deal with the problems confronting Spanish migrant families, the first associations were established in the late sixties. In 1973, twenty-four local associations founded the Confederaciä de las Asociaciones Espanolas de Padres de Familia en la RFA. By 1977 ninety local associations had been established. In 1986, one hundred and twenty associations had arisen all over West Germany, with most Spanish family members participating.

The associations' activities include education, lifestyles, juridicial problems of their status in Germany, and other vital questions. For example, when Spanish families came to Germany, there was still a shortage of kindergartens. The Spaniards, like the majority of guest worker groups, wanted bilingual education for their children. These associations were most influential in the school system, supporting full integration of their children into the German schools.[12] Today Spanish students have the highest test scores.

---

[11] This movement was a fundamentalist sect founded by Süleyman Hilmi Tunahan (1888-1959).

[12] German government opposes this because of its policy that the workers and

Greek Workers

The Greek workers have a long and important tradition of emigration, marked by a sense of the continuity of emigration and of the necessity of preserving the national identity. While the Spanish associations in Germany are interested in integration into the German school system, the Greeks insist on the preservation of their "national schools."

In Germany, *Griechische Gemeinden* (koinotita, community) which unite all the leftists, are clearly the most important organizations. (Schlumm, 1984; Katsoulis, 1983) These associations are truly political in nature and have rightist opponents, as well as the Greek Orthodox church. The majority of Greek workers have membership in either the Griechische Gemeinden, the rightist organizations, and the Orthodox church is only a formal organization.

The informal structures of the Greek community should also be taken into consideration. This ethnic group, more than any of the other groups, tends to migrate collectively. That is, the Greek population of a given German city is made up mainly of migrants from a few towns or villages. Greeks also tend to migrate inside Germany to strengthen these kinship and village relations.

Although the organizational patterns differ considerably among the various ethnic minority groups, the differences are all equally important in facilitating adaptation to the environment in Germany. Despite the difficult legal situation, the low social status of the migrant workers, and the lack of material resources, these groups have been able to form significant meaningful autonomous organizations. These organizations seem equally important for the migrants' adaptation to the new situation.

---

their families are on a temporary basis there and should be equipped to go home when they are no longer needed for employment in the country.

Concluding Remarks

African Americans do not recognize themselves as migrants, but practically every black person in the North will likely tell you where his or her family comes from in the South. The older generation is the one to tell us of the experiences during the "hard times." It is this generation that shares similarities with the first generation of adult migrant workers living in Germany today. The subsequent generations are left to deal with the problems created by the migration process.

Although first-generation African Americans might appear to have adjusted "relatively well" to their new linguistic environments, an apparent longing to go "back home" to the quiet life is present among the majority of them. In addition, the wish to return to the South is evident among many black families in the North and West to this day.

It has become quite obvious to African American language scholars that the Great Migration to the North and West in search of better job opportunities, better education for children, and an improvement in the quality of life also meant modifications in the nature, style, and presentation of language. Of course, in the end the various conditions in the North and West dictated new metaphors, similes, and icons. Charles, who had left Alabama to go to Detroit, soon discovered the meaning of "the hawk." And Vladimir, from Bosnia, found in Germany difficulties in explaining himself as he confronted an entirely new language. The language development of both African Americans and ethnic minorities in Germany became by virtue of experience a new revelation based upon new associations, connections, and resources a positive act hammered out on the anvil of the people's collective will.

REFERENCES

Blackshire, Carol Aisha. (1991) *Language Contact: Verb Morphology in German of Foreign Workers*. Tübingen: Gunter Narr Verlag.

Castles, Stephen and Godula Kosack. (1985) *Immigrant Workers and Class Structure in Western Europe*. Oxford: Oxford University Press.

Griffin, John Howard. (1961) *Black Like Me* Boston: Houghton Mifflin Company.

Herbert, Ulrich. (1986) *Geschichte der Ausländerbeschäftigung in Deutschland 1880 bis 1980*. Berlin: Verlag J. H. W. Deitz.

Katsoulis, Haris. (1983) (1983) *Burger zweiter Klasse: Ausländer in der Bundesrepublik*. Frankfurt: Campus.

Malcolm X. (1970) *The Autobiography of Malcolm X.* New York: Penguin.
Sable, Anton. (1966) *Magnet Bundesrepublik.* Informationstagung der Bundesvereinigung Deutscher Arbeitgeberverbände (B.D.A.). Bonn: Köllen Verlag.
Schlumm, Hans. (1984) *Eine neue Heimat in der Fremde: Die Entwicklung der griechischen Gastarbeiter zu Angehörigen einer Einwanderungminorität in der Bundesrepublik.* Frankfurt: Campus.
Wallraff, Günter. (1985) *Ganz Unten.* Cologne: Verlag Kiepenheuer and Witsch.

6

African Languages in the African American Experience
Alamin Mazrui

African societies, including those of Arab origin in the northern part of the continent, are known to have concepts of ethnic identity that are quite liberal and assimilative.[1] "Purity of the bloodline," for instance, is a notion that is relatively alien to the relational universe of African peoples. To be a member of any European ethnic group, both parents would normally have to be European. But maternal or paternal parentage alone in the case of most African peoples would normally be sufficient to qualify the offspring for membership in a particular African ethnic group. Mazrui dramatizes this difference between Afro-Arab and European conceptions of identity in the following hypothetical terms:

> If the white citizens of the United States had, in fact, been Arab, most of the coloured citizens would have become Arab too. It has been estimated that over seventy percent of the Negro population in the United States has some "white" blood. And the "white" blood was much more often than not derived from a white father. Now given the principle that if the father is Arab the child is Arab, most of the Negroes of the United States would have been Arab had the white people of the United States been Arab too. But the white Americans are Caucasian and the dominant culture is Germanic. And so if either of the parents is

---

[1] I am indebted to Professor Jaffer Kassamali of Hunter College, New York, for providing stimulation and views and ideas about certain issues discussed in this essay.

non-Germanic, the offspring cannot be Germanic either. (1964:22)

But the liberalism and assimilative essence of the Afro-Arab concept of identity are by no means limited to the area of genetics. It also extends to the sphere of culture, and, more relevant to our present discussion, to the phenomenon of language. Anyone who speaks Hausa as a first language, for example, would under normal circumstances be regarded as ethnically Hausa. The same can be said of virtually all other African languages. This stands in marked contrast to European languages, which do not admit into their ethnic fold people who are not genetically European. European languages may be acquired by all and sundry; but when it comes to linguistic definitions of European ethnicity, European languages have failed to neutralize genetic boundaries. African languages, on the other hand, defy genetic boundaries in their contribution to ethnic identities.

Making another hypothetical projection, then, had the American *lingua franca* been Swahili, for example, instead of English, the entire African American population that, for generations has been speaking English as a first and often only language, would have been ethnically Swahili. Likewise, if the mother tongue of African peoples throughout the world were Swahili, then the entire African diaspora would again have been Swahili.

It is perhaps in view of this assimilative tendency of Swahili and other African languages that Julius Nyerere, the first president of Tanzania, sometimes used the term "Swahili" to refer to any person of African origin. Nyerere thus made Swahili, in the collective consciousness of the Tanzanian people, a local equivalent of a transcontinental, Pan-African identity. It was as if Nyerere was anticipating the development of Swahili into a language of global Africa. Inadvertently, Nyerere was also pitting the liberal humanist boundaries of African languages against the narrower racial boundaries of the European languages at the stadium of international politics of human relations.

The restricted genetic (or "racial") boundaries of the English language, a phenomenon that may have emerged with the rise of imperial capitalism in the northern hemisphere, have made it impossible for African Americans to become fully a part of the American "mainstream." It was natural, therefore, that language too would become a factor in the struggles for equality in the Civil Rights Movement of the sixties. But if the system ultimately capitulated, to some degree, in the political-economic sphere, it was not about ready to do the same in the arena of linguistics. No matter how extensively "assimilated" African Americans were, in cultural and linguistic terms, the system ensured that they would remain "black," that they would remain American with qualification. At the frontier of linguistics of identity, therefore, the English language simply failed to forge a nation that is truly one.

Apart from its segregative ethno-linguistic "nature," however, the English language has sometimes been regarded as inherently racialist. With words that evoke all sorts of negative images, the English language is supposed to have served as an instrument of racism against people of color. It is in this regard that Ossie Davis once declared that the English language was his enemy and indicted it "as one of the prime carriers of racism from one person to another in our society" (1973:72).

In an instructional manual on racism in the English language, Robert Moore (1976) outlines some of the ways in which the English language has contributed to conditioning racial attitudes in American society. These range from the association of blackness with evil, ignorance, and death, to the employment of passive constructions to blame African victims of racial prejudice. And, in conclusion, Moore calls for what amounts to a deracialization of the English language, arguing that "while we may not be able to change the language, we can definitely change our usage of the language" (1976:14).

The ethnic exclusiveness and racial invocativeness of the English language naturally led to a quest for alternative sources of ethno-linguistic identity. But for African Americans this search was not without its problems. African Americans remain the only minority group in the United States whose African linguistic background has been completely obliterated by centuries of European slavery and oppression. From which source, therefore, could they derive a sense of independent ethnolinguistic identity? The growing consciousness of themselves as an African people in the particular racialist setting of the United States, and of their heritage in a continent that was engaged in a major struggle for liberation in a more global political context, ultimately prompted a bifocal approach to the question of ethno-linguistic identity.

The first dimension of this approach was one of reaffirming the autonomy and uniqueness of African American English, or "Black English" as it has often been called. If "Black English" had hitherto been considered a mere corruption of the "European brand" of English, a corruption that is unworthy of any dignified status in American civil society, it now became a cherished symbol of African American identity. Even the term "Black English" now became racially suspect and new names like *Palwh*, an acronym for Pan-African Language in the Western Hemisphere (Twiggs, 1973), and *Ebonics* (Williams, 1975) were coined to refer to the African American tongue.

The attempts to reappraise the status of "Black English" were not merely symbolic. Scholars trained in linguistics took the initiative to demonstrate that "Black English" was not a corruption of anything but an autonomous, internally logical and coherent linguistic organism, with a strong continental African linguistic heritage that the Middle Passage was unable to destroy. "Africanisms" thus became a point of emphasis in some linguistic descriptions of "Black English." In the words of Imamu Amiri Baraka, "It is absurd to assume, as has been the tendency, among a great many Western anthropologists and sociologists, that all traces of Africa were erased from the Negro's mind because he learned English. The very nature of the English the Negro spoke and still speaks drops the lie on that idea" (1963:9).

Perhaps the most extensive study of linguistic Africanisms is that of Lorenzo Turner (1949) in which he gives a comprehensive list of words from the so-called Gullah dialect, which he traces to an African linguistic origin. And in a prefatory note to the 1969 reprint, Turner indicates that the decision to reproduce the study was essentially prompted by the desire to make it more generally accessible in the wake of growing African American interest in their African heritage.

Following Turner's line of inquiry, J. L. Dillard argues that there "is hardly any reason to assume that any of the Africanisms listed by Turner were limited to the Gullah area in the eighteenth and nineteenth century" (1972:117). Dillard admits that the African linguistic contribution to American English may seem proportionately small, but he regards it as being no smaller than that of Native American words if place names are excluded. "When it is considered that American Indians survived in essentially monolinguial tribal groups while Africans in the New World did not, the 'contribution' to American English by Africans begins to seem impressively large" (1972:119). In fact, in Dillard's opinion, a much larger proportion of Africanisms could probably be discovered in (African) American English if the academic establishment was not unduly resistant to this kind of research (1972:123).

6. African Languages in the African American Experience

Expanding the scope of this inquiry, Molefi Asante has argued that the most enduring evidence of the African essence in African American speech can be obtained, not from the lexical domain as Turner and others have tried to demonstrate, but from the domain of linguistic pragmatics. "Retention of lexical items constitutes one part of this linguistic continuity with Africa, but the major burden," argues Asante, "has been carried by communicative processes, i.e. African American manners of expression, supported in the main by verb serialization and the unique use of tense and aspect" (1990:250).

Both symbolically and substantively, therefore, "Black English" and its "inherent" Africanity became markers of a new kind of consciousness among sections of the African American population. To some extent this situation can be compared with that of the Irish. As Deane explains with regard to Irish nationalism:

> At its most powerful, colonialism is a process of radical dispossession. A colonized people is without a specific history and even, as in Ireland and other cases, without a specific language. The recovery from the lost Irish language has taken the form of an almost vengeful virtuosity in the English language, an attempt to make Irish English a language in its own right rather than an adjunct to English itself. (1990:10)

This linguistic exercise among African Americans, the Irish, the Kurds, and other "colonized" people can be seen as one modest attempt among many to repossess their histories.

The second dimension in the bifocal quest for ethnolinguistic identity among African Americans was the attempt to relink, in a more direct manner, with continental African languages. The demand for civil rights, therefore, sometimes came to include the right of access to the African linguistic heritage in the corridors of American academia. The existence of several African languages in American educational institutions that we now seem to take so much for granted is one of the products of those major battles for civil rights on American campuses in the 1960s.

Today African languages are taught widely in American universities and in some high schools, even though Swahili has remained by far the most popular.[2] The right of African Americans to pursue the study of African languages is now widely accepted in the United States. It is, in fact, explicitly recognized in the National Language Policy of the United States, which describes one of its objectives as: To foster the teaching of languages other than English so that native speakers of English can rediscover the language of their heritage or learn a second language.[3]

The African American quest for an alternative ethno-linguistic symbol of identity rooted in the African continent, however, has not been without its detractors. In my experience, teaching Swahili in the United States since 1969, I have often been confronted with two arguments seemingly intended to deride the African American ideological motives for studying African languages. It is argued, first, that if the African American interest in African languages has been prompted by the instrumental quality of English as a language of racism and European slavery, then African languages themselves have not been completely innocent of a similar charge. It is suggested that African "middlemen" used African languages as the media of communication with their African brethren when pursuing or mobilizing captives for the transcontinental European slave trade. How, then, it is asked, can such African languages be considered any more liberating than the European languages inherited from the "enslaved" tradition?

There are two fundamental problems with this argument. First, it unjustifiably puts the African middlemen in the European slave trade at

---

[2] It has been estimated by Juma Mutoro of the State University of New York, Albany, that in 1988, for example, there were over a hundred African language programs in American universities and that almost invariably Swahili was one of those languages.

[3] This policy was developed by the Conference on College Composition and Communication (CCCC)--an affiliate of The National Council of Teachers of English (NTE)--and adopted during its Executive Committee meeting on March 16, 1988. The other two main objectives of the policy are specified as:

1. To provide resources to enable native and non-native speakers to achieve oral and literate competence in English, the language of wider communication.

2. To support programs that assert the legitimacy of native languages and dialects and ensure that proficiency in the mother tongue will not be lost.

6. African Languages in the African American Experience

par with the European owners of Africans who were enslaved in the New World and elsewhere. Coming from a more humane tradition of indigenous "slavery,"[4] these middlemen did not even have a sense of the multifarious horrors of the transatlantic European slavery system. They were no more than peripheral and transient "entrepreneurs" in this new human commodity whose contact with other African peoples, except in very few instances, did not lead to linguistic dislocations of any magnitude. In essence, it is the linguistic experience in the Americas, and not the contact with African middlemen, that led to the African American's loss of a continental African ethno-linguistic identity. And it is against this particular experience that African Americans now seek to establish a linguistic re-connection with the African continent.

The second problem with this argument is its historical staticity, which renders it superfluous and even void. Language is not a mass of lifeless molecules. It is, in a sense, a living organism that responds dynamically to changing politico-economic stimuli. Thus the language of Russian tsardom also became the language of Bolshevik socialism; the language of English feudalism also became the language of its liberal capitalism. So, if Swahili or Yoruba, for example, were used in the European slave trade at some point in history, they "moved on" to become important media of struggle against, and opposition to, European imperialism. On the other hand, even after the abolition of European slavery, the English language in the United States has continued to be the language of a racialist, oppressive class that continues to articulate its legitimating ideology through this particular linguistic medium. There continues to be a cultural dimension to the legacy of European slavery, which has included African Americans' experience with the English language, which has sometimes induced a re-emphasis on cultural continuities and a re-establishment of cultural links, with continental Africa.

---

[4] The anthropologist Lucy Mair, for example, made the following observation with regard to "slavery" among the Baganda of East Africa: "Certain duties, it is true, were specifically allocated to slaves, but, for the greatest part, they shared in the ordinary life of the household, were described by the head as 'his children' and a stranger would not be aware that they were his slaves unless this was expressly explained by him (1934:31)"

The second argument against the African American quest for a linguistic "return to the source" has tended to be targeted specifically against Swahili. By the 1960s Swahili was second only to Arabic as the most widely spoken African language on the continent. It was already spoken across several national boundaries. In Kenya, Tanzania and Uganda it was beginning to acquire some national and official status. It had demonstrated its ability to serve as a common medium of communication among African people of diverse ethnic origins in their struggle against European colonial rule in eastern Africa. Later, it was increasingly to be heard in radiobroadcasts throughout the world. In Tanzania, Swahili was also beginning to acquire a reputation as a counter-idiom to class oppression, as a linguistic medium of African-based socialism or *Ujamaa*. It was also in the heartland of Swahili political culture that transcontinental Pan-Africanism found its "resurgence" with the convening in Tanzania of the Sixth Pan-African Congress. And it is the combination of these and other political reasons that rendered Swahili the most popular language among African Americans.

But as the momentum for the study of Swahili was growing, opinions reminiscent of the divide-and-rule policies of the colonial era in Africa began to emerge in the United States. Swahili, it has sometimes been pointed out, is an eastern African language, while Africans in the Americas originated from West Africa. It is suggested, then, that their search for an ethno-linguistic identification with Africa should be directed at western African languages like Yoruba and Wolof, and not an eastern African language like Swahili. After decades of attempts to divide peoples of continental Africa along ethno-linguistic lines, a similar rationalizing equation was brought into play at the level of global Africa.

First, it is not completely true that east Africa did not feature in the European slave trade across the Atlantic Ocean. There were Portuguese, Spanish, and French connections in eastern Africa that contributed in no small measure to the translocation of Africans. The Portuguese are known to have procured Africans to be enslaved from the east African coast from the very beginning of their encounter with the region in the fifteenth century. At first the Portuguese also supplied enslaved to the French. But as a result of recurrent Swahili struggles against the Portuguese, the French turned their attention to the east African port of Kilwa and made their own arrangements for procuring slaves. The Spanish are also known to have taken thousands of Africans to be enslaved from the Swahili coast around the cape to South America

(Nicholls, 1971:200). Furthermore, raids from the enslaved from western Africa sometimes went deep into the Congo, where Bantu languages akin to Swahili were spoken. All in all, the Swahili speaking region of Africa was not altogether excluded as a source of European slavery.

But to attempt to justify the promotion of Swahili or any other African language in the United States of America on the basis of these demographic features of the European slave trade is to succumb to a Eurocentric vision. It is a line of reasoning that completely misconceptualizes the nature of African Americans' consciousness of their Africanity. The ethno-linguistic divisions in continental Africa that Eurocentric scholarship is wont to highlight do not exist, nor need they exist, in the African American collective imagination. African consciousness in the Americas has always placed emphasis on the continent's *unifying qualities* and not on its *divisive attributes*; and it is perhaps for this reason that transcontinental Pan-Africanism, though inspired by the "motherland," was born in the African diaspora before it established roots on the African continent. There is some sense of shared destiny among peoples of the African diaspora that seeks a common political expression which may, of course, vary in degree and form. In the process Africa has become fused and homogenized to a point where any of its languages could serve as a shared source of inspiration and symbolic expression of a new consciousness among African Americans. And for reasons mentioned earlier Swahili turned out to be the natural choice for this purpose.

At another level this particular African American linguistic initiative can be seen as an extension of the growing pro-Swahili sentiments within continental Africa itself. Swahili is offered as a university subject not only in eastern Africa, but in some western African universities, in places like Nigeria and Ghana. It is also the declared continental language of the Organization of African Unity (OAU). And distinguished creative writers from eastern Africa (like Ngugi wa Thiong'o) and western Africa (like Wole Soyinka) have, at different times, campaigned for its establishment as a Pan-African language of the continent. There is a sense, then, in which African Americans are inadvertently responding to the silent throbbings of a continental African quest for unity whose linguistic manifestation has tended to revolve mainly around the Swahili language.

I have so far discussed the question of African languages in the African American experience at a macro-linguistic political level. What, then, are some of its micro-linguistic political manifestations? There is no doubt that the micro-dimension of this issue is bound to vary a great deal from place to place, from experience to experience, from individual to individual. It is nonetheless possible to make at least two generalizations.

The first generalization has to do with naming. The demise of European colonial rule in Africa brought with it an entire naming "revolution." This was part and parcel of the wider African consciousness movements variously called "African nationalism" in some places, "Negritude" in others, "Authenticity" in places like Zaire and so forth. In clusters of domino effect, people began to drop their Euro-Christian names and "return" to more indigenous naming systems abounding in various African languages. And since these naming systems are founded on a deep-rooted gnosis that defines human relations with people, history, or the environment, their re-adoption has been, in effect, a wider cultural embrace between Africa and its sons and daughters.

The naming revolution that has been going on in Africa, however, has also found expression among African Americans. Since the 1960s and 1970s many African Americans have looked upon African languages as a source of symbolic affirmation of their African identity as an increasing number came to discard their baptismal names and acquire African names. In the words of Molefi Asante,

> During the 1960s and 1970s, we came to terms with our collective name and chose to be either "African," "Afro-American," or "black" rather than "Negro" or "colored." We must certainly sooner or later make the same observation on a personal level that we have made on a collective level. In the future there is no question that this will be undertaken on many occasions. It is not only logical, it is practical and we have always responded to logic and pragmatism. The practical value of changing our names is in identification of names with people. We are an African people and it is logical for us to possess African names. Already we are on the verge of a breakthrough. Young black parents are seeking African names for their children in an attempt to assign meaning to their identity. (1988:27-28)

Euro-Christian names, however, have been seen not only as a method of negating the Africanity of African Americans, but also of inflicting racial blows against them. As Livingston pointed out: "Names have been used not only to identify a human being but also to villify, depersonalize and dehumanize. Sam and Sambo, which Dr. Puckett identified as common names for enslaved of the seventeenth century, became racist slurs in the twentieth century when black men were commonly summoned by these names" (1975:v). These racial politics of naming in fact came to inspire Puckett (1975) to undertake an extensive study of the origins and usage of different names in the African American experience, tracing some to the American enslavement context and many others to African languages from various parts of the continent.

Unlike their compatriots on the African continent, however, many African Americans who opt for African names do not select them in accordance with any specific African ethnic tradition. Often names have been selected for their symbolic and semantic content even if they are at variance with the ethnic naming systems from which they are derived. First and last African names among African Americans have sometimes come from different ethnic groups and even different countries, for example, Kwame Toure (a Ghanaian first name and Guinean last name). What we are witnessing among African Americans, then, is the Pan-Africanization of Africa's naming systems as a result of the particular political circumstances of their space and time, circumstances that have forged an African consciousness that transcends the narrower continental ethnic lines of Yorubaness, Zuluness, Amharaness, and the like. The African naming system among African Americans is yet another example of how political economy can be the mother of culture.

But "what is in a name?" one might ask. European slavery and racialism in the United States of America have generally reduced African Americans to a rootless state with skin pigmentation as the essence of their being. Their identity became "black" and their personal names became a reminder of their ruthless severance from their roots. The struggle for civil rights, therefore, had to include an affirmation of their Africanity, of the historicity of their being; and this new sense of African identity had to be raised to the realm of public knowledge.

Like material objects, however, identities do not become "public knowledge" until they are named. Without a label to capture our conception of them, they have little social relevance because there is no awareness of their existence in the first place. The emergence of a new label, therefore, carries with it the elevation of a new sense of identity to the domain of "public knowledge." It is this important function of bringing their historical Africanity and political Pan-Africanity to the public sphere that names from African languages came to serve in the African American experience.

The second generalization on the impact of African languages in the African American experience has to do with the area of ceremony. People generally have a very strong attachment to ceremonial activities, especially of a religious nature. Such activities are important symbolic expressions of valued ideas, events, institutions, struggles, and sometimes the entire ideological orientation of a people. As a result, ceremonial activities can be very important to enhancing a sense of collective identity, and their demise may not augur well with the collective consciousness of a people. There is also a sense in which the infusion of "foreign" ceremonial symbols undermines some of the binding elements of an independent identity of a particular society and signals its cultural capitulation to the "other." And it is against this backdrop that we must understand the emergence of the *Kwanza* ceremony among African Americans.

The legacies of European slavery and colonialism have been some of the most important factors in the spread of Christianity and in rendering Christmas and the New Year supreme ceremonial symbols of Euro-Christian pre-eminence among large sections of global Africans. But the growing African consciousness among African Americans ultimately led to the birth of *Kwanza* as a direct antithesis to Christmas/New Year. Inspired by African harvest ceremonies as markers of new temporal cycles, an entire idiom,[5] drawn mainly from Swahili, came into existence to designate *Kwanza* principles, practices and artifacts.

The *Kwanza* ceremony is, of course, itself rooted in a wider ideology of nationhood propounded by Maulana Karenga (1978). This ideology, *Kawaida*, with its various concepts and principles, is again based on an idiom that is entirely Swahili and seeks to unfold a creative motif for African American identity. Once again, therefore, African languages came to serve as a source of counter-symbols to European predominance in American society, as a source of symbols of African American counter-consciousness that positively affirms their Africanity.

---

[5] The idiom includes principles like *umoja* (unity), *kujichagulia* (self-determination), *ujima* (collective responsibility), *nia* (intention), *kuumba* (creativity), *ujamaa* (socialism/communalism) and *imani* (faith). Molefi Asante's *Afrocentricity* (1988) also, to some extent, relies heavily on an African linguistic idiom. Swahili concepts like *Kawaida* (Tradition), *Njia* (The Path), *Msingi* (Foundation), and others form important pillars of his philosophy.

Conclusion

We have seen how the racial circumstances that led to the cultural dis-Africanization of African Americans may also have been responsible for the emergence of a new African consciousness. This naturally led to a quest for counter-philosophies, counter-ideologies, and counter-symbols, often inspired by Africa, to give substance to this new consciousness. In this search African languages too came to play an important role. Linguistic Africanisms in certain African American dialects of English and the use of aspects of African languages for naming and ceremonial purposes all came to serve as contributing features to a neo-Africanity in the African diaspora. But precisely because Eurocentricity always attempts to universalize its paradigms, it regards any counter-insurgency as necessarily provincial, subjecting it to attack and decisions. "Afrocentricity," "Negritude," "Africanity," and so forth can be regarded as manifestations of a nationalism whose essence is rooted in metaphysics and utopianism. On the other hand, nationalism must also be seen as an indispensable dialectical social stage toward liberation. There has been a tendency among (both European and African) Marxists, in particular, to diminish the importance of this kind of African nationalism in favor of the class struggle, but as Terry Eagleton notes:

> Nationalism . . . is in a sense like class. To have it, and to feel it, is the only way to end it. If you fail to claim it or give it up too soon, you will merely be cheated, by other classes and by other nations. Nationalism, like class, would thus seem to involve an impossible irony. It is sometimes forgotten that social class, for Karl Marx at least, is itself a form of alienation, canceling the particularity of an individual life into collective anonymity. Where Marx differs from the commonplace liberal view of such matters is in his belief that to undo this alienation you had to go, not around class, but somehow all the way through it and out the other side. To wish class or nation away, to seek to live sheer irreducible difference now in the manner of some contemporary post-structuralist theory, is to play straight into the hands of the oppressor. (1990:23)

Africans, therefore, must continue to strive to set their own terms of definition and discourse on the global arena, and the attempts to deride their efforts in this regard must be seen as an ideological offensive that needs to be resisted.

But African Americans must not be seen merely as *recipients* in their cultural and linguistic relationship with Africa. They have also been and may continue to be *donors*. African Americans have made important philosophical and political contributions to the formation of movements like Negritude, Pan-Africanism, and the African personality. Their African heritage led to the emergence of a distinctive type of music, which has in turn been feeding back to Africa. Even hair styles like "Afro," though arguable that they originated in the United States of America, became popularized in Africa partly through the African American link. In other words, the global children of Africa have long had a give-and-take relationship with their mother continent.

What, then, are some of the language-related contributions that African Americans can make to Africa? One important contribution may be in the area of national languages. Many African countries are still grappling with the problem of choosing appropriate national languages from their indigenous languages. There is usually a felt need that the European languages inherited from the colonial tradition should be replaced with local languages at the national and official levels of operation. But the internal politics of ethnic pluralism have not always made it easy for African policy makers to "elevate" one language to national and official status over other languages. In many instances, there has been the concern that the choice of one ethnic language over others may generate fears of ethnic dominance that may propel the countries toward political instability.

The African American quest for a linguistic link with Africa, however, may help internationalize certain African languages from individual African countries. If the trend to study African languages like Hausa, Lingala, Wolof, Zulu, and so forth continues to becomes more firmly established, the languages may acquire an international image that may help reduce their ethnic "essence." In this way they may eventually become more acceptable as national languages by speakers of other African languages in their respective countries. Likewise, the popularization of a language like Swahili among African Americans may increase its chances of becoming a Pan-African language.

The other language-based contribution to Africa is connected with the *Kwanza* ceremony. As indicated earlier, this is a ceremony that has been articulated and brought into the sphere of public knowledge through an African language--Swahili. In Africa there is today a quest for a cultural Pan-Africanism, and it has sometimes been suggested that different cultural practices could be adopted from different parts of Africa: Swahili from eastern Africa, a mode of dress from West Africa, a cuisine from north Africa, music from Zaire and the diaspora, and so forth. Is it possible that *Kwanza*, with its African idiom, will one day become a spiritual component of this potent potential cultural pan-Africanism? Perhaps. It is too early to tell, but let us not forget that great achievements often have humble beginnings.

REFERENCES

Asante, Molefi Kete. (1988) *Afrocentricity*. Trenton, N.J.: Africa World Press.

Asante, Molefi Kete. (1990) "The African Essence in African American Language." In: M. K. Asante and K. W. Welsh, *African Culture: The Rhythms of Unity*, pp. 47-81. Trenton, N.J.: Africa World Press.

Baraka, Imamu Amiri. (1963) *Blues people; Negro Music in White America*. New York: W. Morrow Press.

Davis, Ossie. (1973) "The English Language is My Enemy." In Robert H. Bentley and Samuel D. Crawford, eds., *Black Language Reader*. Glenview, Ind.: Scott, Foresman and Company.

Deane, Seamus. (1990) "Introduction." In Terry Eagleton, Fredric Jameson and Edward Said, eds., *Nationalism, Colonialism and Literature*, pp. 3-19. Minneapolis: University of Minnesota Press.

Eagleton, Terry. (1990) "Nationalism: Irony and Commitment." In Terry Eagleton, Fredric Jameson and Edward Said, eds., *Nationalism Colonialism and Literature*, pp. 25-39. Minneapolis: University of Minnesota Press.

Karenga, Maulana. (1978) *Essays in Struggle*. San Diego: Kawaida Publications.

Livingston, George J. (1975) "Forward." In Newbell Niles Puckett, *Black Black Names in America: Origins and Usage*, pp. 74-93. Boston: G.K. Hall and Company.

Mair, Lucy Phillip. (1934) *An African People in the Twentieth Century*, New York: Russell & Russell.

Mazrui, Ali A. (1964) "Political Sex." *Transition* 4 (17): 19-23.

Moore, Robert. (1976) *Racism in the English Language: A Lesson Plan and Study Essay*, New York: The Racism and Sexism Research Center for Educators.

Puckett, Newbell Niles. (1975) *Black Names is America: Origins and Usage*. Boston: G.K. Hall and Company.

Turner, Lorenzo. (1949) *Africanisms in the Gullah Dialect*, Chicago: University of Chicago Press.

Twiggs, Robert D. (1973) *Pan-African Language in the Western Hemisphere*. North Quincy, Mass.: The Christopher Publishing House.

Williams, Robert L., ed. (1975) *Ebonics: The True Language of Black Folk*. St. Louis, Mo.: Institute of Black Studies.

7

Kitchen Table Talk: J. California Cooper's Use of Nommo—Female Bonding and Transcendence

Barbara J. Marshall

The current thrust toward examinations of the works of African American female writers has demanded both theoretical and critical paradigms. Because of the many and varied forms female texts have taken, because of the extent of these literary contributions, scholars have sought to critique works from many viewpoints. Scholars have used narratology, deconstruction, and Marxism for critical insight. Narratology, as a theory of narrative texts, analyzes the text in terms of fabula: events, actors who resemble characters from life, and aspects or techniques the writer employs to move the text forward. The deconstructionist breaks the text apart and analyzes the parts rather than the whole, while the Marxist examines the text in terms of an on-going struggle between the classes.

Despite these various forms of analysis, black female writers are demanding a "say" in their own criticism. Critics, such as Barbara Christian, call for black feminist criticism, while Audre Lorde insists that the lesbian view point is also viable and necessary. Afrocentric scholars are expanding horizons: an African centered worldview is used to analyze the female writer's expression. We question whether the text expands from an African center. This new field of analysis opens doors to an energetic and historically correct examination of the literature of African American female as well as male writers.

My aim is to utilize an Afrocentric paradigm that focuses upon the themes of *Nommo*, female bonding, and transcendence in the short stories of J. California Cooper. To make this critique, I will exam the three texts: *A Piece of Mine* (1984), *Homemade Love*, (1986), and *Some Soul to Keep* (1987). The following issues will be discussed: male/female relationships, mother/daughter relationships and other mother relationships. Finally, I will explore the position J. California Cooper holds in an Afrocentric paradigm.

J. California Cooper has been neglected in the canons of African American female writers; for example, in *Wild Women in the Whirlwind*, she is only mentioned in the forward: "In the United States, J. California Cooper continues to distinguish herself as one of the most prolific and talented young black women short story writers and playwrights" (Braxton, 1990: xxxiii). Yet her works are seldom analyzed; serious analysis is heaped upon the mighty thirteen: "Hurston, Walker, Morrison, Brooks, Angelou, Shange, Evans, Marshall, Sanchez, Hunter, Bambara, Giovanni and Naylor, who are continuing to bring a sorely needed vitality to American literature" (Braxton, 1990:248-249).

We may speculate upon the neglect of Cooper by suggesting that readers do not tend to gravitate toward the short story as reading material. Perhaps public sentiment holds that plays too are to be seen, not seriously read. Whereas, readers who gravitate toward poetry do so because its simplicity is appealing. The novel reader may feel that only novels contain the necessary intricacies to gain his/her attention and sustained interest.

Copper stated her preference for writing short stories in an interview: "Playwriting is more work for me because you have to separate the dialogue from the directions, and so on. Whereas in a story you can have everything in the same paragraph" (Gray, 1985:1).

In considering Cooper's preference for strong paragraphs, one may note how she develops memorable male and female characters. The characters of all three books are often middle-aged women and men; the less-complicated people of the Southern backwoods. Or they are poor people living in the substrata of the city. Since Cooper's men and women appear to speak in tones of the South, their dialect is often associated with the unlettered and therefore uncultured. Yet, these characters have wisdom--an innate "mother wit." Their humor is akin to that of Langston Hughes when he allows Simple to tell tales. According to J. California Cooper, "It is not a Southern dialect, as many people have said. It is an uneducated dialect. I really believe the less words you know to be ambiguous with, the closer to the truth you have to stay" (Gray, 1985:12).

The relationships in Cooper's short stories are between men and women. An overview of how the relationships are presented shows that

7. J. California Cooper's Use of Nommo

they lack "sacrifice, inspiration, vision and victory" (Asante, 1980:145). These relationships are often stilted by the pressures of poverty. The women are described as sickly, beaten down, old. These women are not totally weak; they are simply lost. They have spent their lives giving to their children and husbands, sacrificing both mentally, morally, and physically, half of their lives to discover their only reward is to give more. Thus, they do not expect a "Thank You."

The men, in contrast, are virile; they date and have affairs with women half their age. Cooper is not kind to her male characters; these men are often vindictive and cruel. They tear up their wives' Bibles, sell their most precious possessions, and spread their wives with verbal and physical abuse. At times the reader gets the impression that if it were possible these men would castrate their wives!

Since Cooper's characters lack an education, often they simply do not know how to express any emotion other than lust. The voices of mothers are often heard as daughters speak about their lives as young women.

In an interview I had with Cooper in 1989, she commented: "Use the Bible, the ten commandments are the only themes you need; I use them all the time." Therefore, her female characters find a way to make spiritual choices about their future. In the form of a praise song or morality play, Cooper is prone to allow hope to remain though the characters may seek solace in graveyards or die.

Using spirituality as a form of transcendence or liberation, the female characters are able to survive in otherwise painful situations. Often a dear friend is able to guide the female character through survival techniques. Each short story in *A Piece of Mine* (1984) has a summation in which the main character is shown transcending her situation; thus, she achieves peace of mind. There is both physical and spiritual movement toward peace, affirmation of self, and achievement of a higher good. The characters move forward, Bible in hand, and seek their own self-appointed salvation. This salvation is achieved without the benefit of a minister; it is self-salvation, which is accomplished by the character realizing her self-worth.

Also *In a Piece of Mine*, Cooper experiments with two different endings in a story entitled "The Free and the Caged," thus allowing the reader to discover which ending he/she finds acceptable. Those readers who expect a happy ending will be pleased to know that they can create their own, while those who tend toward realism cannot when the man and woman separate forever.

Homemade Love, according to the author's note, is love that cannot be bought; it is grandmother's cookies, baked when she could afford the flour. Homemade anything lasts longer than store bought (Cooper, 1986). Therefore, we are given homemade love in a series of thirteen short stories. In *Homemade Love*, Cooper experiments with style again. She writes a story shaped like a *Y* and says: "Two paths lead to one road, I got to tell you two things, or stories before I get to the main road where it all comes together" (Cooper, 1986:61). Throughout the stories in *Homemade Love*, we hear mothers warning their children and providing lessons in learning. Yet, we see the girls often repeating the same mistakes their mothers warned them against: "they marry the wrong man, take up house keeping in the same community and raise their own children to repeat the cycle" (Subryan, 1988).

In *Some Soul to Keep*, the stories get longer and more powerful. The reader is able to observe the growth of two generations. Cooper extends her themes of education, religion, sexuality, and race. She also expands her treatment of male-female relationships and sisterly bonding. She seems to be drawing toward novel format.

What Cooper does within the context of her short stories is a matter of her style and presentation. In my opinion, she is able to weave into her story quilts, a sense of *Nommo* and its power, sisterly bonding, and the motif of transcendence. I posit that though her stories are not completely Afrocentric, she brings to the reader the following elements of the African American experience, which are worth discussing:

NOMMO:

I HEAR you . . . but, are YOU listening?

Both Richards (1980) and Asante (1987) have discussed *Nommo*, the power of the word. This generative power is African in both a historical and spiritual context. Richards explains: "Nommo is signs of the African Spirit; the ability of Muntu (human beings, the ancestors, the spirit, the Creator) to make use of the force within the universe in order to affect other beings" (Richards, 1980:40). Asante addresses the communal interaction of *Nommo* and its functionality: "to be an artist means that the creation and its function in society are uppermost . . . even a performance becomes a collective experience" (Asante, 1987:64-66).

Nommo as spirituality, functionality, communalism are all concepts contextually presented in J. California Cooper's short stories. This particular use of *Nommo* has always been a major tradition of African culture dating back to the story of Isis and Osiris. When Isis needed to express her grief over Osiris's death, she spoke to her sister Nephthys, who listened, sympathized, and assisted. Our historical use of *Nommo* can be traced throughout our history both on the continent of Africa and in the diaspora:

> If there is a single distinguishing feature of the literature of black women . . . women talk to other women in this tradition, and their friendships with other women--mothers, sisters, grandmothers, friends, lovers are vital to their growth and well-being. . . . Women (usually two) gather together in a small room to share intimacies that can be trusted only to a kindred female spirit. (Washington, 1990: xxi)

The kindred female spirit and literary foremother one hears when reading Cooper is Zora Neale Hurston. In Hurston *Their Eyes Were Watching God*, Janie and Pheoby are kindred female spirits. Hurston through Janie, exercises *Nommo* and Pheoby listens. Thus, Janie relates the story of her own life as it grew through a relationship with three men: Logan Killicks, Joe Starks, and Tea Cake. As Janie says: "You can tell 'em what Ah say if you / wants to. Dats just de same as me / cause mah tongue is in mah friends / mouf"

Pheoby responds: "If you so desire Ah'll tell / 'em what you tell me to tell em'" (Hurston, 1978:17).

Thus, the use of *Nommo* is transferred from the main character to the secondary character; we have no way of knowing if Pheoby retold Janie's story. However, if the story were to be retold, Pheoby would have been the best equipped to retell the tale with compassion, empathy, and TRUTH!

Thus *Nommo*, the power of the word, is extended. Copper manipulates this skill by taking Hurston's style, which is as old as the pyramid texts, and shaping it into a uniqueness of the female voice: the sister informant. Therefore, we envision women sitting on porches, at kitchen tables, or on plastic covered sofas talking the good talk. This type of talk would be considered to be words of wisdom by some and experienced warnings by others. The reader can expect to hear homespun wisdom and mother wit.

FEMALE BONDING

We acquire "mother wit" from our mothers. Cooper in each of her stories, includes the mother's presence or a message from the mother. In African American female literature, bonding or socializing characteristics fall into several patterns: turbulence or tenderness (Troester, 1984), difficult survival (Pettis, 1987), ritual healing (Davies, 1985), or circles (Subryan, 1988). We recognize women spoken about and the women informants. Listen: "Mothers are something ain't they? They mostly the one person you can count on! All your life . . . if they live. Most mothers be your friend and love you no matter what you do!" (Cooper, 1986:1) and "The Bible warn people bout strangers in their life and he had heard that warning from his mama just like the rest of us" (Cooper, 1986:113).

However, if the mother provided a negative role model, the daughter attempted to best her mother in negative mores: "My mama had a baby when she was fourteen so she can't tell me nothin! She had her fun and I know why!" (Cooper, 1986:80). This daughter is repeating the mistakes of the mother and more than enjoying herself. Sometimes, the mother abandoned her child and bonding of any type was impossible, as demonstrated in *A Piece of Mine*. Subryan has suggested: "It is a signal tragedy that in learning to conquer adversities, the daughter sometimes experiences the same pain and agony which her mother experienced. In many cases a daughter becomes a part of her mother, their lives comprising one circle" (1988:123).

In another instance, the daughter has a mother whose spirit is strong and who instills in her daughter a love of life: "My mama was a happy person, liked to laugh. She could help your sore fingers and cut knees, or fusses with your friends, away. She always told me, 'If you laugh at things, they get lighter and you can bear em better!' (Cooper, 1987:66)." However, the mother is white and the black daughter grows up in a orphanage, an even deeper problem emerges; the relationship becomes one of turbulence (Troester, 1984:13-16): "They were both stunned! Cause the girl, Victoria, had thought her mama was black and her daddy was white. She was a militant young woman with race pride. Marchin and all! The first time they met each other, their minds almost flew away!" (Cooper, 1987:34).

In contrast, the black mother explains the African concept of motherhood: "When a black Negro woman have a white baby, by rape or not, we keep it; we raise it and love it. Cause that's our baby" (Cooper, 1987:35).

OTHER MOTHERS

In the African community the presence of an "other mother" is felt (Troester, 1984). Historically "other mothers" have been an integral part of the black family structure and provided the necessary elements for rites of passage and preparation for femalehood. "Other mothers" are female bridges between biological mothers and daughters. These "other mother" bridges were traditionally cousins, aunts, or grandmothers. In the black community, what a biological mother could not provide, an "other mother" could.

If the relationship between mother and daughter is a stormy or empty one, the bonding is supplied by the tenderness of an "other mother" (Davies, 1985): "Aunt Ellen was a husky-looking mannish-looking woman who wore pants, a straw hat and a red flowered blouse. I will always remember that. I was crying when she came . . . scared. I stared at her . . . our new mama.. . . She picked me up and held me close to her breast, under her chin and she felt just like I knew my mama did" (Cooper, 1986:3). Often, this tenderness contains the element of healing--the "laying on of hands."

LAYING ON OF HANDS

The ritual motif of the "laying on of hands" by "other mother" healers is an African symbol of unity. The healing may be motivated by illness as the result of a physically or psychological beating. For Cooper this healing can be soothing. Some readers would view elements of healing as lesbianism. Cooper, however, presents the "laying on of hands" as a need between "sisters," a motif that allows the one needing healing to transcend the lowly life of the psychologically undernourished and emotionally alienated in *A Piece of Mine*.

Most of Cooper's stories are told by women; only one story is told by a man. He uses *Nommo* and reminds one of Jesse B. Semple, created by Langston Hughes. In "Living" Seymor decides he is tired of the country and his wife is just all right; she looks old and beat out: "You ain't pretty no more! Fact about it, you is pretty doggone ugly!"

(Cooper, 1986:19). Seymor goes to the city to find himself: "So I said, 'Facts about it, Seymor, that's my name, it's time for you to sip from the glass of life.'" (Cooper, 1986:21).

While sipping from the glass of life, Seymor is beaten, robbed, and acquires the clap. But, he learns that life in the city isn't all he has heard and that living near the land is the best place to be: "My wife was at the door watching me make my way. She came out and ran to me, her arms stretched out and I was yearning, trying to hurry to get to 'em! When I got inside the gate, that little picket gate, I had built and put there, I made her help me get down on my knee, only one was useful, and let me kiss my ground!" (Cooper, 1986:25).

Seymor returns to his wife with a deeper appreciation of what it means to remain in a relationship and have a woman who sincerely cares. In learning a lesson of life, Seymor heals himself. A man apparently also can have the ability to "lay on hands," but not in the same manner that women do.

TRANSCENDENCE

According to Asante (1980), transcendence takes us from traditional awareness to revolutionary consciousness. The breakdown occurs first; the person tears away from mental and psychological habits that held the individual to European concepts. For Cooper's women, transcendence is there; she uses rain as a metaphor to symbolize the trouble one must endure before the sun shines and a rainbow appears. Though Cooper's transcendence is not connected to an Afrocentric center, there is a tendency for her women to rise above the mundane elements in their lives. Moreover, Cooper's women make breaks with their abusive husbands. In fact, Cooper speaks of liberation in her short stories: "I think real liberation starts in the heart. In men and women. I think the truth sets you free or at least gives you a direction to go in to get free. Some people don't need to be enlightened or educated to know they are not free" (Gray, 1985:12).

J. California Cooper puts the edict of transcendence and liberation into a framework in the following short stories: "$100.00 or Nothing!," the wife suffers constant verbal abuse from her husband, as Cooper vividly demonstrates in *A Piece of Mine*.

J. CALIFORNIA COOPER AND THE AFROCENTRIC PARADIGM

Asante has written: "When a writer seeks to write about life, death, birth, love, happiness or sadness, the first thing that should come to mind is himself, his people, their motifs. If he writes about his own people, he is writing about a universal experience of people" (Asante, 1980:47). Therefore, as black people we cannot be dictated to by European forms of expression or experience. However, though Cooper writes about black people, she allows herself to become entrapped by the European definition of universality and at times seriously falls away from having an Afrocentric approach to writing. She says: "They're black people, but its not about what happens to black people alone. It's about love, lying, defeat, sincerity, fear, loneliness, deceit, those kinds of things; it wouldn't matter if they were white, Mexican, Chinese, whatever. They do all those things" (Gray, 1985:12).

I posit that unless one has lived a particular ethnic background or culture, he/she cannot possibly, with true, authenticity, tell what he/she can do. Thus, the manner in which an Afrocentric story is presented must find its center in the experience of the African experience of that writer. Anything less means that the writer is writing a story about people who just simply happen to carry the color black as a part of their baggage.

In "Color Me Red," for example, at issue is a mulatto who marries a white. Era, the main female character, grapples with her blackness. When she finds her white husband in bed with a black woman, Era produces pictures of her mother, confessing her blackness. Her husband beats her and files for divorce.

Next, Era marries a black man who thinks she is white. When, at a cocktail party, he begins, which is his usual practice, to demean the black woman, Era explodes and admits her blackness again. Her second husband beats her, kicks her out of the house, and files for divorce. Neither husband is able to accept her for what she is.

This issue is quite African in its context; yet Cooper insists that it holds universal connotations. For some undisclosed reason, Era cannot continue to pass; therefore, when her African center emerges, she can no longer deny who she is. Finally she marries a man who accepts her for the woman she is, not because of the color of her skin.

By far the most Afrocentric of Cooper's short stories is "Sisters of the Rain." In this longer short story, Cooper explores the issue of education as a method for survival in the black community. The first voice is that of a teacher, the second the teacher's daughter. Therefore continuity is maintained between women and across families.

Cooper presents three generations of a family with strong ties. The story begins with a twelve-year-old girl whose only company, after her mother dies, is an old geography book. Her mother insisted that she go to school and take a note with the word "Please" written on it. That way, the girl would be able to bring home a used book to read. Before the girl returns, her mother dies. But, the love of learning does not die.

The girl marries at sixteen, becomes a mother, and has one child every year until she is nineteen. She names her children from the geography book: "her sons, Africa and Pyramid. Her daughters, Egypt and Lake Superior." (Cooper, 1987:6). The mother and daughter's lives are an interwoven circle and the young girl, now called "Mud Dear," is laid to rest at twenty-six. The daughter Superior takes up the torch of education and the school teacher's daughter tells Superior's story.

The remainder of the story is Superior's for she marries a man who wants her simply because she does not sleep with him. Superior feels that sex will keep her from finishing school. Superior appears to hear her mother's voice. Soon after her marriage, she begins to have babies and Rudy, Superior's husband, starts to have affairs. When Rudy has a stroke, Superior cares for him for eighteen years, until he dies. While she is caring for her wayward husband, she "remembers her mama's dreams. She intends for all her children to go to college!" (Cooper, 1987:27).

Superior's strength and perseverance enable her first three children to go to college--poor but proud. Her last and youngest son chooses to become a master builder. Each child provides for their "Mud Dear," to the point that she has everything she could possibly want.

Most of Cooper's themes are decidedly African in orientation, primarily reverence for the mother: "Affection for one's mother and especially the respect with which it was necessary to surround her were the most sacred of duties" (Diop, 1959:62).

In conclusion, though J. California Cooper writes about the black experience and uses black characters, she is grappling with her identity as an African American and as a writer. Much like Era in the short story "Color Me Red," J. California Cooper appears to be attempting to write for the sake of writing and not to inform the people. Yet, in essence, because Cooper's short stories reflect our lives, they are also motifs by which we, African American women, can design our lives.

We have always depended upon the voices and healing powers of our mothers and "other mothers." In fact, an article by Millroy entitled "Sisters Helping Sisters: Support and Caring from 'Kitchen table self-help groups,'" in *Essence*, October 1990, discusses that black women across the country are forming help groups whose main functions are to help themselves and to help others. These women talk, discuss books, and "heal" the wounds of domestic violence. The Chicago-based group called Sturdy Black Bridges states that its goal is "working on being positive, honest, respectful and nurturing to themselves--then sharing the spirit with others" (Milloy, 1990:126).

What the sisters are doing in actuality J. California Cooper is doing in narrative text. Hers is a voice we must hear; if we students of Africalogy read and critique her works based upon our paradigm, we may find more than Cooper is willing to share in a public forum. We must allow J. California Cooper to join us at the kitchen table, for she has stories to tell.

REFERENCES

Asante, Molefi Kete. (1980) *Afrocentricity: The Theory of Social Change*. New York: Amulefi.

Asante, Molefi Kete. (1987) *The Afrocentric Idea*. Philadelphia: Temple University Press.

Braxton, Joanne M., ed. (1990) *Wild Women in the Whirlwind: Afro-American Culture and the Contemporary Literary Renaissance*. New Brunswick, N.J.: Rutgers University Press.

Chamberlain, Basil Hall. (1902) "Basho and the Japanese Poetical Epigram." In *Asiatic Society of Japan Transactions*, vol. 30, pp.243-362.

Cooper, J. California. (1984) *A Piece of Mine*. Stanford, Calif.: Wild Tree Press.

Cooper, J. California. (1986) *Homemade Love*. New York: St. Martin's Press.

Cooper, J. California. (1987) *Some Soul to Keep*. New York: St. Martin's Press.

Davies, Carole Boyce. (1985) "Mothering and Healing in Recent Black Women's Fiction." *Sage: A Scholarly Journal on Black Women*, vol. 2, no. 1 (Spring):11-17.

Diop, Cheikh Anta. (1959) *The Cultural Unity of Black Africa*. Chicago: Third World Press.

Gray, Lynn. (1985) "Interview: J. California Cooper": *FM Five.* (November/December): 1, 12.

Hurston, Zora Neale. (1978) *Their Eyes Were Watching God.* Chicago: University of Illinois Press. (First published in 1937.)

Milloy, Marilyn. (1990) "Sisters Helping Sisters." *Essence.* vol. 21, no. 6:83-84;126.

Pettis, Joyce. (1987) "Difficult Survival: Mothers and Daughters in The Bluest Eye." *Sage: A Scholarly Journal on Black Women.* vol. 4, no. 2:26-29.

Richards, Dona Marimba. (1980) *Let the Circle Be Unbroken: The Implications of African Spirituality in the Diaspora* Trenton, N. J.: Redsea Press.

Subryan, Carmen. (1988) "Circles: Mother and Daughter Relationships." In Toni Morrison's "Song of Solomon." *Sage: A Scholarly Journal on Black Women.* vol. 5, no. 1 (Summer): 34-36.

Troester, Rosalie Riegle. (1984)" Turbulence and Tenderness: Mothers, Daughters, and 'Other Mothers'" in Paule Marshall's "Brown Girl, Brownstones." *Sage: A Scholarly Journal on Black Women*, vol. 1, no. 2. (Fall): 13-16.

III

Literary Analysis: Style and Substance

8

Dilemma of the Dutiful Servant: The Poetry of Jupiter Hammon

Lonnell E. Johnson

Since the First Century when Paul wrote of the paradox of freedom and servitude, Christians have been continually striving to understand the oxymoronic relationship of enslavement and freedom expressed in the Epistle to the Corinthians: "For he that is called in the Lord, being a servant, is the Lord's freeman: likewise also he that is called, being free, is Christ's servant (I Corinthians 7:22). " In 1520 in a tract "On the Freedom of a Christian Man," Martin Luther (1957:7) wrestles with the paradox of freedom in Christian service, whereby he declares: "A Christian man is free lord over all . . . [yet] dutiful servant to all." Two centuries later Jupiter Hammon, the first known African American to publish a literary work, exemplifies the same duality. Indeed, Hammon embodies the dilemma, since he is not only a Christian but enslaved in eighteenth-century Century America.

Born in 1711, Jupiter Hammon has achieved a place in African American literature with the publishing of "An Evening Thought (Salvation by Christ, With Penetential [*sic*] Cries)," a broadside printed on Christmas Day, 1760. Other works include "An Address to Miss Phillis Wheatly' [*sic*]" (1778); two prose pieces "Essay on the Ten Virgins" (1779), a copy of which is yet to surface, and "An Address to the Negroes in the State of New York" (1787); "A Winter Piece," which includes "A Poem for Children with Thoughts in Death" (1782); and "An Evening's Improvement," to which is added "A Dialogue Entitled the Kind Master and the Dutiful Servant" (1783).

The poetry of Hammon reveals a devoutly religious man who assimilates the predominant religious views of colonial New England. Because of this he has been accused of being too conciliatory in his attitude toward enslavement. While he does not always speak out against enslavement, he does speak for equality and unity of both the enslaved and master. Upon close examination, the poetry of Hammon reveals his ability to absorb the basic tenets of Christianity, yet use those precepts to mediate a stronger response to enslavement. In his "A Dialogue Entitled the Kind Master and the Dutiful Servant" Hammon employs a subtle strategy to unify master and the enslaved before God. The poet's life of service reflects a man totally committed to the cause of Christ. Above all else his works reveal a man trying to resolve the dilemma of being a committed servant of God, yet dutiful servant of a man.

All the works of Hammon mirror a man absorbed in religious matters. His identification as a Christian believer colors his poetry, as Ransom comments on the religious aspect of Hammon's verse: "His poetry is sincere and enthusiastic, and it is primarily religious: Hammon's poetry reflects his great intellectual and emotional involvement with religion to the point where it approaches intoxication " (1970:12).

With regard to more secular matters, such as the issue of enslavement, Hammon is more moderate in his attitude. His response in "A Winter Piece," however, indicates that while he does not desire freedom for himself, he firmly believes that the young enslaved should be set free. For Hammon true freedom is a spiritual matter: "And ye shall know the truth and the truth shall make you free. If the Son therefore shall make you free, ye shall be free indeed" (John 8:32, 36). In his "Address to the Negroes of New York," Hammon elaborates on the freedom that most concerns him: "But this [earthly freedom], my brethren is by no means the greatest thing we have to be concerned about. Getting our liberty in this world is nothing to our having the liberty of the children of God" (Ransom 1970:113). It is precisely Hammon's preoccupation with spiritual matters, rather than with his state of bondage, for which he is vehemently criticized.

To more clearly understand Hammon and his development as a poet and proponent of the Bible, it is important to understand the sociocultural background that gave rise to his outpourings in poetry and prose. One must examine the environment out of which his works took root. The portrait of Hammon must be viewed against the backdrop of colonial New York that Higginbotham (1978: Chapter 4) describes as progressing from "Half-Freedom to Slavery."

The region of Hammon's birth was originally settled by the Dutch in 1610. Under Dutch rule in New York, enslaved blacks were often accorded rights usually reserved for white indentured servants. Among the

8. Dilemma of the Dutiful Servant: The Poetry of Jupiter Hammon

Dutch, in fact, the distinction between freedom and enslavement was at times more social than legal. The casual attitude of the master class, together with the ill-defined legal status of the enslaved, tempered the system to such an extent that it resembled in many ways an indentured servant system. In the Dutch courts, "the status of an enslaved was nearly the same as that of a free man or woman." Records of status were not even kept until 1640 (Higginbotham, 1978).

The war with England in 1664 changed the colony to a British possession, which took its name from the Duke of York. Under English rule, however, enslavement codes were more developed: "As a rule, a slave code was an accurate reflection of the fears and apprehensions of the colony. Hence the more numerous the blacks, the more strict the slave code" (Quarles, 1969:15).

In 1712, the year after Hammon's birth, an enslavement uprising in New York City resulted in harsher restrictions upon the enslaved of the colony, as the number of enslaved increased to more than 9,000 adults--the largest enslavement force in any English colony north of Maryland (Quarles, 1969). When Hammon was born on the prominent Lloyd Family estate, located on Lloyd's Neck, a "promontory on the Long Island Sound between the towns of Huntington and Oyster Bay" (Vertanes, 1957), enslaved had been in that area for more than fifty years.

McManus points out what was probably the condition of enslavement in New York during Hammon's lifetime: "The slaves lived quietly, enjoyed good treatment, and often looked forward to eventual freedom as a reward for loyal service. All evidence available indicates that master-slave relations were good, often marked by mutual affection and respect" (1966:15). The mild form of servitude under which most of the colonists lived suggests the privileged state of Hammon, whom Schomburg describes as "the gentleman slave" (1930:14). Hammon describes how well treated he is in his address to the blacks of New York: "I have great reason to be thankful that my lot has been so much better than most slaves have had. I suppose I have had more advantages and privileges than most of you who are slaves, have ever known, and I believe more than many white people have enjoyed" (Ransom, 1970:107).

Hammon's status as an enslaved mirrors that of the household servant as seen in the Old Testament. In eighteenth-century America, perhaps the most effective means of introducing Christianity to the enslaved was by means of participation in religious observances in the master's household. The enslaved, such as Hammon, were part of a household and participated in religious observances, for "family worship was an important feature of the Puritan household. . . . It is probable that most of the Christianized Negroes in colonial New England received their first religious impulse in the family worship of their master's household" (Greene 1942:76).

Because the Puritans based their institutions on the pattern outlined in the patriarchal Old Testament, they drew two classes of bondmen: "Hebrew servants" and "Gentile slaves." Both forms were adopted by the Puritans and changed into an enslaved system where the status of the enslaved was somewhere between the two. Greene mentions, "As such the Negro was considered part of the Puritan family and, in keeping with the custom of the Hebraic family, was usually referred to as a 'servant' rarely as 'slave'" (1942:168).

As the servant of Christian masters who instructed their enslaved in the same religious doctrine of the evangelical movement begun in the Church of England and which spread to America, undoubtedly Hammon was profoundly influenced by the Bible. His poetry and prose reveal a man very knowledgeable of the Scriptures. Schomburg believes him to have been "a missionary and lay preacher" (1930:14).

Records from the Lloyd estate reveal that Hammon purchased a Bible from his master in 1733. The source of income for such a purchase may have been from hiring out himself to work or from profits from "Jupiter's Orchards." The Lloyds hired out their enslaved for periods of time. Such resourcefulness would have allowed Hammon the financial means and time to learn to read and write and cultivate the impetus to write poetry (Vertanes, 1957). That Hammon was a literate household servant in colonial New York was not particularly rare during his lifetime, for Whitlow paints this picture of eighteenth-century New England:

> Many blacks, slave and free, were quite well educated . . . blacks were successful artisans and planters, and . . . some themselves owned slaves. In short, blacks were generally better treated in the 18th century than in the 19th, partly because of the influence of religion in the northern colonies, where it was generally held that blacks should be educated at least enough to understand Christianity. (1973:16-17)

Given the religious climate in New York and New England, it is not surprising that religion dominates the poetry of Hammon. It is also not sur-

8. Dilemma of the Dutiful Servant: The Poetry of Jupiter Hammon

prising that Hammon would be literate as a household servant in eighteenth-century New York. Wealthy landowners often maintained private tutors who instructed family members. Conceivably Hammon may have received such tutelage.

Another possible explanation can be seen in examining a major movement to educate colonists, particularly the enslaved, during Hammon's lifetime. The precedent for the education of the enslaved goes back to Cotton Mather's reminder that some enslaved might be "the elect of God placed in their hands by Divine Providence" (1706:4-5). Mather established a school to instruct "Negroes and Indians, in reading the Scriptures and learning their catechisms." He not only favored but actually fathered enlightenment of the enslaved, saying:

> I will put Bible and other good and proper books into their hands; will allow them time to read and assure myself that they do not misspend this time. (Mather, 1706:42).

Hammon echoes these words in his address to the blacks of New York:

> Those of you who can read, I must beg you to read the Bible; and if you can get no other time, spare some of your time from sleep, and learn what the mind and will of God is. . . . In hopes of this, I will beg of you to spare no pains in trying to learn to read. If you are once engaged, you may learn. Let all the time you can get be spent in trying to learn to read. Get those who can read, to learn you; but remember, that what you learn for, is to read the Bible. (Ransom, 1970:113-114)

Following the lead of Cotton Mather, the most concerted effort to educate and indoctrinate the enslaved was promoted by the Society for the Propagation of the Gospel in Foreign Parts, which had support of the highest civil and ecclesiastical officials in England and was probably the most powerful branch of organized philanthropy in England. Founded to save souls, black and white, the society provided much of the drive and most of the money behind the missionary effort in New York (McManus, 1966). From 1702 to 1785 the society sent missionaries, catechists, and teachers to America to convert the enslaved. Activities began in New York in 1702 and soon covered the province, especially New York, Westchester, and Queens counties (Vertanes, 1957). The society also recruited local contacts to serve as catechists for the enslaved in the colonies.

According to Klingberg, the Oyster Bay area, around which the Lloyd estate was located, received attention from the society:

> In 1733, the schoolmaster at Oyster Bay, Thomas Keble, reported thirty scholars, four of whom were Negroes, another instance of teaching white and black together. In 1734, the school increased to thirty-one children. The curriculum included reading, writing, arithmetic, and Church Catechism. Enrollment increased to thirty-seven in 1735 at which level it remained for the next decade, with Negro enrollments small. (1942:159-160)

Instruction was not limited to religious teaching, however; the society also provided courses in reading and writing. The organization carried out its efforts both to educate and to proselytize since literacy facilitates proselytizing. In fact, the emphasis of the society was upon education, more than indoctrination. Generally those enslaved under their direction were fed a bland diet of homiletics seasoned with exhortations about the hereafter and the need to submit to lawful authority. The only remotely radical idea advanced by the missionaries was the brotherhood of all men under the fatherhood of God. Although the proselytizers of the society failed to attack the institution of slavery directly, they boldly asserted the enslaved's spiritual equality with the rest of the population. This assertion was ultimately of greater importance than the failure of the proselytizers to win converts (McManus, 1966).

Since the society was quite active in the area of New York where Hammon grew up, conceivably he might have come under its influence. Certainly he espouses the same egalitarian view throughout his poetry and prose. The verse of Scripture he selects to introduce the printed version of his address to the blacks of New York encapsulates Hammon's attitude toward master and servant, indeed toward all mankind: "For I perceive that there is no respect of persons with God; but he hath created all nations of one blood to dwell together upon the face of the earth" (Acts 17:28).

The religious convictions of Hammon are most clearly expressed in "A Dialogue Entitled the Kind Master and the Dutiful Servant." Written in ballad form, with quatrains of alternate iambic tetrameter and iambic trimeter lines with *a* -*b* -*a* -*b* rhyme scheme, the format is similar to the hymn stanza, often employed eighteenth-century colonial America in the popular hymns of Watts and Wesley. Hammon uses the form to skillfully take the reader on an exercise of "follow the leader." The thirty stanzas

8. Dilemma of the Dutiful Servant: The Poetry of Jupiter Hammon 111

open with Master and Servant alternately exchanging remarks for the first fifteen stanzas, with stanzas 16 to 23 offering "A Line on the Present War" and with the Servant closing with the last seven stanzas.

Stanza one opens with an invitation from the Master:

> Come my servant, follow me,
> According to thy place;
> And surely God will be with thee,
> And send thee heav'nly grace.

(59)

With great irony the Servant is bid to follow "According to thy place," as if he has any choice in the matter. Yet before the poem ends Master and Servant will have changed places.

The Servant responds by pointing out the conditions for following, as he relates the essence of the message of the entire poem:

> Dear Master, I will follow thee,
> According to thy word,
> And pray that God may be with me
> And save thee in the Lord.

(59)

The poem emphasizes the importance of following, as the term is used or implied in fifteen of the first twenty-four stanzas. The second stanza gives the basis for following "according to thy word." The Master who bids the Servant to follow, likewise, is told to follow by Christ, the Master, who said, "Follow me."

As the dialogue continues, the poet subtly brings Master and Servant to the same level. Beginning in stanza 9, the poem employs the pronouns "our," "us," and "we." Both Master and Servant speak of "King" and the Master acknowledges "My servant, we are sinners all."

MASTER

My Servant, follow Jesus now,
　　Our great victorious King;
Who governs all both high and low,
　　And searches things within.

SERVANT

Dear Master, I will follow thee,
　　When praying to our King;
It is the Lamb I plainly see,
　　Invites the sinner in.

MASTER

My servant, we are sinners all,
　　But follow after grace;
I pray that God would bless thy soul,
　　And fill thy heart with grace.

(60-61)

The Servant closes the poem, addressing the readers as "friends," a term mindful of Jesus' exhortation to his disciples in John 15:14, 15: "Ye are my friends, if ye do whatsoever I command you. Henceforth I called you not servants . . . but I have called you friends." The poet also uses the term to describe himself and addresses his readers as "Christian friends": "Believe me now my Christian friends, Believe your friend call'd Hammon: You cannot to your God attend, And serve the God of Mammon."

The context of the passage to which Hammon alludes reminds followers of Christ that no man can serve two masters: "No man can serve two masters: For either he will hate the one, and love the other; or else he will hold to the one, and despise the other. Ye cannot serve God and Mammon" (Matthew 6:24).

In referring to himself as "friend," which is an elevated status above a servant, the Servant does not demote his master, but both Master and Servant are placed on the same level as equals before Christ, who is their lord and king (yet also a servant). Matthew 10:24, 25 make clear this position: "The disciple is not above his master, nor the servant above his lord. It is enough that he be as his master, and the servant as his lord."

8. Dilemma of the Dutiful Servant: The Poetry of Jupiter Hammon 113

As the reader progresses through the dialogue, one may ask who follows whom? The Master opens with a call for the Servant to follow him. The Servant responds by establishing the basis for following "according to thy word." Before the poem ends, both Master and Servant are reminded to follow Christ, "our King," thus both become "fellow followers." At the end of the poem Master and Servant have switched places, as the Servant takes the lead and closes the poem. The poet ultimately becomes a good follower by being a good leader as he concludes the dialogue. Although the piece appears to be simple and straightforward, there is a subtle strategy at work whereby Hammon gives a masterful demonstration of "follow the leader."

Just as the sweeping influence of the Society for the Propagation of the Gospel may have touched the life of the poet Hammon, so might another movement that overwhelmed New England during his lifetime also have produced a profound effect upon this early black writer. Inspired by Jonathan Edwards in 1735, The Great Awakenlng or New Light Movement inaugurated a series of revivals, sweeping America in a wave of great religious emotionalism, touching whites and blacks alike. The powerful sermons of Edwards, Whitefield, and Wesley thundered with the words "regeneration" and "conversion," as thousands of people had deeply personal experiences with God. Such an experience may have been the inspiration for Hammon's "An Evening Thought (Salvation by Christ with Penetential [*sic*] Cries)," which opens with:

> Salvation comes by Christ alone,
> The only Son of God;
> Redemption now to every one
> That love his holy word.

(45)

The poem opens with the word "Salvation," as the poet hammers away with the term twenty-three times throughout the work. "An Evening Thought" is also the only poetic work of Hammon's to use the word "slave."

> Salvation now comes from the Lord,
> He being thy captive slave.

(46)

The poet does not use the term *enslaved* to refer to himself, whom he designates with the milder term *servant*. But the poet reserves the harshest designation of servitude and ladens the couplet with irony and paradox, as he points out the source of salvation, which comes from the Servant of Servants, the Lord, who is not merely enslaved, but "captive slave" to those whom He serves.

Hammon's conscious repetition of the term *salvation* may also have been a means of facilitating memorization, in the same way that Wigglesworth's "Day of Doom" was designed as a didactic tool for Puritan doctrine. Loggins discusses the possible influence of "Day of Doom" upon Hammon's "A Poem for Children with Thoughts on Death," which he describes as a "Methodist Commentary" on the rigid Calvinism expounded in that section of "Day of Doom" describing the Last Judgment of children who died in infancy and who are not God's elect. (1931:369). Both works are structured the same way, with four-line stanzas followed by the scriptural reference alluded to in that stanza. Because of his use of the same format, conceivably Hammon could have been exposed to Wigglesworth and other such writers.

Hammon undoubtedly had access to some of the noted writers of his day. He speaks of "Mr. Burkitt" [*sic*] in his "Winter Piece," where he also mentions "Bishop Beverage" [*sic*]. Books by Burkitt and Beveridge were part of the extensive library of Henry Lloyd. Conceivably Hammon had the opportunity to read these works and others, for his master not only imported books for sale but lent books to tenants on his property and to the inhabitants of the nearby towns of Huntington and Oyster Bay. Records indicate that Lloyd amassed an impressive collection of "primers, horn books, catechisms, Bibles, Testaments, Psalters, prayer books, a law book, pictures, ink horns, paper, and such titles as *The Twelve Patrlarchs. The Young Mans's Companion.* Hodder's *Arithmetic* Dolittle's *Lord's Supper.* Watt's *Song*" (Vertanes, 1957:29).

Access to the library of the family was undoubtedly a great factor in Hammon's development as a poet. Such exposure, together with diligent reading and study of the Bible and personal devotion, participation in family religious observances, and attendance at church were also factors contributing to the poet's growth. In addition some schooling and catechetical instruction, either from the family tutor or perhaps from the Society for the Propagation of the Gospel, plus the encouragement he probably received from his benefactors also amply account for his degree of intellectual maturity and the literary intensity motivating the poet to write and publish.

8. Dilemma of the Dutiful Servant: The Poetry of Jupiter Hammon

Unquestionably numerous influences must have contributed to his writing ability. That he published a poem in colonial America is truly an awesome accomplishment in itself. Not only did he publish poetry but prose as well. Without the assistance of the Lloyds and other supporters, he could not have done this. Relying on such support, Hammon could not offend those whites who encouraged him in his writing endeavors. He assimilates their views; yet he maintains his own integrity, as he attempts to become a dutiful servant who leads his master to the truth. He himself said, "Good servants frequently make good masters" (Ransom, 1970:7).

Examining the cultural background of Hammon's time and recognizing his personal religious commitment, one can sense the dilemma he faced in his efforts to reconcile his position as a servant of God with being a servant of man. Although he contributed to African American literature with the publishing of his first poem, his contribution goes beyond this singular accomplishment. He is a significant figure whose method of composing must have been similar to those who fashioned spirituals from their souls; yet his poetry is original.

> It would seem likely that he was strongly affected by the renaissance of religious fervor which swept Long Island in the middle 18th century, for he expresses the deep evangelical feelings of the time. Yet the medium and form of expression, while owing much to the poetic forms of hymn writers, is his own, with stirring similarities to Negro spirituals and other religious folk poetry. (Ransom, 1970:12)

Hammon's poetry can be described as roughhewn and rugged, rhythmically heavy with at times awkward, forced rhymes. Nevertheless, the poetry does mark a transition leading from the artless beauty of spirituals to the more formal verse of the poets following Hammon. Wagner speaks of "An Evening Thought" as "a halfway stage between the guileless art of the unknown composers of spirituals and the already much wordier manner of the popular preacher" (1973:17).

Although Hammon's verse lacks the refinement and fluency of his contemporary, Phillis Wheatley, there are many admirable qualities to be noted in his works. Loggins states that Hammon's verse was composed to be heard with "that peculiar sense of sound, the distinguishing characteristic of Negro folk poetry" (1931:12). Robinson classifies Hammon as an oratorical poet whose works are best suited for oral renderings. (1971:xv) Porter sees Hammon's verse as "seldom matched by such occasional expressions as hymns, spiritual songs, or didactic verse, however impassioned, on the subjects of freedom, slavery, or worldly bliss" (1971:3). Thus in his unrefined yet engaging manner, Hammon strives in his poetry and indeed in his life to resolve the dilemma of being a servant to God, yet a dutiful servant to man.

REFERENCES
Greene, Lorenzo Johnston. (1942) *The Negro in Colonial New England, 1620-1776*. New York: Columbia University Press.
Higginbotham, A. Leon, Jr. (1978) *In the Matter of Color--Race and the American Legal Process--The Colonial Period*. New York: Oxford University Press.
Klingberg, Frank J. (1940) *Anglican Humanitarianism in Colonial New York*. Philadelphia: n.p..
Loggins, Vernon. (1931) *The Negro Author in America*. New York: Columbia University Press.
Luther, Martin. (1957) *Treatise on Christian Liberty (Freedom of a Christian)*. Philadelphia: Fortress Press.
McManus, Edgar J. (1966) *A History of Slavery in New York*. Syracuse, N.Y.: Syracuse University Press.
Mather, Cotton. (1706) *The Negro Christianized*. Boston: n.p..
Porter, Dorothy B., ed. (1971) *Early Negro Writing*. Boston: Beacon Press.
Quarles, Benjamin. (1969) *The Negro in the Making of America*. New York: Collier Macmillan.
Ransom, Stanley A., Jr., ed. (1970) *America's First Negro Poet: The Complete Works of Jupiter Hammon of Long Island*. Port Washington, NY: Kennikat Press, 1970.
Robinson, William H., ed. (1971) *Early Negro Writing*. Boston: Beacon Press.
Schomburg, Arthur A. (1930) "Jupiter Hammon, before the New York African Society." *Amsterdam News*, 14.
Vertanes, Charles A. (1957) "Jupiter Hammon, Early Long Island Poet." *Nassau County Historical Journal*. Winter, 1-17.
Wagner, Jean. (1973) *Black Poets of the United States*. Urbana: University of Illinois Press.
Wegellin, Oscar. (1969) *Jupiter Hammon, American Negro Poet: Selections from his Writings and a Bibliography*. Freeport, N.Y.: Books for Libraries Press. (First published in 1915.)

8. Dilemma of the Dutiful Servant: The Poetry of Jupiter Hammon   117

Whitlow, Roger. (1973) *Black American Literature: A Critical History*. Chicago: Nelson Hall.

9

The Blue/Black Poetics of Sonia Sanchez

Regina B. Jennings

As a poet, Sonia Sanchez has evolved since her first book *Homecoming* published in 1969 during the heart of the Black Power Movement. Back then her poetics included a strident tropology that displayed a matriarchal protection of black people. Today, after publishing twelve books of poetry, including the acclaimed *Homegirls and Handgrenades* and *Under a Soprano Sky*, one can still discover poetic conventions developed during the Black Arts Movement. The purpose of this artistic movement involved challenging the Eurocentric hegemony in art by developing a new aesthetic that represented the ethos, pathos, and expression of African Americans. These neo-renaissance artists were inspired by the rhetorical eloquence and activism of Rev. Martin Luther King, Jr. and Malcolm X. From this era of intense political activism, artists such as Sonia Sanchez wrote poems illustrating a resistance to inequality best described in "Black Art" by Imamu Amiri Baraka (1969).

It is obvious that revolutionary fervor characterized some of Sanchez's work, but it is essential for understanding her poetics, as well as the neo-aesthetic of the sixties, to recognize that anarchy was not the goal. These poets considered themselves to be word soldiers for black people, defending their right to have equality, honor, and glory. In each of Sanchez's volumes of poetry, for example, one finds the artist handling themes that include love, harmony, race unification, myth, and history. Her poetic personas are diverse, incorporating themes from China, to Nicaragua, to Africa. Yet, there is a pattern in her figurative language that blends an African connection. In this article, I shall examine the Afrocentric tropes that embody Sanchez's poetics. To use Afrocentricity in this regard is to examine aspects of traditional African culture not limited by geography in Sanchez's work. A body of theory that argues such an African commonality is in Kariamu Welsh's *The Concept of*

Nzuri: Towards Defining an Afrocentric Aesthetic. Using her model will enable this kind of topological investigation.

Houston Baker, Jr. presents a different aesthetic in *Blues, Ideology, and Afro-American Literature.* This book is a point of departure from Africa, concentrating solely on discussions of African American art from a black American perspective. On the back cover of *Under a Soprano Sky,* Baker maintains that blue/black motif appears in selected works by Sanchez. Baker's definition of the blues constitutes a transitory motion found precisely in this motif. The blues manifests itself in Sanchez's prosody in varying degrees and in differing forms. It determines shape and category, directs the vernacular, and informs the work. To demonstrate this specific vitality in Sanchez's poetry, Baker's construct of a blues matrix is an apt qualifier.

One can identify the blues as matrix and Afrocentric tropology in Sanchez's literary vision when one understands the significance of her axiology. Her ethics informs not only her creativity but her essays and articles as well. Her focus is to inscribe the humanity of blacks to challenge the Eurocentric perspective of black inferiority. Her particular axiology emerged during the greatest period of social unrest between whites and blacks. In the sixties, African American artists deliberately fused politics and art to direct social change. That Sanchez's axiology influenced her ethics has to be considered in order to understand why her poetry inverts the tropology of "white" and "black." The artists of the Black Arts Movement were at war with America. Their tone and perspective encouraged black people to rethink their collective position and to seize control to direct their destiny. Consider this Sanchez poem entitled "Memorial":

>   i didn't know bobby
>   hutton in fact it is
>   too hard to re
>   cord all the dying
>   young/blks.
>   in this country.
>   but   this i do know
>   he was
>   part of a long/term/plan
>   for blk/people.

9. The Blue/Black Poetics of Sonia Sanchez 121

>   he was denmark
>   vesey.
>   malcolm
>   garvey. all the
>   dead/blk/men
>   of our now/time
>   and ago/time.
>   check it out. for
>   bobby wd be living today.
>   Panther/jacket/beret
>   and all.
>   check it out & don't let
>   it happen again.
>   we got enough
>   blk/martyrs for all the
>   yrs to come
>   that is, if they
>   still coming
>   after all the shit/
>   yrs of these
>   white/yrs   goes down

(Sanchez 1969:30)

The ethics in "Memorial" involve the dichotomy between "white" and "blk" (black). By positioning Bobby Hutton historically in the pantheon of heroic black men who died fighting against racial oppression, Sanchez elevates him. In death, she has magnified the significance of how he lived. The conditionality of being black in this poem denotes heroism against tyranny. In fact, D. H. Melhem (1990) argues that heroism exists in Sanchez's poetry. In the ideology of black people, Panthers are resistance leaders (Foner, 1970; Brisbane, 1974). Thus, by capturing the humanity of heroes in the first five stanzas, the persona suggests to the reader that he or she too can incorporate Hutton's heroics.

The term "white" adjectivally expresses the racism in America responsible for all the "years" of heroic deaths. White is now an inverted symbol, the antithesis of its traditional meaning of purity and goodness. Imamu Amiri Baraka, one of the definers of the black aesthetic, along with Larry Neal, "modernized the black poem by fusing it with modernist and postmodernist forms and ideas (Harris, 1985:136)." William Harris writes that poets such as Sanchez learned from Baraka to invert poetic techniques. "Even the most cursory reading of contemporary black poetry reveals the extent to which it was influenced by projective form and avant-garde" (Harris, 136). However, Sanchez herself states that her inversion of symbols derived directly from the Muslims and Malcolm X (Braxton, 1990:357). The meaning of avant-garde has to broadened to include the philosophy of Malcolm X. To adopt a projective form was crucial to the sixties poet who stood before audiences during this politically tense era. Poets such as Sanchez were in the forefront of reshaping the ideology and activism of black people. Elements of the avant-garde challenged the status quo in society and in art. Welsh writes: "the idea of art for the sake of art has firm roots in European culture. Africans, for the most part, do not believe in the concept of art for art's sake (Richards, 1985). The life force is the motivating factor in the expression and the product of art (Barrett, 1979:5)."

In "Memorial," the lines "check it out & don't let it happen again" speak directly to the reader, suggesting three modes of action. First, it encourages the reader or listener to review the situation inherent in the poem. Second, it expresses the need for a defensive and offensive posture against oppression. Third, it speaks of black control. This utterance of action points to the passivity of the audience. In this matriarchal persona, using accusatory language and tone in such lines as "part of a long/term/plan," Sanchez infuses the fracture that has historically wounded African American advancement. Likewise, the concept of black annihilation is in the denotation of the final terms "goes down."

Annihilation is a seminal notion in the collective black psyche based upon African enslavement (Kardiner, 1967; Kovel, 1984; Cress-Welsing, 1991). Therefore, Sanchez's linguistic war with America comes out of the ethos of black people. Conversely, another seminal theme throughout her body of work is one of racial solidarity. Using this theme, her persona as matriarchal protector assumes mythic dimensions. The following untitled poem from *We a BadddDDD People* is an example:

9. The Blue/Black Poetics of Sonia Sanchez

>   i am a blk/wooOOOOMAN
>   my face.
>   my brown
>   bamboo/colored
>   blk/berry/face
>   will spread itself over
>   this western hemisphere and
>   be remembered.
>   be sunnnnnnnNNNGG.
>   for i will be called
>   QUEEN. &
>   walk/move in
>   blk/queenly/ways

(1970:6)

Here one can see that the ontology of "blk" has mythological and historical advantages. Male and female deities enrich the mythology of traditional Africa. As "queen," the black woman is an avatar, possessing extraordinary powers, stretching her "face" across the continents (Thompson, 1984:79-83). To be black in this archetypal voice is to be potent, omnipotent, and good. In "Memorial" and in the above black woman poem, a feature of deictics, (verb tenses, adverbials, pronouns, demonstratives) (Culler, 1975:165) is similar, in particular, the concept of time. Both poems converge the timeless present with the future. However, in this black woman poem, the power of myth determines a success that will occur in the future. This sense of continuity depicts power, harmony, and victory. Welsh writes: "It is the consciousness of victory that produces in cyclical fashion an aesthetic will. The consciousness of victory will involve redefinition and reconstruction and a fundamental understanding of the creative processes, historical factors, and cultural legacies of Africa" (8-9).

In the above poem, the aesthetic will is victorious because of the "redefinition" of black that has broadened into a nationalistic "consciousness." This nationalism that challenges Eurocentricism in art and society is an utterance that welcomes its own distinctiveness. It has a concern for all black people distinguished in the gradations of hue. Pragmatics this deliberate demonstrate how deeply Sanchez's poetics emerge from the concept of race solidarity. Unlike black poets of previous decades such as Countee Cullen and Claude McKay, Sanchez finds victory in being black. The ontology of black in the poetry of Cullen and McKay, on the other hand, involves one or all of the following declensions: inferiority, shame, denial, and escape (Bell, 1989; Davis, 1974; Cooper, 1973). Form is another difference in Sanchez's poetry. She does not write poems in traditional taxonomy, imitating and revising established meter, versification, and rhyme. Her poetic patterns are avant-garde.

The theme and genre of the black woman verse show a definite African connection. This is a praise poem popular in Africa since 2000 b.c. (Lomax, 1970:xx). By writing the above poem, Sanchez gives honor to the power of the female principle which will not only be "remembered" but be "sunnnnnnnNNNGG." Song and its traditional significance in African culture has already been established (Bebey, 1975; Chernoff, 1979). From the mundane to the extraordinary, it is interwoven within traditional African culture. When a child cuts its first teeth, the people sing. When a king is coronated, the people sing. Larry Neal writes: "Most contemporary black writing of the last few years has been aimed at consolidating the African American personality. And it has not been essentially a literature of protest. It has, instead, turned its attention inward to the internal problems of the group" (*Black Fire*, 647).

Pigmentation problems have plagued African Americans since their sojourn in this country. Sanchez suggests this problem by lyrically presenting the solution. Her presentation demonstrates the realism inherent in an Afrocentric aesthetic because it must be "representational of the ethos of black people" (Welsh, 1990:3). Sanchez continues:

> and the world
> shaken by
> my blkness
> will channnNNNNNNGGGGGEEEE
> colors. and be
> reborn.
> blk. again.

(1970:6)

To be reborn black again is a prelude to collective self-reliance. The final two lines suggest that blacks were in power prior to whites; therefore, seeking control is in concert with past behavior. Her historical reference probably points toward the ancient Egyptians or Kemitans (Asante, 1990). This reach back to Africa for a common past is a commonality argued in *The Concept of Nzuri*: "Numerous writers have expounded on the historical and cultural bond between continental and

9. The Blue/Black Poetics of Sonia Sanchez

diasporan Africans. It is not based solely on color, but the bond exists because of a common African heritage that dates back to predynastic Egypt" (3).

Sonia Sanchez's poetic voice is visionary and archetypal. She wrote the above black woman poem twenty-one years before scholars in a focused manner textualized the notion of a common African aesthetic. Another facet of this theoretical aesthetic is found in the staggered formation of letters in particular words. This formation is an element of the avant-garde, introduced during the 1960s. For example, consider the spelling of the sign "change." Its orthographic repetition signals a specificity in quality and energy of expression (Richards, 1989:11-12). Dona Richards defines this energy as *ntu*, a manifestation of the energy informing our ontology. By transforming the orthography of "change," Sanchez causes her listeners and readers to enter a textured relationship with the sign's denotation, connotation, and sound. To hear or read a word formulated this way gives an unsettling tension. This orthography for the effect of sound is a poetic praxis that demonstrates the Black Arts Movement's theory of audience involvement, which can be traced back to traditional Africa. David Miller writes that some of Sanchez's poetry is "in essence, communal chant performances in which [she] as poet, provides the necessary language for the performance. The perceptions in such poems are deliberately generalized, filtered through the shared consciousness of the urban black" (Evans, 1984:16). It is here where Sanchez's style sharply contrasts the performances of other sixties poets. Houston Baker would compare this technique to that of the blues or jazz singer making and improvising the moment simultaneously. To compare Sanchez to a more traditional poet is like comparing how singers Patti LaBelle and Paul Simon hit high notes. Thus, Sanchez's "quality of expression" as defined by Welsh, produces an energy that electrifies audiences, involving them in the experience of the performance.

An Afrocentric artist does not view society impartially because "society gives visions and perspectives to the artist" (2). This interrelationship between poet and audience can also be examined in this next poetic praxis. Sanchez prefaces her poetry in a manner that warms the audience. Before she recites, she generally talks informally to her public. By the time she actually reads a poem, they have come to know her as friend, mother, sister, or guide. The following selections demonstrate how Sanchez speaks directly to and with her audience, requesting guidance, direction, companionship, and leadership. The first short excerpt is from a poem entitled "blk rhetoric" and the second is from "let us begin the real work":

> who's gonna make all
> that beautiful blk/rhetoric
> mean something...

(1970:15)

...

> with our
> minds/hands/souls.
> with our blk/visions
> for blk/lives.
> let us begin
> the begin/en work now.
> while our
> children still
> remember us & looooooove.

(1970:65)

"Blk rhetoric" begs for an answer. The reader can be silent or the listener can shout the answer. It doesn't matter; the question encourages a response. Here the poet is asking for direction and guidance. She is asking either to join or to be joined in the task of building a better future for black people. In "let us begin the real work," the deictics (pronoun usage) illustrate further the nonseparation between poet and audience. The pronoun "I" is absent. Jonathan Culler writes that the artist constructs a "model of human personality and human behavior in order to construct referents for the pronouns" (1975:165). Sanchez's "human behavior" is represented in the possessive case pronouns throughout the work. They bind the artist not only to her creation, but also to her audience. She takes responsibility for the behavior she calls forth in the poem. The use of "our" in particular shows the respect and interrelatedness the artist has for the audience, and by extension, society. She is "with" them, representing their ethos and pathos in poetry and performance. Terminology such as "our" visions and "our children" creates a commonality of purpose and strongly indicates her position as one of the people. The pragmatics suggest that she is not a leader but an utterer and clarifier of what is already known. To paraphrase Malcolm X in a 1972 film about his life, Sanchez is only telling the people what they already know.

9. The Blue/Black Poetics of Sonia Sanchez

Similarly, the blues is a creative form indigenously American that has always been known. In selected poems from Sanchez's collection, one finds, as Houston Baker points out, a blue/black motif.

> we are sudden stars
> you and i exploding in
> our blue black skins

(1984:9)

To the redefinition of "black" as aesthetically and mythically good, Sanchez adds the color blue. This blue motif changes meaning in different poems, but it consistently demonstrates itself as a literary engagement issuing specific denotations to expression. Houston Baker defines the blues as matrix. It is an impetus for the search for an American form of critical inquiry. The blues is, of course, best known as a musical art form removed from linguistics and semantics. Naturally when one thinks of the blues perhaps one conjures up a grits and gravy black man fingering his guitar or a whiskey brown woman moaning about her man leaving town. Baker extends these cultural metaphors. In *Blues, Ideology, and Afro-American Literature*, his theoretical blues matrix informs African American literature, giving it inventive play in symbol and myth. Its expression gives the literature an emotive of music. The blues emerges out of black vernacular expression and history. It is the motion of the enslaved American Africans bringing coherence to experience.

In the above poem entitled "Haiku," Sanchez gives us the energy of the blues "exploding" inside a distinctive American couple. Being both black and blue is an American duality that symbolizes the tragic institution of European slavery and the vital energizer that reformed the tragedy. It is significant that in Sanchez's collection of poetry, she frequently writes symbolically in sharp and brilliant haiku that form a "locus of a moment of revelation" (Culler, 175). "Haiku" reveals the heights of cosmological love, one boundless as the universe, with energies constantly in transformation and motion. Baker writes:

> To suggest a trope for the blues as a forceful matrix in cultural understanding is to summon an image of the black blues singer at the railway junction lustily transforming experiences of durative (increasingly oppressive) landscape into the energies of rhythmic song. The railway juncture is marked by transience. (7)

Only a radically altered discursive prospect--one that dramatically dissociates itself from the "real"--can provide access to the blues artistry. (121)

To adjectivally describe "stars" as "sudden" marks this transience. Considering that the blues is always in motion contextualizes the differing modes of exploration that Sanchez creates when this motif appears. Using "blue" to denote mythic propensities, she creates it as a healing force, not just for her own personal self, but as a remedy for the distress that disturbs humanity. Consider this excerpt from "Story."

> when will they touch the godhead
> and leave the verses of the rock?
> and i was dressed in <u>blue</u>
> <u>blue</u> of the savior's sky.
> soon, o soon, i would be worthy.

(1984:9)

Notice that the voice is restrained and reverent as if in prayer. The mythical elements are obvious, giving a timeless quality to the poem, but a certain deictic movement signaled by the word *when* quietly reaches back into antiquity. For a specific effect, Sanchez's typography moves inward in the final three lines. This kind of typographic movement alerts the reader that something special is occurring in those lines. It is the persona, perhaps being either ritualized or anointed for the job of saving souls. The comparison of "blue" as the color of the garment worn with the "blue" of the "savior's sky" dramatically accentuates the healing potential of "blue" as color and as spatial covering of the universe. This blues matrix is undertoned with a subtle sadness; yet it is not the sadness normally associated with the blues singer. It is more like the melancholy of a holy person relinquishing her personal wants to be able to fulfill an ordained prophecy. Larry Neal called it the Blues God that survived the Middle Passage: "The blues god is an attempt to isolate the blues element as an ancestral force, as the major ancestral force of the Afro-American. It's like an Orisha figure" (Baker, 1988:157-58).

Orisha are African deities that can interact with mortals through prayer, sacrifice, and dance. They are either male or female, each controlling specific powers that inform human existence (Thompson, 1983; Jahn, 1961). In traditional African culture, one of the ways people can become avatars is through ritual where those chosen dress in the colors

9. The Blue/Black Poetics of Sonia Sanchez

of the god and adorn themselves or are adorned in natural objects of the diety's habitat. For example, the riverain goddess Oshun heals with water and carries a fan crafted in a fish motif because her spirit moves through fish. In "Story," the persona's spirit is placated and made reverential through blue as motif. This shows a specific example of how the blues matrix influenced Sanchez's poetics. From the mythic to the commonplace, it can determine content, category, and form. A point of contrast is in the next selection where Sanchez writes a blues poem written in black vernacular expression.

> will you love me baby when the sun goes down
> i say will you love me baby when the sun goes down
> or you just a summer time man leaving fo winter comes
> round.

(1987:74)

This poem entitled "blues" can be sung or recited in the style of a blues song. Its mimesis is in the melody and lyric of music. Repetition is a poetic as well as a blues convention reifying the stated question. The terms "i say" merely add stress, signifying the importance of the initial inquiry. Langston Hughes gave the concept of the "blues-singing black" prominence in poetry. As a folk poet or a poet of the folk Hughes's works have marks of orature. According to Richard Barksdale in *Black American Literature and Humanism*, Hughes poetry contains naming, enumerating, hyperbole, understatement, and street-talk rhyming. Plus, Hughes's has a recurring motif of a "sun down" image. Sanchez in a real sense is a disciple of the Hughesian school. In her repeated line is a signifying "sun down" image.

An examination of the deictics of verb tense demonstrates the converging of the present with the future. The speaker is asking a question that can only be answered in the future. Baker refers to blues translators as those who interpret the experiencing of experience (1974:7). The persona is allowing the readers to partake of her knowledge of distinct circumstances that ended in grief and loss.

Metaphorically ingesting her "man" demonstrates the music in lyrical and figurative language. Cannibalistically, this man is very much a part of the persona. Yet, an irony is in the final two lines: the persona is not going to suffer grief and loss again. Larry Neal writes: "even though the blues may be about so-called hard times, people generally feel better after hearing them or seeing them. They tend to be ritually liberating in that sense" (Baker, 1988:158).

Aware of experiencing experience, the persona, "sees" the probability of sorrow lying before her. In the seeing is the "liberating" because she is free to make choices about her life. She can choose to continue her present course, or she may redirect her situation, excluding the danger signal in front of her, or she may take some other mode of action, keeping the situation in tact but with some element of difference. This series of options in this folksy expression is heightened because of the final stanza.

This is the inventive play of the blues. Was the persona teasing us all along? Will she indeed start a brand new life? Will she continue to question the stability of her mate, or is she preparing him for the difference, the changes that life automatically brings? The answer rests in the mystery of the Blues God, always in motion, forever in productive transit.

The poetry of Sonia Sanchez continues to be in productive transit. She is a poet spanning over two decades, creating a new aesthetic that fused politics and art. She believes that the artist is the creator of social values (Sanchez, 1983) and her legacy and artistry indicate that single purpose. As the co-founder of the Black Studies Program at San Francisco State College, in 1967 she has been the antithesis of the ivory tower scholar. Sanchez's activism is difficult to equal. Not only did she fight for a Black Studies Program, but she is the first person to develop and teach a course concerning black women in literature. Sanchez has lived and created in an Afrocentric perspective before this way of knowing became textualized. Creating a protective matriarchal persona, she has through versification, plays, and children's books inscribed the humanity of black people. Being our champion and critic, she has forged a blue motif that cleanses, heals, mystifies, and rejoices.

REFERENCES

Asante, Molefi Kete (1987) *The Afrocentric Idea*. Philadelphia: Temple University Press.

Asante, Molefi Kete (1990) "The African Essence in African American Language." In M. K. Asante and K. W. Asante, *African Culture The Rhythms of Unity*, pp. 233-252. Trenton, N.J.: Africa World Press.

Baker, Houston A., Jr. (1988) *Afro-American Poetics: Revisions of Harlem and the Black Aesthetic.* Madison: University of Wisconsin Press.

Baker, Houston A., Jr. (1984) *Blues, Ideology, and Afro-American Literature.* Chicago: University of Chicago Press.

Baker, Houston A., Jr. (1974) *A Many-colored Coat of Dreams: The Poetry of Countee Cullen.* Detroit:Broadside Press.

Bebey, Francis. (1975) *African Music: A People's Art.* New York: L. Hill.

Bell, Bernard. (1989). *The Afro-American Novel and Its Tradition.* The Amherst: University of Massachusetts Press.

Braxton, Joanne M. and Andree Nicola McLaughlin, eds. (1990) *Wild Women in the Whirlwind: Afro-American Culture and the Contemporary Literary Renaissance.* New Brunswick, N.J.: Rutgers University Press.

Brisbane, Robert H. (1974) *Black Activism: Racial Revolution in the United States, 1954-1970.* Valley Forge, PA: Judson Press.

Chernoff, John Miller. (1979) *African Rhythm and African Sensibility.* Chicago: University of Chicago Press.

Cooper, Wayne, ed. (1973) *The Passion of Claude Mckay: Selected Prose and Poetry 1912-1948.* New York: Schocken Books.

Cress-Welsing, Frances. (1991) *The Isis Papers.* Chicago: Third World Press.

Culler, Jonathan. (1975) *Structural Poetics: Structuralism, Linguistics, and the Study of Literature.* New York: Cornell University Press.

Davis, Arthur P. (1974) *From the Dark Tower: Afro-American Writers, 1900-1960.* Washington, D.C.: Howard University Press.

Evans, Marie, ed. (1984) *Black Women Writers 1950-1980: A Critical Evaluation.* New York: Anchor Books.

Foner, Philip S., ed. (1970) *The Black Panthers Speak.* New York: J. B. Lippincott.

Harris, William J. (1985) *The Poetry and Poetics of Amiri Baraka.* Columbia: University of Missouri Press.

Jahn, Janheinz. (1961) *Muntu: The New African Culture.* New York: Grove Press.

Jones, LeRoi and Larry Neal, eds. (1969) *Black Fires.* New York: William Morrow.

Kardiner, Abram and Lionel Ovesey. (1967) *The Mark of Oppression.* Cleveland, Ohio: Meridian Books.

Kovel, Joel. (1984) *White Racism: A Psychohistory.* New York: Columbia University Press.
Lomax, Alan and Raoul Abdul, eds. (1970) *3000 Years of Black Poetry.* New York: Dodd, Mead & Company.
Malcolm X. (1972) *The Autobiography of Malcolm X.* Warner Bros Studio.
Melhem, D. H. (1990) *Heroism in the New Black Poetry.* Lexington: University Press of Kentucky.
Sanchez, Sonia. (1983) *Crisis and Culture: Two Speeches by Sonia Sanchez.* New York: Black Liberation Press.
Sanchez, Sonia. (1969) *Homecoming.* Detroit: Broadside Press.
Sanchez, Sonia. (1984) *Homegirls & Handgrenades.* New York: Thunder's Mouth Press.
Sanchez, Sonia. (1987) *Under a Soprano Sky.* Trenton, N.J.: Africa World Press.
Sanchez, Sonia. (1970) *We A BaddDDD People.* Detroit: Broadside Press.
Thompson, Robert Farris. (1984) *Flash of the Spirit: African and Afro-American Art and Philosophy.* New York: Vintage Books.
Welsh, Kariamu. (1991) *The Concept of Nzuri: Towards Defining an Afrocentric Aesthetic.* Westport, C.T.: Greenwood Press.

10

Afrocentric Aesthetics in Selected Harlem Renaissance Poetry
Abu Shardow Abarry

Due to the persistent inability of Eurocentric literary paradigms to fully understand and explicate the artistic and literary creations of peoples of African descent, scholars have once again responded with a variety of innovative and interesting alternatives. Probably the best known and most interesting of such new ideas is Afrocentricity, especially as defined by its Temple University proponents like Asante, Keto, Azibo, and Welsh; and other intellectuals like Maulana Karenga, Jacob Carruthers, Dona Richards, Carol Aisha Blackshire, Wade Nobles, and Naim Akbar. According to Asante, for example, Afrocentricity is the placement of African peoples, both continental and diasporan, at the center of any literary or artistic creations and analysis (1987:6). In other words, literature by African or African American writers must reflect and treat African peoples as subject, not object; and African ideals, values, culture, history, traditions and worldview must inform any such creation, analysis, or presentation. (Asante, 1989:5).

By deductive reasoning the Afrocentric aesthetics then becomes a reference to the values, criteria and perspectives of beauty and goodness derived from the African and African American's cultural ideals, social and historical realities, and traditions. As such, it is an aesthetics distinguished by what Keto calls its Africa-centeredness (1989:5). It is complex, existing in the cultures of peoples of African descent all over the world. But it may also be specific, derived from a particular locale, region, or group, or a set of locales or groups, either on the continent or in the African diaspora. It may be composite, or Pan-African, drawing on features common to all African cultures and peoples. But irrespective of its locale, region, or group of derivation, when critically digested, the aesthetics yields the following characteristics, patterns, and values: spirituality, harmony, repetition, call and response, balance, rhythm, communalism, and functionality (Thompson, 1974:16). Other dimensions of the aesthetics, especially in the performing arts have been brilliantly articulated in Welsh's Nzuri model as consisting of polyrhythm, polycentrism, curvilinearity, dimensionality, holism, and epic memory (1990:74-82).

The foregoing then is what Afrocentric aesthetics means. It consists of a set of specific values, characteristics, and perspectives that arise from the historical circumstances, cultural imperatives, and legitimate aspirations of all themselves and other people of African descent. Its meaning, ethos, motifs, technique, and form all emanate from the worldview of African peoples and reflect their own sense of beauty, goodness, and transcendental truth. It is imbued with the generative power of African orature, the Spirituals, the work songs, the blues, jazz, tales, and Ebonics (Asante, 1990:8-44). There is no room in such aesthetics for "art for art's sake" as we see in the arts of Western cultures. Nor is the individual seen to be separate from, or deemed more important than, his society. It is humanistically derived, spiritually inspired, and commually oriented, with the individual lending his knowledge, special talent, and skills in the formulation and articulation of group sensibilities, goals, and aspirations (Obiechina, 1975:53-65).

As such any artist or writer who utilizes this aesthetics should endeavor to "speak victoriously, dispense with resignation, create excellence and establish victorious values for his or her African community" (Asante, 1990a:42-73). It should also be seen to uphold the Ma'atic principles of truth, fairplay, and righteousness. Though different, the Afrocentric aesthetics is not supposed to be superior or inferior to any other variety of racial or cultural aesthetics. But it consists of a special framework, values, and perspectives that should be taken seriously into consideration by any African American or European American, or Europeanized African critic or writer who embarks on a critical interpretation of a literary or artistic work based on, or emanating from, any part of the African world. If this is done, hegemonistic and ethnocentric creations and analysis may be averted, paving the way for truth, harmony, mutual respect, and intercultural understanding.

Now that we seem to understand what is meant here by Afrocentric aesthetics, let us attempt a review of some of the African American literary works that appeared during the Harlem Renaissance period and to assess the extent to which the foregoing ideas of truth, beauty, goodness,

10. Afrocentric Aesthetics in Selected Harlem Renaissance Poetry

and pleasure are reflected in them. Though the writers and critics of the Harlem Renaissance period have been severely criticized by certain succeeding generations of critics, particularly members of the Black Arts Movement of the 1960s, for going through "the stage of affirming their personal and national identity by aspiring to the ideals of high art" (Bell, 1974:11). Such negative comments, as Bernard Bell has rightly argued, tend to tell us more "about the politics and sensibilities of the critics than about the aesthetic qualities of specific works" (1974:11). Indeed, the period has remained one of the most significant in African American literary history. This was the time when the works and activities of older scholars like W. E. B. DuBois, Alain Locke, James Weldon Johnson, C. L. R. James, Charles S. Johnson, Carter G. Woodson, and Marcus Garvey helped to galvanize young African Americans into a higher consciousness of themselves as a people, their culture and destiny to a level hitherto unknown. As rightly noted by Charles S. Johnson, this was the period when African American writing showed confident self-portraiture, a "more widespread effort in the direction of art than was possible in the two previous centuries" (Bontemps, 1969:vii). Alain Locke saw the African Americans of the day inevitably moving forward under the control largely of their own objectives in an effort to re-establish the connection between peoples of African descent the world over. (1925:3-16). The upshot would be a rejuvenated black culture and self-esteem. As Huggins says, the period "produced a phenomenal race consciousness and race assertion, as well as unprecedented numbers of poems, stories, and works of art by black people" (1971:82-83).

However, the specific aesthetic agenda for the period was first articulated in 1926 by one of the then younger writers, Langston Hughes:

> We young Negro artists who create now intend to express our individual dark-skinned selves without fear or shame. If white people are pleased, we are glad. If they are not, it doesn't matter. We know we are beautiful. And ugly too. The tom-tom cries and the tom-tom laughs. If colored people are pleased, we are glad. If they are not, their displeasure doesn't matter either. We build our temples for tomorrow, strong as we know how, and we stand on top of the mountain, free within ourselves. (85)

Energized by this innovative agenda, the young artists and writers responded by turning to their cultural and historical past for exploitable models. The popular misconception of Africa as a shameful and savage land was transformed into a reconnecting symbol of pride, beauty, and inspiration. Consequently African and African American history, legends and myths, music and folk speech became elements of a re-usable past. But the Afrocentric aesthetic also demands how well the artist has portrayed the folk culture, utilized folk forms and ethos to reinterpret the community, myths, and project their collective vision. (Fowler, 1981:5-12). Not all of them were able to do that, given their individual talents, personalities, and vision. Thus while gifted poets like Countee Cullen and Claude McKay echo the culture in their works but cling to the European aesthetic as a validating stamp, others like Jean Toomer, Langston Hughes, and James Weldon Johnson show a sincere attempt at self-definition through cultural and historical explorations in the path of Afrocentric consciousness.

It is paradoxical that the author of the book *Cane* who was first to capture the real spirit of the new aesthetic American of mixed racial heritage, had previously insisted on being recognized only as "an American," not white, not black (Bontemps, 1969:viii-ix). The key to this ironic twist may be seen in Toomer's relocation:

> Within the last two or three years, however, my growing need for artistic expression has pulled me deeper and deeper into the Negro group. And as my powers of receptivity increased I found myself loving it in a way that I could never love the other (white). It has stimulated and fertilized whatever creative talents I may contain within me. A visit to Georgia last Fall was the starting point of almost everything of worth that I have done. I heard folksongs come from the lips of Negro peasants. I saw the rich dusk beauty that I had heard many false accents about. And a deep part of my nature, a part that I had repressed, sprang suddenly to life and responded to them. Now I cannot conceive of myself as aloof and separated. (Bontemps, 1969:viii-ix)

Being thus relocated in the culture and traditions of his people, Toomer was able to produce a work that reflects the ethos of the African American in the Southern setting in an unprecedented manner. The main source for his artistic creation then became African American history and culture, orature, the spirituals and work songs as well as the interdependence of spirit, man, and nature. However, because of the author's relocation and enhanced vision, many critics and commentators of the time, including the perceptive and talented Arna Bontemps, found it difficult to

10. Afrocentric Aesthetics in Selected Harlem Renaissance Poetry

fully understand his work: "Toomer's *Cane* is as hard to classify as its author. At first glance it appears to consist of assorted sketches, stories, and a novelette, all interspersed with poems. Some of the prose is poetic, and often Toomer slips from one form into the other almost imperceptibly. The novelette is constructed like a play" (viii-ix).

The elements that Bontemps has cited above are in fact what links Toomer's *Cane* strongly to the African aesthetic tradition. In traditional African orature there is no rigid separation between prose, poetry, and drama. The performance of a prose piece may include poetic pieces, dialogue, music, dance, and dramatization. All such elements may be fused into a homogeneous artistic whole that comments on man, community, nature, and spirits. Thus in theme and form *Cane* is deeply rooted in ancestral tradition. It captures the experience of an American writer in the quest for artistic liberation and self-fulfillment. That journey acquaints the hero with the spiritual and environmental (natural) beauty of the African American Southern folk life as it is contrasted with the dingy landscape of black Northern urban life. In the South, he is assailed by beauty "perfect as dusk when the sun goes down," exalted and rocked by powerful folksongs, and hushed by "corn leaves swaying, rusty with talk" the force of epic memory compels recognition that "the Dixi Pike has grown from a goat path in Africa, helping to reconcile the artist passionately with his rich cultural heritage" (Bontemps, 1969:76). Though the work is critical of aspects of that heritage, it is unyielding in its applause for its beauty and spiritual values whose gradual demise the poet laments and tries to stem up. For instance, in the poem "Song of the Sun"[1] Toomer mourns the tragic erosion of African American Southern folk life by the rapid industrialization that has made many people emigrate to such Northern cities as Chicago, Washington, D.C., and New York in the late nineteenth and early twentieth centuries. Below the poet tries to capture and preserve for us some of the vestiges of the idyllic life before it completely disappears:

---

[1] This and all subsequent poems by Jean Toomer were taken from *Cane* (New York: Harper and Row, 1967).

> O Negro slaves, dark purple ripened plums,
> Squeezed, and bursting in the pine-wood air,
> Passing, before they stripped the old tree bare
> One plum was saved for me, one seed becomes
>
> An everlasting song, a singing tree,
> Caroling softly souls of slavery,
> What they were, and what they are to me,
> Caroling softly souls of slavery.
>
> (21)

Though aspects of the poem, such as the poet's almost exclusive interest in the pre-Emancipation life may seem ambivalent, it is right on target in calling on African Americans to explore their historical past for clues to their identity and guidance for future development. One of his other interesting poems, "Cotton Song," is an exercise in victorious thought:

> Come, brother, come. Let's lift it;
> Come now, hewit! roll away!
> Shackles fall upon Judgement Day
> But lets not wait for it.
>
> (15)

The poem is a call to oppressed African Americans to look within themselves, not only for the apt instruments of their liberation, but also on how to use them. He enjoins them to set their own liberation agenda and if necessary to utilize counter-violence against aggression rather than turn the other cheek. The poet asserts that the oppression of the black humanity amounts to oppression against God in whose image the former were also created:

> God's body's got soul,
> Bodies like to roll the soul,
> Cant blame God if we dont roll
> Come, brother, roll, roll!
>
> (15)

The poem also subtly ridicules the Euro-Christian concept of "original sin," which finds no echo in ancestral African religion and notes that though "weary sinners" have been promised a heavenly "cotton-bale" comfort, such a myth is not meant for earthly oppressed people like the group to which the poet belongs:

> Cotton bales are the fleecy way
> Weary sinner's bare feet trod,
> Softly, softly to the throne of God,
> "We aint agwine wait until the Judgement Day!"

(15)

But the publication of *Cane* also created a foretaste of future realities. It presaged Toomer's anguished search for self-identity and fulfilment that lasted until his death in 1967. (Baker, 1975:53-80). The book is therefore Toomer's answer to the probe that required the retracing of steps back to the ancestral heritage. Consequently a few writers who were his contemporaries, like Arthur Fanset and Zora Neale Hurston, began to work with African American orature from various perspectives. The use of such material and the concurrent promotion of spirituals by black intellectuals then became an index of the latter's sophistication and self-confidence in their urbanity (Huggins, 1971:72-75). Paradoxically, they had previously avoided them due to the stigma of enslavement with which it was associated. But as DuBois has stressed in his discussion of "The Sorrow Songs" in *The Souls of Black Folk*, no self-respecting African American would deny such vital and unique achievements of his race (1979). These songs, which reflect the personality and the collective experience of African peoples, also contain mystical and emotive forces that strongly bind them together. Subsequently, some attempts were made by a number of people to collect them. They were "discovered" for European American audiences through the performances of the Fisk Jubilee Singers (Huggins, 1971:75-76). By the second decade of the twentieth century, a growing body of literature on them had begun to appear, all made in the attempt to preserve aspects of African American life and history. But the more perceptive writers of the Harlem Renaissance period went beyond this concern with the genre as the historical account of the emotional and imaginative experience of African Americans. They saw the songs, together with the other genres of African American orature like the blues, jazz, and the sermon, as fertile sources for the reconstruction of the artistic and literary heritage of the race.

One of the talented writers to successfully tap the above mentioned sources, especially the spirituals and the sermon in their artistic and literary works, was James Weldon Johnson. In 1925 and 1926 he and his brother Rosamond had been among the earliest to collect and edit spirituals (Johnson, 1990). In later years he experimented with folk idioms, exploiting the rhetorical vehemence and the captivating imagery of the folk preacher's sermons and prayers as raw material for his poetry. These companion genres to the spirituals, together with their profound religious faith and tremendous emotional power, are what Johnson sets out to capture in his second volume of poetry, *God's Trombone* (1969).

In writing these poems, Johnson tried to capture for art a basic African American expression--the sermon--but not in the manner of Dunbar. He portrays, in a free verse typical black figures of speech and a realistic vision of their Christian feelings and customs. It is true that, as Huggins has noted, Johnson extended the syllables, and included unorthodox expressions, these effects are euphonic and rhythmical, not the dialect poetic. He goes on to explain that he chose "a loose rhythmic instead of a strict metric form" because it was the first that could accommodate itself to the movement, the abandon, the change of tempo, and the characteristic synchopation of the raw indigenous form. To him dialect connotes the minstrel or plantation tradition, unworthy of the serious dignity with which those time-honored sermons and preachers should be treated. Moreover, traditional dialect is difficult for the modern reader to understand, and the beauty of the thought would be lost if it were couched in such archaic verbiage.

The poetry of Johnson possesses a considerable degree of "true and high seriousness" and high poetic craftmanship. It exudes a spiritual and moral quality that grips the mind of all his readers. In *God's Trombone* he provides ample evidence that the voice of the black folk was a suitable medium of artistic expression. The book blazed a new trial for American writers of African descent. Through this and other works he promoted the social interests of his people by "subverting the conventions of literary discourse" (Smith et al., 1991:26-37). He also forged a link between black art and artists to the currents of the vital literary and cultural change that took place in the first three decades of the twentieth century. He may have began his life of leadership thinking of writing as an activity engaged in for its own sake; he ended it along an Afrocentric path in the service of both private pleasure, community interest and public principle.

Another talented poet of the period who successfully transformed black folk speech and musical idioms into poetic diction was Langston Hughes (Barksdale, 1977). He was also one of the earliest writers of the period, together with Countee Cullen, to turn to Africa for identification and artistic inspiration. Their poems "The Negro Speaks of Rivers" and "Heritage" respectively reflect the romantic attraction of Africa as a remote, strange, and forbidden place. But while Hughes's poem reveals his sincerity and sense of epic memory, Countee Cullen's "Heritage" articulates mostly his emotional turmoil, confusion and ambivalence:

> What is Africa to me
> Cooper sun or scarlet sea,
> Jungle star or jungle track,
> Strang bronzed men, or regal black
> Women from whose loins I sprang
> When the birds of Eden sang?
> One three centuries removed
> From the scenes his fathers loved,
> Spicy grove, cinnamon tree,
> What is Africa to me?

(36)

The answer to the recurrent question may be seen in the pejorative terms the poet uses to describe Africa: "barbaic birds," "unremembered bats," and circling "cats" (Baker, 1974:34-35).[2] In spite of the recurrence of the question and the poet's enumeration of Africa's supposed enchanting qualities, the questioner comes off as insincere in his questioning. Africa, therefore, appears to be romantic and exotic in the poem. This lapse, coupled with the use of a rigid tetrametic verse form and rhyme scheme reminiscent of Vachel Lindsay's poem "Congo," constitutes an index to Cullen's aesthetic dislocation. In much the same way, the Afrocentric integrity of Claude McKay's brilliant and empowering pieces, especially the famous "If We Must Die," is jeopardized by the poet's excessive reliance on the sanctity and efficacy of the European poetic forms, particularly the sonnet. In the case of Langston Hughes, however, both in theme and technique, the poem reveals a higher sense of Afrocentric consciousness.

---

[2] See also Arthur P. Davis, *From the Dark Tower: Afro-American Writers: 1900-1960* Washington, D.C.: Howard University Press, 1974), pp. 75-76 and *When Harlem Was in Vogue*.

Though Hughes's symbolic treatment of the Mississippi River may be traditional as Huggins (1971) and others have noted, the poet shows that it is only in conjunction with the other great rivers of the African world experience, such as the Euphrates, the Nile, and the Congo, that it functions effectively as a powerful and enigmatic symbol of perseverance and eternity. Apart from life, nature, and civilization, these rivers are also linked with African peoples, free or enslaved, who have not only known, observed, and interacted with them for centuries, but have also derived from them a sense of strength, inevitability, and eternity. The poet suggests that no matter where they are, the blacks will survive, persist, persevere, and triumph because they have attained harmony with the great streams of life. The identification of the persona with eternal forces that may help in the transcendence over worldly conditions reflects the force and beauty of the spirituals that we have already noted. The poem reveals the centrality of the African world in the process of creation. It celebrates Africa's prime position in the history and civilization of humankind, and it reveals her people's sense of balance between spiritual, natural, and human entities. It is also victorious and empowering because it echoes the transcendental qualities of the blues and the spirituals that have enabled African Americans to overcome pain, suffering, and oppression in the search for self-actualization, truth, freedom, and justice. It also evokes the phenomenon of epic memory by which peoples of African descent are linked subconsciously throughout the world. It is curilinear and positively repetitive.

Some critics might, however, view the poem's references to the Euphrates and Abraham Lincoln as evidence of the poet's dislocation. But such a reading would be off the mark for in classical times considerable interaction and collaboration existed between the Kemetic people of the Nile Valley and the Mesopotamians across whose land the Euphrates flowed. As such, both are parts of the poet's proper center, which he revisits through epic memory. The reference to Abraham Lincoln too is defensible, given his image in the minds of many African Americans as the kind and courageous Emancipator. Such allusions and imagery, therefore, suggest the poet's familiarity with the physical, historical, and spiritual landscapes of his people, whose primordial ancestry, indomitable spirit, and profound humanity he cherishes, highlights, and celebrates in the oft repeated lines:

> I've known rivers ancient as the world and older than the flow
> of human blood in human veins.
> My soul has grown deep like the rivers.
>
> (151)

At the time of its appearance, the poem certainly occupied a crucial niche in the history of African American literature, for in theme and technique it was marked a departure from the ethnography-oriented literature of previous generations. In other words, it was not one of those works of the period that Molefi Asante has described as "speaking of us to others" (1989: 94). Indeed, it was poems like "The Negro Speaks of Rivers" that inspired Alain Locke to write in *The New Negro* that "We have lately had an art that was steadily self-conscious, and racially rhetorical rather than racially expressive. Our poets have now stopped speaking for the Negro--they speak as Negroes. Where formerly they spoke to others and tried to interpret, they now speak to their own and try to express (themselves)" (Hughes, 1927b:33).

The Weary Blues, the collection from which "The Negro Speaks of Rivers" is taken, also features poems of similar aesthetic qualities like "The Weary Blues" and "Afro-American Fragment" (1927b). Some of the poems in this first volume also marked the broadening of concern by Hughes from Africa to the day-to-day life of ordinary black people and their church-oriented tradition. Consequently, such inspirational pieces as "Mother to Son" and "Song for a Dark Girl" appeared in his next volume, *Fine Clothes to the Jew* (1927a). The poems in this collection reflect the dignity of black people, whom the poet exhorts to keep striving for self-fulfillment, victory, and excellence in spite of pain, obstacles, and setbacks. This trend continues into his fictional works, especially *Not Without Laughter* (1930).

Hughes's ability to portray the aesthetic liberty of African peoples as they express their epic memory, personality, and heritage in art during and after the Harlem Renaissance has been praised by almost everyone who has written about him. Thus his works have remained faithful to the meaning and spirit of the Afrocentric declaration that he made at the dawn of the renaissance.

The works of Hughes during the period clearly shows him to be well located within the history, culture, and tradition of his people. Though the whole world was his audience, his main subject was ordinary African Americans, whose speech, character, and humor became part of his poetic idiom, just like the blues and jazz. His "Homesick Blues," for example, is a delightful transformation of a blues lyric into an original poetic creation. He exploits blues rhythm in "Weary Blues" and manipulates its phrases for articulation and stress. The music of his poetry has been described as "the sound of Lennox Avenue, and Seventh South Street," and his language "Harlemese: vibrant, rhythmic, direct and racy" (Bell, 1989:130).

This preoccupation with the common African American folk arises from Hughes's deep personal conviction that it is through the artistic capturing of their experience that authentic Black art would be made possible:

> These common people are not afraid of the spirituals ... and jazz is their child. They furnish a wealth of colorful, distinctive material for any artist because they still hold their own individuality in the face of American standardization in spite of the Nordicized Negro intelligentsia and the desire of some white editors, we have an honest American Negro literature today with us. (1926:67-8)

Hughes's faith in the common people's ability to produce art was underguarded by their "acceptance of what beauty is their own without question?" From what we have seen so far, it is clear that the works of Langston Hughes appear to be the closest to the Afrocentric aesthetic ideal, above those of James Weldon Johnson, Jean Toomer, Claude McKay, and Countee Cullen. This is obvious in the themes, values, and techniques of his poetry. Moreover, whereas the latter four poets tend generally to view external reality largely on the basis of their personal conscience and consciousness, which offered them "a universal criterion," Hughes's vision seems almost always to move in the opposite direction. He lives basically in terms of the extenal world, and in unison with it, making himself one with the community and refusing to stand apart as an individual. Consequently, his poetry reflects the collective states of his people's minds in which he simultaneously participates. This overwhelming immersion in his African and African American heritage easily establishes Langston Hughes as the people's poet. Indeed, it is in his works that ordinary African Americans find their voice and the Afrocentric aesthetics its most glorious expression.

REFERENCES

Asante, Molefi Kete (1987) *The Afrocentric Idea* Philadelphia: Temple University Press.

Asante, Molefi Kete (1988) *Afrocentricity: The Theory of Social Change.* Trenton, N.J.: Africa World Press, Inc.

Asante, Molefi Kete (1990a) "Afrocentricity and the Critique of Drama." *The Western Journal of Black Studies* 14 (2):136-141.

Asante, Molefi Kete (1990b) *Kemet, Afrocentricity and Knowledge.* Trenton, N.J.: Africa World Press.

Baker, Houston A., Jr. (1975) "Journey Toward Black Art: Jean Toomer's *Cane*" In *Singers of Daybreak: Studies in Black American Language*, pp. 53-80. Washington, D.C.: Howard University Press.

Baker, Houston A., Jr. (1974) *A Many-colored Coat of Dreams: The Poetry of Countee Cullen.* Detroit: Broadside Press.

Barksdale, Richard. (1977) *Langston Hughes: The Poet and His Critics.* Chicago: American Library Association.

Bell, Bernard W. (1989) *The Afro-American Novel and Its Tradition.* Amherst: University of Massachusetts Press.

Bell, Bernard W. (1974) *The Folk Roots of Contemporary Afro-American Poetry.* Detroit: Broadside Press.

Bontemps, Arna. (1969) "Introduction." In *Cane* by Jean Toomer. New York: Harper and Row.

Davis, Arthur P. (1974) *From the Dark Tower: Afro-American Writers: 1900-1960.* Washington, D.C.: Howard University Press.

DuBois, W. E. B. (1979) *The Souls of Black Folk: Essays and Sketches.* New York: Dodd and Mead.

Huggins, Nathan Irving. (1971) *The Harlem Renaissance.* London and New York: Oxford University Press.

Hughes, Langston. (1927a) *Fine Clothes to the Jew.* New York: Knopf.

Hughes, Langston. (1926) "The Negro Artist and the Racial Mountain." *The Nation 122:692-694.* Reprint 1976 in Nathan I. Huggins, ed., *Voices from Harlem.* New York: Oxford University Press.

Hughes, Langston. (1927b) *The Weary Blues.* New York: Knopf.

Johnson, James Weldon. (1990) *Along This Way: The Autobiography of James Weldon.* New York: Viking Penguin.

Johnson, James Weldon. (1969) *God's Trombones: Seven Negro Sermons in Verse.* New York: Viking.

Keto, C. Tsehloane. (1989) *Africa-Centered Perspective of History.* Blackwood, N.J.: K. A. Publications.

Locke, Alain. (1925) *The New Negro: An Interpretation.* New York: Albert and Charles Boni.
Obiechina, E. (1975) *Culture and Tradition in the West African Novel.* London: Cambridge University Press.
Smith, Valerie, Lea Baechler and A. Walton Litz, eds. (1991) *African-American Writers.* New York: Charles Scribner's Sons.
Thompson, Robert Farris. (1974) *African Art in Motion.* Los Angeles: University of California Press.
Toomer, Jean. (1969) *Cane.* New York: Harper and Row.
Welsh, K., ed. (1990) *African Culture: Rhythms of Unity.* Westport, Conn.: Greenwood Press.

IV

Reflective Designs in Literary Works

11

Folk Idiom in the Literary Expression of Two African American Authors: Rita Dove and Yusef Komunyakaa
Kirkland C. Jones

Many of the younger African American writers will admit that they have been influenced by such figures as Langston Hughes and Zora Neale Hurston, an influence that may be seen clearly through the types of language these younger poets select as vehicles for their ideas. Hughes's "Simple Tales" catalogs the speech habits of the everyday, working-class black man, which are similar to the kind of speech patterns Hurston displays in her book *The Sanctified Church*, a posthumous collection of essays on African American folk language, folk lore, and popular mythology. Both of these works, along with most of what their respective authors have published, provide a great deal of insight into the speech patterns of black America, rural and urban, and have preserved these speech customs for posterity. Similarly, Yusef Komunyakaa and Rita Dove to a lesser extent have adapted particular forms of African American speech to impart vitality and humor to their works. Both of these young authors use language that may be described, à la Toni Cade Bambara, as the speech of "blacksouth folks" (1981:7).

Hurston understood how fundamental black speech is to African American literary expression and that dialect, as authors use it, influences not only form but message as well. She wrote in her essay "Characteristics of Negro Expression": "The Negro's universal mimicry is not so much a thing in itself as an evidence of something that permeates his entire self. And that thing is drama. His very words are action words. His interpretation of the English language is in terms of pictures. One act described in terms of another. Hence the rich metaphor and simile" (1981:49). Both Komunyakaa and Dove, like many other authors of

African American roots, appreciate the uniqueness and power of this black speech as Hurston has described it. Arguing along the same line with Hurston, Henry Louis Gates asserts that a "Literary text is a linguistic event," and he would have students and teachers of African American literature and linguistics to understand that the literary critic must come to terms with this linguistic element before or, at least simultaneously with, any close reading of African American texts (1978:44-69). Ochillo also appreciates this peculiar balance between form and meaning as she perceives it in the poetry of Gwendolyn Brooks (1988:15-30).

Most contemporary African American poets would say about the folk element in their works what their colleagues Marilyn Nelson Waniek and Rita Dove have said in their collaborative essay, "A Black Rainbow: Modern Afro-American Poetry":

> Black poets have created their own tradition, rooted in song fundamentally different from its white counterpart. Modern black poetry is nourished by the work of earlier black poets, and draws much of its sustenance from the folk sources which have nurtured the race since slavery. These sources include black music, black speech, the black church, and the guerilla techniques of survival--irony, concealment, double-entendre, and fable (1990:171).

In this statement, the Pulitzer Prize laureate (Dove) and her colleague Waniek are acknowledging with pride the dialect tradition in African American poetry that in the forties and fifties, and even into the sixties, was an element in African American literary expression that the Black academy tried, erroneously, to deny. Dove and Waniek would have us applaud the song-like black speech preserved on our behalf by Horton, Harper, Johnson (JWJ), Dunbar, Toomer, Hughes, Cullen, and Sterling Brown, to name only the greats. These earlier poets link us with Brooks, Walker-Alexander, Baraka, Giovanni, and many other black poets after modernism. Rita Dove, born in 1957, and Yusef Komunyakaa, born a decade before her, have their individual and unique ways of becoming keepers and extenders of that speech flame in poetry

11. Folk Idiom in the Literary Expression of Two Authors

that "grins and lies," hiding innumerable "subtleties."[1] And Dove and Waniek are right on time when they insist that this "broken tongue," as Dunbar and others have described black idiom in American literature, stems from the peculiar concept of audience in these African American works. They explain the phenomenon in the following passage:

> The most pervasive influence on modern black poetry has been the idea of audience. . . . The idea of the audience has affected black poetry in several ways. The choice of language is one . . . the black poet must consciously choose to write either in the standard English preferred by the white audience, or in . . . dialect or colloquialisms. Early in this century, black poets tended to alternate between the two modes . (1990:171)

African American literary artists still find themselves addressing more than one audience at once. And this view of audience and of appropriateness may be seen in the idiom in which these authors, their personae, and their characters speak, not only in their poetry, but in their literary prose as well. The truth of this statement is borne out in the short fiction of Rita Dove as it is in some of her poems. In her 1983 collection of eight short stories, the reader appreciates Dove's sparkling voice as she lends it to her characters and to her narrators.[2] The idiom of her characters, most of them just into puberty, becomes a profound source of meaning in these creations in prose fiction. As do the characters in *Thomas and Beulah* (1986), that prize-winning sequence of narrative verse that won Dove the Pulitzer Prize for poetry in the following year, her short story characters use a culturally transmitted dialect from which the poet derives her ideolect.

The stories in *Fifth Sunday* illustrate Dove's linguistic and formal versatility, a quality in her poetry and prose that places her within the ranks of America's most laudable contemporary writers. But more important for the present study, the linguistic quality of her literary expression marks and, yes, celebrates an undercurrent in her works that is

---

[1] This allusion is to a frequently anthologized poem, "We Walk the Mask" by Paul Laurence Dunbar.

[2] *Fifth Sunday* (Lexington: University of Kentucky Press, 1985.) All references to Dove's stories are to this edition.

distinctly African American. The themes of these eight stories range from puberty and its onset, to adolescent courtship, to the emergence of self through a simultaneous emergence of the selves of significant others, to the displacement and oddity that American blacks have felt upon venturing into Europe, to the flowering of womanhood and manhood, to sex and reproduction, to the blossoming of mature relationships as these young characters learn to play skillfully on life's instruments to produce the music that is life itself. The language that the characters of these stories use is the speech of a youthful Rita Dove and her peers growing up together in the African Methodist Episcopal Church, the first and oldest of America's black Protestant denominations, and which tangibly represents through its traditions all other African-American Protestant sects. The volume's title, *Fifth Sunday*, represents the tradition of the black church and its inherited pattern of naming. Indeed, Dove's use of special language in this work first strikes the reader through the sounds of the names and nicknames the characters wear: Valerie, Virginia, Vandalia, Zabriah, Diana, and Christie; and Andrew, Sam Rogers, Swoop, Matt, Damon, Jerry Murdon, Jeremiah Morgan. The youthful female and male personalities who wear these appellations possess experience and insight worthy of their names, for Dove understands the drama and rhythm of traditional naming. These characters represent a worldview that is at once romantic and realistic, black and non-black. Dove takes these common people-sounding names and nicknames and elevates them, through their spoken sounds and through their literary contexts, above the mere prosaism that mars much of contemporary poetry.

In Dove's poems, dramatic monologue and compressed narrative are the primary contexts through which the language of the people is presented. In her short stories, though they are often very brief, the dialogues and musings of her characters are set forth in authentic speech patterns. Moreover, Dove has a keen sense of history. She links the past and the present through her characters names and through the appropriateness of their speech, revealing Dove's brilliant cross-cultural perceptivity, as her characters' voices move in and out of the centuries, simultaneously transcending the local and the mundane. "Catecorner," an expression found in the volume's title story, is a folksy way of describing the site of the church building, along with the phrase "let loose," meaning to set free. And the language of the black church adds enough flavoring to join the generations of worshippers with their inherited family and community traditions--"the junior ushers," "the junior choir,"

11. Folk Idiom in the Literary Expression of Two Authors

as they stand up to sing, "their blue silk robes swaying slightly as they rocked to the beat." The marching choir, the little-girl "gleaners," the fat officious women in white, all fit the story's "Fifth Sunday" language, modern enough to be Methodist and familiar enough to impart a quality of agedness and blackness.

Aunt Carrie, in the story that bears her name, speaks long dramatic monologues, and her speech is almost correct enough to match her assumed primness, allowing her to communicate with her young niece to whom she recounts more than one interesting story. Aunt Carrie is the type of matron who sprinkles her addresses with "dear." But she lapses occasionally into the remembered language of her parents and grandparents--"Don't go apologizing to me . . . makes me blush," she exclaims, and later in a much more relaxed, more confiding tone, she admits to her niece, "I didn't think about nothing at all." But on a whole, dialect is more subtle in the prose vignettes than in the author's most representative poems.

Dove's latest volume of verse, *Grace Notes*, is a good place to examine her verse, for in it appear some of her most polished poems from such earlier books of hers as *The Yellow House on the Corner* and *Museum*, and in some of her chapbooks. The language and situations of these poems further document Dove's cultural perceptivity and her sense of literary decorum, a sense of what works well with what. The range of subject matter is wide and her characters and their voices transcend boundaries of time and place. The views these voices articulate concerning the universe and of humanity are always reliable and never lack propriety.

In her poem "Crab Boil" we laugh as we read a poetic reference to the "Crab-barrel" myth transmitted by black culture and that is almost always a source of humor in spoken contexts:

> Why does Aunt Helen
> laugh before saying "look at that--
>
> a bunch of niggers, not
> a-one get out' 'fore the others pull him
> back."
> "When do we kill them?"
> "Kill 'em? Hell, the water does that.
> They don't feel a thing . . . no nervous system."

(14)
Here the poem's rhythm is reminiscent of black folk music. In another poem "Arrow," Dove acknowledges the humor and dramatic power of black speech without actually employing it:

> The eminent scholar "took the bull by the horns,"
> substituting urban black speech for the voice
> of an illiterate cop in Aristophanes' Thesmophoriazusae.
> And we sat there.
> And the answer came as it had to;
> humanity--celebrate our differences--
> the virility of ethnicity.

(21)
In "Genie's Prayer Under the Kitchen Sink," Genie, black male fashion, raps and signifies and plays the "dozens" simultaneously:

> Yes, I'm a man born too late for
> Ain't-that-a-shame, I'm a monkey
> with a message and a heart like
> my father who fell laughing to his knees
> when it burst and 24 crows spilled
> from his mouth and they were all named Jim.

(17)
Other poems in the volume *Grace Notes* in which the rhythms of black speech are adopted by the author's persona are "Canary," "The Island Women of Paris," and "The Royal Workshop." Fast becoming a favorite among anthologizers is Dove's poem "Parsley," in which she laments the persecution of people who, because of their ethnic backgrounds and speech habits, tend through no fault of their own--to mutilate the sounds of a received or second language, or of a contrasting dialect of their own language. Dove is aware of the ways in which a shared dialect can produce a sense of community between the sexes or among persons of contrasting socio-economic backgrounds, as seen every now and then in her poems. This is especially true of a few well-placed lines: *Thomas and Beulah*, Dove's tale of her family's history, the work for which she won the Pulitzer Prize. Her reader expects more black speech from the grandparents than he actually finds. Only occasionally does a phrase come through, for the poet is always in control of her voice. Notice these lines--"Swamp she born from, swamp / she swallow, swamp she got to

sink again" ("The Greater Palaces of Versailles"); "put her in the mind of" ("Pomade"). But in this biographical sequence speech peculiarities are generally more Southern and rural than African--"Them's chestnuts, I believe" ("The Event"); "He sure plays / that tater bug / like the devil" ("Jiving"); "I ain't dead" ("The Charm"); "The possum's a greasy critter / that lives on persimmons and what the Bible calls carrion" (Roast Possum). In *Thomas and Beulah* there are no utterances as clearly African American as Zora Hurston's "bref and britches," or "Ah take you out de white folks kitchen and set you down on yo royal diasticutis and you take and low-rate me," and "Scuse mah freezolity" or "Lawd a'mussy honey, . . . Umph! Umph! Umph!" from *Their Eyes Were Watching God.* Like Hurston, Dove shifts her idiom occasionally through the contrasting speech patterns that she places in the mouths of her characters, changing thereby her authorial voice to meet the demands of her narrative.

In an early poem, "The House Slave," Dove evokes a preconceived atmosphere and historical time frame by employing a single word, "Massa." In "Corduroy Road" from *Ten Poems* she creates a frontier setting by using archaic diction and syntax: "What prevails a man to hazard his person in the Wisconsin Forests."

African American literature--before it is anything else--is performance, and it is primarily the sound of the speaking, singing black voice that imparts this dramatic quality. This vernacular sound undergirds the ritual importance of the literary event, and the sounds and sound pictures that the writers display have at least two levels of value: the African value and the American value. This is one reason that the spiritual and the gospel, with their statement-response patterns, have exerted so much influence on black literary expression. Their bipartite design brings together the author and his audience in much the same way that Langston Hughes communicates through his blues poems and jazz poems, and through the *Simple Tales.* The linguistic markers used in this tradition create boundaries that facilitate at once intra-group and inter-group understanding. But the African American author must first learn to communicate with his primary audience (other blacks) before reaching out to the secondary audience (non-blacks). This ability to reach out by evoking received speech patterns is also seen in the fiction of Ralph Ellison, especially through such folk characters as Peter Wheatstraw, "The Devil's own Son-in-law," of *Invisible Man.* One cannot interpret the rhythms, pitches, and junctures of Wheatstraw's speech by simply looking at his language on the page. The reader, to interpret his passages orally, must shift into Northern black urban speech superimposed upon traditional Southern black rural speech.

Comprehending this function of Negro idiom in African American literature, Waniek and Dove have written:

> Those black poets who address the black audience often resolve this problem by writing poems intended to be performed, rather than silently read. The older tradition of the griot, or storyteller, has been kept very much alive by poets who perform their works on street-corners, at political gatherings, and anywhere they can find an audience willing to listen. Indeed, the oral nature of much black poetry is one of the reasons critics and teachers often find it difficult to discuss more than the sociological background of individual poems. (1990:172)

Maya Angelou's frequent public performances of her works, for example, make her poetry and prose more effective for audiences than when they lie silent on the page. This is not to imply that they are entirely lost in silent readings. But Angelou's performances, and those of Baraka, Giovanni, and many others, are made vivid through the literary conventions of an African communal society.

Returning to the topic at hand, Dove's concept of poetry has been shaped by the idioms and rhetorical devices of such American poets as Robert Frost, Langston Hughes, and Gwendolyn Brooks. But a search for dialectal pecularities in Dove's verse cannot be separated from an examination of structural design in her poems. Her use of language is exciting, and as her reader learns early on, she frequently melds time-tested devices to shape an original idiom, her own and fresh. Dove's humor resides primarily in her memorable characters who *rap* and *testify* and *signify* individual texts, making them "speakerly" texts as Gates would say, as only African American speakers can do. In a word, they live up to their especially dramatic names. Through these well-named rappers and their voices Dove strives for originality through the commonplace, for her intent is always to create something special, a historical reality that happens once in a great while. The speech of Dove's characters adds a textural dimension to her multi-layered technique, a method that shows the poet constantly seeking a voice with which to address both of her audiences, the African American and the European American. Like most successful African American literary works, her narra-

11. Folk Idiom in the Literary Expression of Two Authors 157

tives, in verse and in prose, become examples of Gates's "speakerly" texts, blending the traits of oral literature that Gates calls a "theory of narrative" that is "indigenously African," a kind of "formal revision that is at all points double-voiced" (1988:22). Hence Dove, as do many African American writers, consciously creates and interprets simultaneously--her reason, I am sure, for reverting every now and then to African American idiom. But never is her use of dialect obtrusive or difficult to read. In her poem "The House Slave" from *Ten Poems*, the reader appreciates a profound Africanness that is produced by a subtle blend of slavery images, images of the talking African drum, and of the work song:

> The first horn lifts its arm over the dew-lit grass
> and in the slave quarters there is a rustling--
> children are bundled into aprons, cornbread
>
> and water gourds grabbed, a salt pork breakfast taken.
> I watch them driven into the vague before-dawn
> while their mistress sleeps like an ivory toothpick
>
> and Massa dreams of asses, rum and slave-funk.
> I cannot fall asleep again. At the second horn,
> the whip curls across the backs of the laggards--
>
> sometimes my sister's voice, unmistaken, among them.
> "Oh! pray," she cries. "Oh! pray!" Those days
> I lie on my cot, shivering in the early heat,
>
> and as the fields unfold to whiteness,
> and they spill like bees among the fat flowers,
>
> I weep. It is not yet daylight.
>
> (56-57)

Here the interplay between history and imagination produces a poem that is typical of Dove.

Yusef Komunyakaa is stylistically different from Rita Dove; this is not to imply that he is the thoroughgoing formalist that we have in Marilyn Waniek. Komunyakaa's Louisiana Creole idiom is sometimes his most depended-upon medium, especially in his poems that celebrate the experience of the black soldiers of the Vietnam War and in his autobiographical verse--with themes of childhood and young adulthood in Louisiana. Yet his other war poems and those on non-maturation themes show his mastery of other idioms, creating thereby the multi-audience, multi-voiced poetry that we see in Dove and in many other young African American poets. Occasionally, though, in his war poems he employs black speech, but it is an adult speech, a more hardened dialect than that used in his childhood poems.

Born in Bogalusa, Louisiana, Komunyakaa attended the public schools of that village, graduating from high school in the mid-sixties. Immediately after graduation, he entered the United States Army and did a tour in Vietnam. Forced by circumstances to grow up earlier than do most youths in his age bracket, and affected by the turbulent 1960s, the period during which he began publishing his poems in literary journals, Komunyakaa has a stark realism in his poetic voice, indicated by the very titles of his early poems--"Intermission," "Rituals and Rides," "Sideshows," "Testimonies," "Passions," "Family Skeletons" in *Lost in the Bonewheel Factory* (1984). From the beginning of his career until the present, much of Komunyakaa's uniqueness has resided, not only in his subject matter, but also in the cultural levels and functional varieties of the language he has employed. Komunyakaa has not been afraid to experiment with form and voice. He believes, as his poetry shows, that the author's tongue must be the vehicle for revealing the beauty of the human spirit and the reality, and even the grotesqueness of human experience.

In his second volume titled *Copacetic* (1984), he presents jazz poems and blues poems in the manners of Hughes and Baraka. The *Copacetic* of the book's title is a word that has become a difficult-to-translate idiom that was contributed by black jazz musicians in their effort to describe a musical mode that is *mellow,* or *groovy,* or totally *together.* Like *cool, copacetic* has come to mean in less-restricted contexts a state of mind that is acceptable, an ambience that is desirable, a situation where everything is all right. Perhaps the closest English phrase of European origin to *copacetic* would be the archaic expression *hunky-dory.*

The poems in *Copacetic,* like many of the poems in *Magic City* (1986), hearken back to his boyhood and to early manhood. These poems examine folk concepts, folk beliefs, folk sayings, songs and the terminology of two traditionally African American musical genres, the blues and jazz. Typical of the volume's first sequence are "Blackmail Blues," the book's first poem, and "Mojo," named with a decidedly African

11. Folk Idiom in the Literary Expression of Two Authors

idiom, used as the rubric of the second and final sequence. Other titles that reflect the book's central theme include "Fake Leads," "Jumping Bad Blues," "Woman, I Go the Blues," "Street Cool Clara," and "Blues Chant Hoodoo Revival." The familiar mirror images of the first book are maintained, and his settings are decidedly Southern: "piney woods" and "cottonmouth country." The reader encounters the bloodhounds and "freight train hopper" of Richard Wright's fictionalized settings, elements that impart a narrative quality even to Komunyakaa's lyrical poems. Such typical phrases as "milkweed & blackberries," "the rope dangling from / a limb of white oak," "rope and blood," the mourning of crickets (cicadas) and his references to cornfields call forth the rural settings in Toomer's *Cane*.

In the mode of Gwendolyn Brooks's "We Real Cool," but minus Brooks's marcado, Komunyakaa has penned "Jumping Bad Blues," a work that also has a hint of Eliot's "Prufrock":

> I've played cool,
> hung out with the hardest
> bargains, but never copped a plea.
> I've shot dice heads-up
> with Poppa Stoppa
> & helped him nail
> his phenomenal luck
> to the felt floor with snake eyes.
> I've fondled my life in back rooms,
> called Jim Crow out of his mansion
> in Waycross, Georgia, & taught
> him a lesson he'll never forget.

(15)

In this volume, the poet's story comes across as if sealed "inside a wino's bottle," and the poet's story becomes "our story," a "rifle butt / across our heads."

For its candor and its subtle restraint, and for its appeal through its African rhythms to audiences everywhere, "More Girl Than Boy" is the work's strongest piece:

> You'll always be my friend.
> Is that clear, Robert Lee?
> we go beyond the weighing
> of each other's words,
> hand on a shoulder,
> go beyond the color of hair.
> Playing Down the Man on the Field
> we embraced each other before
> I discovered girls.
> You taught me a heavy love
> for jazz, how words can hurt
> more than a quick jab.
> Something there's no word for
> saved us from the streets.
>
> Night's pale horse
> rode you past commonsense,
> but you made it home from Chicago.
> So many dreams dead.
> All the man-sweet gigs
> meant absolutely nothing.
> Welcome back to earth, Robert.
> You always could make that piano
> talk like somebody's mama.
>
> (10)

In this creation the poet captures a rareness of love that is platonic, real, and elemosynary--a love that outlasts frustration, disappointment, death. The breathless rhythms of the jazz saxophonist supports such African American idioms as "mansweet gigs" and "somebody's mama." Komunyakaa refrains here from overusing the black-speech phrase, allowing a few well-chosen ones to identify the poet and his kinship with at least one of his audiences.

In a majority of the poems in *I Apologize for the Eyes in My Head* (1986), Komunyakaa employs metaphors that imply difficult transitions, or the inability to adapt to change and loss. The lover sometimes is forced to straddle a continent with one foot in the piney woods and the other in New York City. Or the lover spans "an empty / space [that] defines itself like a stone's weight" as he adjusts to the loss of love while aimlessly searching for a new love to fill the void. Even the titles in this volume evoke the idiom of the people ("Between Loves") and so do first lines ("Lo & Behold"). Speaking of his dead ancestors who have "disappeared," he creates a powerful poem set in a centuries-old cypress swamp in Louisiana. In a manner reminiscent of the Louisiana cane fields of Toomer and similar to the elegiac tone of Johnson's verse sermon "Go Down Death," Komunyakaa creates a new "Yamacraw" as he recites this litany for his ancestors who have succumbed, long before his speaker was born, to the unhealthful Louisiana climate. The power of this and other poems in the volume resides in collected experience transmitted through a collected language from a culture centuries old and deeply mysterious.

In another significant volume of Komunyakaa's poems, *Dien Cai Dau* (1986). The poet retains the idiom of the African American soldier, as seen in the book's third sequence. The following passage is typical: "we hugged bamboo & leaned / against a breeze off the river, / *slowdragging*"--an intimate, sexy dance done almost in one spot--"with ghosts" (emphasis mine). Furthermore, in *Dien Cai Dau*, Komunyakaa occasionally blends the American G.I.'s experience with that of the black civilian. A good example is "Hanoi Hannah":

>Ray Charles! His voice
>calls from waist-high grass,
>& we duck behind gray sandbags.
>"Hello, Soul Brothers. Yeah,
>Georgia's also on my mind." . . .
>"Here's Hannah again.
>Let's see if we can't
>light her goddam fuse
>this time."
>
>Her voice rises
>from a hedgerow on our left.
>"It's Saturday night in the States.
>Guess what your woman's doing tonight.
>I think I'll let Tina Turner
>tell you, you homesick GIs."
>"Soul Brothers, what you dying for?"

(13)

In "Combat Pay for Jodie," he uses an African American idiom for the "other man" in his woman's life. The poem alludes to the rhythm and blues song popular during the Vietnam era, the refrain of which resounds, "Jodie's got your girl and gone." The poem's climax is made poignant through the rhythms of "hip" speech so popular among black males in American inner-city settings:

>   the city hid her
>   shadow & I couldn't face myself
>   in the mirror. I asked her used-to-be
>   if it was just my imagination,
>   since I'd heard a man
>   could be boiled down to his deeds.
>   he smiled over his wine glass
>   & said, "It's more, man.
>   Your money bought my new Chevy."

(49-50)

Komunyakaa's poems are at their best when read aloud by the author himself--I heard him in Houston two years ago. An evening's performance, built on contrasts, looks ahead to a "Magic City" that is able to save the writer from destruction only as it distracts him--momentarily--from his memories, like those of the "toys in a field," broken machine guns abandoned in Vietnam, like a "bleak and soundless bell." But his most authentic performing voice is that of Bogalusa Creole, his native tongue, as it deliberately intones "charrun" for *children* and "runned into" for *ran into*. The wistful reader's voice re-creates "white only" signs and cats that charm birds, their prey. Komunyakaa's audience sits spellbound as he shifts in and out of Bogalusa, "the Nam," and the professor's Ivory Tower.

Reminiscent of the genealogic sequence in Dove's *Thomas and Beulah* is the poet's preoccupation with relatives and family backgrounds in *Magic City*. Some of the poems in this volume appeared in journals, but the majority of them are new. In "Mismatched Shoes" he writes, "my grandfather came from Trinidad / Smuggled in like a sack of papaya / On a banana boat, to a preacher's / Bowl of gumbo & jambalaya to jazz," (56) and in "Cousins" he asks this provocative question, "Where did the wordless / Moans come from in the dark / Rooms between hunger / & panic?" (117). The rhythm is African indeed.

In a published conversation with Vincent Gotera, a teacher of creative writing, Komunyakaa confided: "My definition of poetry is . . . grounded in everyday speech patterns. . . . It is difficult to define what poetry is . . . . I think it ties into the oral tradition for me, because I grew up with some strange characters around me. You know, storytellers and sorcerers" (1990:58-61). Gotera sees Komunyakaa's use of particular brands of speech as a striving to create "a tension between levels of diction. . . . Yoking . . . Latinate words with everyday ones" (220). Komunyakaa's intent in using language is to link real people with the words and phrases they use, creating the kinds of poetic cliches that are excellently employed because they communicate. He admits that in *Magic City* he is recalling images from his four- and five-year-old days in Bogalusa. But critics, unfortunately, sometimes misunderstand his use of folk speech in his poems as too much striving after effects. (221) His detractors notwithstanding, Komunyakaa is to be praised for his unique ability to connect the psychic domains of his personae with those of his readers. This method he deliberately adopts, for his aim is, in his own words, "to speak to many different people. . . . For example, I can . . . rap with my colleagues, but I have to be able as well to talk with my grandmothers, whom I'm very close to. They're not educated, and yet we can communicate some very heartfelt emotions. I'm still learning a whole lot from them" (221). In his striving for conciseness in language, Komunyakaa admits that he shares in a tradition with other African American poets--McKay, Tolson, Hughes, Sterling Brown, Cullen, Brooks, Helen Johnson. Like these poets, he often brings together the streets and *belles lettres* in a single poem with no unwanted clashing. (222-223). Komunyakaa uses folk speech as adornment. To this versatile poet, language should impart color in literary expression. This philosophy may be seen at work in everything that he writes, but I suspect that he is just beginning to rely on colorful spoken language, for he has lately been experimenting with dramatic sequences, the kinds of verse dialogues that should be performed in theatrical settings. One such creation he published in 1990, and it is his finest work to date. The poem is titled "Changes; or, Reveries at a Window Overlooking a Country Road with Two Women Talking Blues in the Kitchen," and it may well become his benchmark narrative poem.

    To say that both Rita Dove and Yusef Komunyakaa employ folk idiom in their verse is not to imply the kind of speech form known to have once marked the dialect poetry of African American literary figures. Dove's use of dialect, in fact, is not nearly as ethnically identifiable as are the speech forms of the common man in Komunyakaa's poems. Dove's speech idioms tend to place characters in a socio-economic category more than in an ethnic group. Her use of folk idiom also places her characters in age brackets, genders, and so on. The folk idioms that she uses, aside from their meter, are rarely identifiable as African American. In *Thomas and Beulah*, for example, even though it is a story about African Americans, Dove is careful not to impose her language or her sensibility upon their lives (Schneider, 1989:112). In Komunyakaa, though, the use of the African aesthetic is more noticeable, less seemingly incidental than in Dove. Both poets employ the rhythms of black speech more than they employ its words and phrases. Moreover, both are aware of the interrelationships among singing, talking, gossiping, testifying and signifying, and the bodily movements and paralinguistic accessories that accompany their employment; often in their works motion becomes sound and sound becomes motion. Both poets have kept intact the ancestral memory, but each uses it in varying, sometimes contrasting, contexts. Both use linguistic and paralinguistic features of the people--their people--and each thereby creates verisimilitude. Both writers are aware that folk grammar often does not conform to that of the educated speaker, and that sometimes the folk grammar is deliberately chosen by a speaker for expressive purposes. Both poets know how to make effective use of oral traditions in contemporary contexts. Their use of folk speech, when they choose to employ it, is always artistically perceived and artistically contrived. Both rely upon folk speech to help them express a wide range of emotions. Indeed, they both are passionately in love with language, as W. H. Auden would describe their poetic rhetoric (1965:209). Language in both poets comes across as blended, a remarkable fusing of Africanisms with Americanisms.

REFERENCES

Auden, W. H. (1965) "Poetry in the Game of knowledge." In Richard Ellman and Charles Feidelson, Jr., eds. *The Modern Tradition: Backgrounds of Modern Literature*, pp. 27-44. New York: Oxford University Press.

Bambara, Toni Cade. (1981) "Some Forward Remarks." In Zora Neale Hurston's, *The Sanctified Church*. Berkeley: Turtle Island Press.

Dove, Rita. (1985) *Fifth Sunday*. Lexington: University of Kentucky Press.

Dove, Rita. (1989) *Grace Notes*. New York: Carnegie-Mellon University Press.

Dove, Rita. (1977) *Ten Poems*. Lisbon, Iowa: Penumbra Press, Manila Series, no. 4.

Dove, Rita. (1986) *Thomas and Beulah.* Pittsburgh: Carnegie-Mellon University Press.
Gates, Henry Louis, Jr. (1978) "Preface to Blackness." In Dexter Fisher and Robert B. Stepto, eds. *Afro-American Literature: Reconstruction of Instruction,* pp. 44-69. New York: Modern Language Association of America.
Gates, Henry Louis, Jr. (1988) *The Signifying Monkey: A Theory of Afro-American Literary Criticism.* Oxford: Oxford University Press.
Gotera, Vincent F. (1990) "Lines of Tempered Steel." *Callaloo* 13:2-22.
Hurston, Zora Neale. (1978) *Their Eyes Were Watching God.* Urbana: University of Illinois Press. (First published in 1937.)
Hurston, Zora Neale. (1981) *The Sanctified Church.* Berkeley: Turtle Island Press.
Komunyakaa, Yusef. (1990) "Changes or Reveries at a Window Overlooking a Country Road, with Two Women Talking Blues in the Kitchen." *Mid-American Review* 10(2):54-56.
Komunyakaa, Yusef. (1990) *Dien Cai Dau.* Middletown, Conn.: Wesleyan University Press.
Komunyakaa, Yusef. (1986) *Magic City.* Middletown, Conn.: Wesleyan University Press.
Komunyakaa, Yusef. (1986) *I Apologize for the Eyes in My Head.* Middletown, Conn.: Wesleyan University Press.
Komunyakaa, Yusef. (1984) *Copacetic.* Middletown, Conn.: Wesleyan University Press.
Komunyakaa, Yusef. (1984) *Lost in the Bonewheel Factory.* New York: Lynx House Press. Middletown, Conn.: Wesleyan University Press.
Ochillo, Yvonne. (1988) "Form and Meaning in the Early Works of Gwendolyn Brooks" *The Literary Griot,* vol.1:15-30.
Schneider, Steve. (1989) "Coming Home: An Interview with Rita Dove." *Iowa Review,* vol. 19:13, 112-123.
Waniek, Marilyn Nelson and Rita Dove. (1990) "A Black Rainbow: Modern Afro-American Poetry." In Robert McDowelkedo, pp. 171-217. *Poetry after Modernism.* (Ed.) Robert McDowell. Three Oaks Farm, Brownsville, Oreg.: Story Line Press.

12

From Nice Colored Girl to Womanist: An Exploration of Development in Ntozake Shange's Writings

Geta LeSeur

> "speak up Ike, an' 'spress yo´se´f?'"
> -Betsey Brown

Ntozake Shange strives to fill a void in the female literary canon. With novels such as *sassafrass, cypress and indigo* (SCI) in 1982 and *Betsey Brown* (BB) in 1985, and her dramatic choreopoem *For Colored Girls Who Have Considered Suicide/When the Rainbow is Enuf* (FCG) in 1977, she has joined the ranks of prominent black women who are giving a voice to their sisters. Through her works, the audience is exposed to the issues facing black women as they develop into adulthood. Issues of racism and sexism must be addressed in order for her characters to grow. Although each of her characters finds a definition of herself as a black woman, the paths taken are unique to the individual. Each woman fulfills herself with a particular interest from which she derives power, be that interest music, dancing, or weaving cloth. These women must also learn to relate to and separate themselves from the men in their lives. With strength of character, Shange's women imprint themselves permanently in our memories. Shange wrote in *sassafrass, cypress and indigo* that the novel is dedicated to "all women in struggle." Within that statement lies the power of her writing. Her works are about black women, but they are indeed for ALL women. She uses Ebonics in a manner that does not exclude any gender, class or culture. Rather it invites all readers to enjoy as well as understand and confront issues facing us.

Shange said in a 1987 interview with Barbara Lyons for the *Massachusetts Review* that "unless black women are writing the pieces, we're being left out in the same way we used to be left out of literature. We don't appear in things unless we write them ourselves" (690). This oppression of black women is addressed by the characters in her writings. Black women are often deprived of their sense of childhood because they must immediately begin striving for recognition in the home and community. In *For Colored Girls...* one of the dancers, a lady in brown, sings solemnly "dark phrases of womanhood / of never havin been a girl" (3) and continues with the realization that the invisibility of black women is like death.

>somebody/anybody
>sing a black girl's song
>bring her out
>to know herself
>but sing her rhythms
>carin/struggle/hard times
>sing her song of life
>she's been dead so long
>closed in silence so long
>she doesn't know the sound
>of her own voice
>her infinite beauty . . .

(FCG,4)

As the choreopoem continues and with the heroines of her novels, Shange sings the black girl's song. Betsey, Sassafrass, Cypress, and Indigo tackle the invisibility of black women and carve their own places in society along with the nameless women dressed in the varied rainbow colors of *For Colored Girls* . . . . This play also explores the never-ending experiences of women--rape, abortion, abuse, love/hate relationships, mothering, death, formulating philosophies of life, third world concerns, what it means to be an Egyptian goddess, and "being colored and sorry at the same time."

The novel *sassafrass, cypress and indigo* is a perfect example of how a homeostatic relationship can be achieved. As creative as Shange is, the book can be analyzed for this formulation on three complimentary levels--culture, education, and the development of four women, Hilda Effania and her three daughters, Sassafrass, Cypress, and Indigo. By examining the importance of customs in the novel, the way in which she wrote the book, and the characters she uses to tell her story, the reader

12. From Nice Colored Girl to Womanist

readily grasps a new alliance in writing which, in essence is the creation of a new subgenre of the female *Bildungsroman*.

Shange's book relies heavily upon the shared heritage from which each of the women grows. First, the importance of cooking, a traditionally feminine activity, is emphasized. Recipes are shared, descriptions of meals and the corresponding preparations are given, and locations are determined by the various aromas from different kitchens.

Second, sewing or weaving is a skill all three daughters possess, a skill taught to them by their mother. Even as a traditional task for women, Shange turns it into an art. From talking about Indigo's dolls, to Sassafrass's weavings, to Hilda Effania's weavings for Mrs. Fitzhugh, each piece is described as an expression from the soul. Here a potentially mundane task becomes beautiful self-expression. Women's culture (manifest in sewing) reinforces feminine roles; yet it is a mode of breaking away from oppression through expression. Third, Shange makes a point of describing the neighborhood in Charleston as all black. She makes the racial and cultural connection even stronger by noting that all of Indigo's dolls are dark-skinned and that she and her dolls will converse only with black folks. To further emphasize the cultural aspect, Shange uses folklore for all occasions, adding richness and depth to the story. For instance, in the beginning, while focusing upon Indigo, Shange tells about Moon Journeys, determining Suitors with the Moon's Blessing, and what to do "If Your Beloved Has Eyes for Another":

> IF YOUR BELOVED HAS EYES FOR ANOTHER
> Sleep on your left side with 6 white roses by your
> head. Fill your pillow with 2 handfuls of damiana
> leaves. . . . Use blue if you merely desire fidelity.
> With the damiana-cubeb berry-filled pouch anywhere on
> your person in the presence of your beloved your way
> shall be had.
>
> (15)

The folklore Shange uses to highlight cultural tenets in the work also acts as a stylistic means by which another level of the book can be analyzed. These devices allow her education and cultural experience to shine through. While her education has helped her to write well, her grounding in who she is adds movement to the work. And while the book can be sociologicaly informative, it also is consistent with the theme of all her writing, which is "what it means to be of color and female in the twentieth century."

By including poetry, recipes, letters, songs, and instruction, Shange creates a different kind of book--not a cookbook, not poetry, not a craft book, and most likely, not entirely fiction. She has created a new medium for expression. This medium is magical in quality and distinctly feminine. By doing so, she has balanced education and various elements of the common female culture and black culture to show that complete expression requires an acknowledgment of our heritage while breaking new creative ground. Additionally, her choice of characters and their development throughout the novel provides another level of analysis.

Shange's first novel, *sassafrass, cypress and indigo*, details the developmental patterns of three sisters. Indigo, the youngest, is the child who possesses the most obvious power. She establishes herself with magic. "Where there is woman there is magic. If there is a moon falling from her mouth, she is a woman who knows her magic, who can share or not share her powers" (SCI,3). That is Indigo. She surrounds herself with dolls that are more than just toys--they are her companions. The dolls have their own thoughts and questions that push Indigo to seek answers.

Shange has blurred the line between reality and a child's imagination to illustrate that Indigo's wisdom goes far beyond her years. Indigo also plays the fiddle and uses that instrument to speak her own language. She creates spells and converses with spirits. "There wasn't enough for Indigo in the world she'd been born to, so she made up what she needed. What she thought the black people needed" (SCI,4). Indigo is fiercely independent and draws on her magic for strength and has a fecund imagination. No one told her she could work this magic; she does it on her own. Because of this inner power Indigo is able to grow on her own as well. She backs off Spats and Crunch with the power of her fiddle and becomes a Junior Geechee Captain, thus gaining for herself access into the behind-the-scenes world of adults in The Caverns. However, she recognizes the time to resign that position and move toward womanhood. She also decides in her own time when to give up her beloved dolls, despite all the previous hounding by her mother. When she finally sends them to the attic, it is with the knowledge that she is saving them from growing up. She has recognized her fate, but she wants to spare her friends the pain involved in the passage to adulthood. She explains this poignantly to her mother: "Being a grown colored woman is hard, ain't it? Just like you tol' me. Just cause I haveta grow up, my dolls

12. From Nice Colored Girl to Womanist

don't haveta. I can save them" (SCI,52). Indigo has a remarkable grasp of life for one so young, and she shares this knowledge with those around her. She is able to gain maturity without developing the hard edges of Cypress or the vulnerability of Sassafrass.

Indigo's escape from the troubles that befall her sisters may largely be attributed to her focus on magic rather than on men. When she announces that she enjoyed the Schuyler's party but liked her fiddle better than the boys she met, her mother is pleased. "There's not be one more boy-crazy, obsessed-with-romance child in her house. This last one made more sense out of the world than either of the other two" (SCI,64).

Cypress and Sassafrass each have special talents to focus on, but both of them allow men to play large roles in their development as women. Indigo is perhaps the strongest of the three sisters, and her story could make its own fascinating novel.

It takes Sassafrass a long time to individuate herself from her man. She lives with Mitch, a chauvinistic musician who dominates her life, and with whom she has a cacophonous relationship. He wants her to pursue her interests but at the same time wants her to wait on him and cook his meals. Because she identifies herself through her man, she endures his attitudes. These interactions among male and female characters expose degrees of sexism, but as Shange says in the *Massachusetts Review* interview, "It's like creating a world of women that's women-centered, so aberrrant male forms really look aberrant" (687). Sassafrass doesn't muster the strength to leave until Mitch's sexist behavior reaches gigantic proportions and with the companionship of two friends, he directs a sexually explicit song at her. She finally explodes: "I am not about to sit heah and listen to a bunch of no account niggahs talk about black women; me and my sisters; like we was the same bought and sold as slave auction . . . breeding heifers the white man created cause y'all was fascinated by some god damn beads he brought you on the continent" (SCI,89).

Her long overdue self-defense is awarded by a beating from Mitch, and so she moves in with Cypress. Yet, even after all of the abuse and humiliation she has endured because of Mitch, she believes that she loves and needs him. "She needed Mitch because Mitch was all she loved in herself" (SCI,98). And with this knowledge, she returns to him as soon as he asks her to come back.

Sassafrass has her weaving and she has her writing, but her man is her way of defining herself. It is not until she and Mitch go to "The New

World Found Collective" that Sassafrass finds a focus that can save her from her destructive relationship. Once she finds completeness within herself, she no longer needs Mitch. She realizes that she lives in her looms and that is enough; self-awareness is complete.

Cypress's road to self-discovery is also a rocky one. She wants most of all to be a dancer. "She knew dancing was in her blood . . . every step" (SCI,135), yet she allows herself to loose sight of her goal by dabbling in alcohol, drugs, and many sexual relationships. She is living the empty life the lady in red describes in *For Colored Girls* . . . :

> you'll have to go no/i've
> a lot of work to do/& i cant
> with a man around/here are yr pants
> there's coffee on the stove/its been
> very nice/but i cant see you again/
> you got what you came for/didnt you

(FCG,34)

Cypress is determined to be a dancer. She studies in New York and travels with an African American troupe to San Francisco. When she returns to New York, she dances herself into two whirlwind relationships that force her to accept herself as a woman and as an artist.

Although Cypress enjoys the company of many men, it is her first love relationship with a woman, Idrina, that derails her sense of self. She allows herself to fall in love even though she knows from the beginning that Idrina has a steady lover. "Idrina knew some things that Cypress didn't know: loving is not always the same as having. And Idrina loved Cypress, but not to have . . . and Cypress didn't know that" (SCI,149). When Idrina's lover returns from Holland, Cypress suffers a devastating blow. After much alcohol consumption, she runs into her old friend Leroy and finds her focus on dance again. As she fulfills herself with her dancing she is able to fulfill her need for love with Leroy and accepts him as part of her life. By the novel's denouement, she has agreed to marry Leroy. Cypress has not defined herself in terms of her man; it is because she has developed her own individual sense of self through her dancing that she is able to have a good relationship with a man.

Hilda Effania, the mother of Indigo, Sassafrass and Cypress is an interesting woman and is depicted uniquely unlike Jane Brown in *Betsey Brown* (1985), who disappears almost completely from her daughter's life. Shange uses Hilda as a catalyst, mixer, a context and frame for the story;

but she definitely has her own story. One can ask some questions, such as why are all three daughters so creative? Why are they so steeped in the South and Southern culture? How come they and she seem to function outside of the ordinary mundane things with which we associate poor black women's lives? What qualifies her to mother such extraordinary women? Do we know her? Hilda Effania had prayed for a husband and got one. Hilda Effania made all the ordinary occasions like Christmas and the onset of menstruation and meals major and creative events for celebration. Hilda Effania essentially got on with life despite single-motherhood. Hilda Effania thinks, "she looked good for a widow with three most grown girls" (SCI,66). Hilda Effania writes nurturing and supportive rather than destructive letters to her daughters no matter where they are, such as this one:

> My two big girls, Sassafrass and Cypress,
>
> Well, looks like you are having a veritable family reunion. I wish I could be there, not just to see you both (which I really would like), but so I could finally be at one of Cypress' parties! Cypress, you be sure to introduce Sassafrass to some nice young men. She doesn't get out like she should. And Sassafrass, watch that your sister doesn't spend up all her money entertaining folks . . .
>
> Well, all I have to do this week is a church supper and a Thursday night bridge game. You two have a good time. Mind what I told you. And dress up pretty.
>
> (SCI,116-117)

Is Hilda Effania a nice colored girl? Is Hilda Effania a self-assured woman? She, in my estimation, although a bit unrealistic (in print and life), is what many of us wish some of our mothers would be more of, that is, compassionate, creative, patient. She, like Jane in *Betsey Brown*, touches her daughters and molds them without seeming to take a proactive part in their lives. It is important, though, that whatever Indigo, Sassafrass, and Cypress become, they become because of what Hilda gave and exposed them to as children. Indigo, the last child, benefits from all who preceded her--sisters, mother and "the geechees, love gone," the South, and Africa and the Ibos. Hilda can be any kind of woman she wants to be because she has been the mother for which her heritage intrinsically deemed her appropriate. It was not effortless, but easy. We also see Hilda and Indigo in a special mother-daughter bonding, and we suspect that the two older daughters have had the same experience and teaching about life and black woman's history from her. Ultimately, Sassafrass, Cypress, and Indigo are wise women. Like their mother, they find out how to live and how to express themselves in a nice/mean world.

Each child thinks that good fortune will follow her. Indigo thinks, for example, that only boys who are "pure of heart, of mind and strong of body" will come to her (SCI,22). When her mother slaps reality to her a feeling of pain and confusion can be felt. The reality of European slave trade and discrimination was brought to life with one sentence: "White men roam these parts with evil in their blood, and every single thought they have about a colored girl is dangerous" (SCI,22). The idea of evil and hatred planted into the mind of innocent Indigo reminds all of us of our slow growth into reality. Prejudice comes alive in Indigo's mind; she has to fear white men. The passage also shows the fierce attachment between Indigo and her mother when Hilda further says, "I would just kill anybody who hurt you" (SCI,22).

Some readers will say that they do not know Hilda at all and that she refuses to let her daughters go by writing those damn letters, but it is an incorrect assessment because what Shange does in those letters is to have the reader see the evolution, although slow, from Hilda's early letters, which are full of worry, anxiety, and concern for their choice of lifestyles, such as this one:

> My Littlest Angel, Indigo,
>
> Wouldn't I look simple, keeping a house full of grown women, aching to be part of the world, from being part of the world, just so I wouldn't be quite so lonely. That's enough of that. You all have your mends to make with the world & so I wouldn't be quite so lonely. That's enough of that. . . . I keep looking for Cypress' face to be on the news, when they talk about those youngsters who have lost their minds in California. I swear, I feel in my soul that she's wandering around San Francisco all painted up with stars & peace symbols. I pray the TV cameras never find her. She might do a dance, then what

would I say to all my neighbors. I got a painted dancing daughter in Haight-Asbury?

(SCI,74-75)

And then this one, where she acknowledges that Cypress's choice of lifestyle is fine with further commentary, which adds rather than admonishes her daughter for her career choice:

My lovely C.,
 . . . I'm so excited about your association with a national touring company . . . please, send me clippings, especially if you play major cities where we have relatives. . . . the Lord will look kindly on the benefits you're going to do for Negro Christians; bless your souls, for taking time from a full season for the race. I'm mighty proud.
Love, Mama

(SCI,209)

The letters show Hilda's slow evolution to wholeness, acceptance, and truth--a process similar to that of her daughters.

Teasing out the different layers of analysis in this book is like an adventure because Shange masterfully weaves all of these elements, characters, genres, poetry, recipes, drama, letters, and cultural trademarks into a beautifully feminine tapestry. As indicated in her previous work history, she dances, writes theater pieces, poetry, weaves, and sews. Furthermore, she is obviously a bit of a dreamer, like Indigo, with a powerful voice of her own. Like Shange, all are complete women through the balance of their education, culture, and art.

Each woman takes her own route to complete womanhood; yet all achieve their definition of all of this. For Indigo, growing into a complete person means giving up her dolls (not entirely, I suspect) and turning toward her brand of music for self-expression, wherein she finds power. At times she abuses the power by using it to entertain white folks or to frighten her G. C. friends. After a time, she realizes that the power in her music is from her self-expression. She has the power, not the fiddle. In developing further, she realizes her ties to the black female community. Her renaissance, this time as a whole woman, occurs as she returns to the black woman's community and aids in bringing life into it. She is a midwife and she loves it.

For Cypress, growing to completeness takes a much rockier road. She must deal with various opposing emotions: fear, jealousy, depression, and guilt. She never tells her mother about her female lover. She knows her mother would be appalled. Still, in her letters she wants to share so much with her. Guilt and pain of this realization accrues. Her lesbianism does, however, teach her about womanness and not being completely male identified. Finally, she becomes whole to herself as she decides to dance for the Civil Rights Movement.

For Sassafrass, most of her development occurs when she is with Cypress and away from Mitch. But her deep love for Mitch prevails. Becoming pregnant, preparing to bring life into the world, makes her feel whole.

Now, the mother, Hilda Effania--she is the one to consider. She is an older woman. She has children who have grown into affirmed womanhood on their own. She did not really grow much until her daughters began their respective journeys. Afraid of the unknown, she kept trying to reel them back into her nest. Still, she was proud of their accomplishments and hence she did grow with them, through them--by proxy. "Hilda Effania couldn't think enough to cook. She looked at Alfred's portrait over the parlor fireplace, a little embarrassed. You know, Al, I did the best I could, but I don't think they want what we wanted" (SCI,225).

Sassafrass, Cypress, and Indigo try to make it on their own, but they are forever linked to Mama. Through her letters, recipes, and weaving, she has a hold on the girls no matter how far away they are. In this novel Shange's poetic sensibilities lend an energetic yet calming lyricism to the book. Her characters have an inherent dignity and are in rhythm with life.

The book closes at a point when the three sisters have achieved self-awareness. They are at various stages in their lives: Cypress is about to be married, Sassafrass is about to have a baby, and Indigo continues to move at her own pace. But they are all strong women, magical women, and talented women who have selected a path for life and will follow it. Shange has shown us what life is all about for these women and created a piece that will endure for the next generation. She says that she doesn't want children brought into this world without a past to hold onto. She wants them to have heard about themselves. "I want to recreate and save what our being alive has been so their being will stay alive, won't be such a surprise" (SCI,690).

12. From Nice Colored Girl to Womanist

Ntozake Shange's first novel, *sassafrass, cypress and indigo*, is a paradox because somehow this shaman of a writer manages to integrate tradition with rebellion, chaos with peace, reality with fantasy, and poetry with life. Meanwhile music, art, and food become literature. The result is a lively/tranquil story that is painful/joyous and real magic.

Shange's novel *Betsey Brown* is about a black family, but it focuses primarily on the struggles of the oldest daughter, Betsey. By virtue of age, comparisons between Indigo and Betsey seem natural. They are also the only two children that Shange has devoted extensive attention to in her works to date. Both girls have an incredible ability to perceive situations and an uncanny grasp of life for their young age. However, Indigo is much more secure in her growth than Betsey, who must deal with constant family turmoil. As Shange says: "Indigo has a knowing sense of what's possible and who she can be. We discover with Betsey what her possibilities are, which is different, I think, from Indigo giving us permission to share what she already knows" (Lyons, 689).

Betsey is a dynamic, imaginative thirteen-year-old beginning to learn about her black heritage. Her mother, Jane, is of a lighter hue and absorbed by fashion. Her father, Greer, is of a darker hue and is trying to instill black pride in his four children, much to his mother-in-law's dismay. "She was most white. Slaves and all that had nothing to do with her family, until Jane insisted on bringing this Greer into the family and he kept making family" (BB,19). Jane herself clashes with her husband's desire to keep the family in touch with its African roots. This creates great turmoil in Betsey, who is experiencing the trials and tribulations of her passage into womanhood amidst this household of conflict. She is also experiencing integration in the St. Louis school system she attends. Because Betsey's parents are affluent, she has never experienced the black culture her father speaks of nor does she understand the prejudices against blacks. "Betsey didn't know yet that white folks could get away with things a Negro'd be killed for. That's what was wrong with this integration talk" (BB,30).

Betsey learns quickly though. She has white girlfriends and knows that something is wrong when she is not allowed to visit their homes while their parents are there. Her friend Susan Linda says that "niggahs" are not supposed to be in their house. This is Betsey's first real experience with the prejudices of whites. She must fight with her conscience over her friendship and the unjust treatment she is receiving. Even more violent clashes with prejudice occur within the integrated school system.

Betsey is left with a helpless sense of frustration when a white teacher tries to rob her beloved writer, Paul Laurence Dunbar, of his merits: "this teacher tried to make me think that being colored meant you couldn't write poems or books or anything . . . she doesn't believe that we're American. I tried to tell them but nobody listens to me cause it's just another nigger talking out the sides of her mouth" (BB,183).

These conflicts often send Betsey to private hiding places on the stairs or up in a tree in order to reflect on life. These secret places are the pathway to her own discovery of self. She has reached the age where she must start to think about her future role as a black woman in a white-dominated society. Her power to acquire knowledge hinges on these stolen moments of solitude. Because of this, she guards her privacy with her life--it is an integral part of her life. When a new housekeeper, Bernice, gives away her secret spot in a tree, Betsey goes to war. The loss of her secret place also signals her loss of innocence.

It is only after Betsey has successfully driven away Bernice that her friend Veejay forces her to confront her privileged living conditions. Veejay says, "That coulda been my mama and you don't care" (BB,67). Betsey suddenly realizes that many black people are doing housekeeping, domestic work, and other less-than-desirable labor in order to support their families. She vowed then never to hurt another black person.

Mixing with the difficult questions that racism is raising in her life are her feelings for Eugene, her first love interest. Betsey watches the maid, Regina, moon over her boyfriend, Roscoe, and ponders the meaning of love. She begins to think of marriage and a family, but at the same time she is torn because her grandmother treats the Regina-Roscoe romance as something that can only lead to trouble. All of this confusion in her young life pushes Betsey to her decision to run away from home. She decides to go to Mrs. Maureen, the hairdresser, to learn a trade and remove herself from the frustrations of love, white people, and to finally immerse herself in black culture. She sees herself as different from everyone else in her family, and the only way for her to discover her identity is to start a new life.

Once again Betsey finds that things are not always the way they appear. There are no ideal worlds. Mrs. Maureen wants to send her home, telling her that she is not living in a manner suitable for a young girl. She is running a brothel and Regina, sans Roscoe, is a part of it. Betsey learns that there are different kinds of colored people--not an easy concept to grasp at the age of thirteen. While she is able to see the good "in all colored people," she finds that others are much more judgmental. "She bet money some of these negroes wouldn't give a stone's throw if something happened to Roscoe, they didn't care what was gonna happen to Regina's baby. 'Niggahs' they's say and leave it to the will of God that people, especially colored people, suffered. Yet, they couldn't go anywhere else to get their hands done but a bordello" (BB,138). Betsey's return home marks a passage for her into true understanding of her situation. She learns through her experiences not only that she is different, but that it is all right for her to be that way. Betsey Brown is her own person, as she is beginning to realize. Her love of black writers and black music does not have to be a setback; instead it can lead to a broader appreciation of her race.

Betsey's mother, Jane, gets a later start on the road to self-awareness, but she, too, runs away. After defining herself as Greer's wife, her mother's daughter, and the mother of four children, she takes out on her own to define herself in her own terms. Having given up control of her household to her husband and the housekeeper, she chooses to reflect and learn about the larger world. When she returns, she has also grown. She is no longer defined by her man, but her identity is enhanced by him--"this man . . . this particular colored man was hers forever and ever . . . those thoughts so provoked her, made her see anew who she was and who they were" (BB,190). She is less disturbed by Greer's interest in everything black because she is coming to an understanding that it is part of her life.

From *Colored girls...* to *Betsey Brown* to *sassafrass, cypress, and indigo*, Shange has created journeys of self-discovery. She has woven tales that reach out to the "searching and yearning" (MR,690) that went on inside her in her own adolescence and extended these stories to touch the lives of all women of all colors. She says that women's novels are like breathing for her, and that seems to capture the essence of her works. The development of women as they struggle to find themselves is as much a part of life as breathing. It is impossible to simply read her works and walk away; they linger in the mind. Shange is "for colored girls who have considered suicide / but are movin to the ends of their own rainbows" (FCG,64). Shange is for women. Shange is for anyone interested in a greater sense of self-awareness. She touches us all.

> "i found god in myself
> & i loved her/i loved her fiercely" - lady in red
> For Colored Girls . . .

(52)

She is also her own universe in which she embraces the mythical, mystical, and the true essence of peoples of color--totally. Consistently and successfully she creates myriad representations of blackness, which celebrate and weave history, heritage, culture, and language. The core of her work is the contemporary experiences of blacks, especially women, but done so uniquely that what we have are revolutionary ways of expression, form, communication--ART!

REFERENCES

Lyons, Barbara. (1987) "Interview with Ntozake Shange." *Massachusetts Review* 687-696.

Shange, Ntozake. (1985) *Betsey Brown*. [BB] New York: St. Martin's Press.

Shange, Ntozake. (1977) *For Colored Girls Who Have Considered Suicide When the Rainbow is Enuf*. [FCG] New York: Macmillan Publishing Company.

Shange, Ntozake. (1982) *sassafrass, cypress and indigo*. [SCI] New York: St. Martin's Press, 1982.

13

De Jure Maurorum in Europa (On the Rights of Blacks in Europe): A Black Civil Rights Activist in Europe in the Eighteenth Century

Reginald Bess

In the Western European tradition, that is to say, the tradition as reflected in Germany, France, England, and Italy and as imported into the United States, there has been a need to create stereotypes. Gilman observes in his critical work that "our need to create stereotypes has given rise to a fantastic variety of images of the Other, some of them quite remote from observable fact but all of them at one time or another solemnly accepted as veritable truth" (1985:11). Indeed, the most powerful stereotypes in nineteenth-century Western Europe (and I hasten to add that the incipience is to be found toward the middle of the eighteenth century) and the United States were those that associated images of race and sexuality. As will be explained later, the stereotyping of the subject of this essay arose when self-integration was threatened. He was viewed as different, and his difference threatened order and control for some. The difference was due to his race. Again Gilman states: "In 'seeing'(constructing a representational system for) the Other, we search for anatomical signs of difference such as physiognomy and skin color. The Other's physical features, from skin color to sexual structures such as the shape of the genitalia, are always the antitheses of the idealized self's" (1985:25). Here the links between "pathology," "sexuality," and "grace" become even more overt: sexual anatomy is so important a part of self-image that "sexually different" is tantamount to "pathological"--the Other is "impaired," "sick," "diseased." Similarly, physiognomy or skin color that is perceived as different is immediately associated with "pathology" and "sexuality."

In his critical work *Black Skin, White Masks* Frantz Fanon has this to say about the West's attitude toward blackness:

In Europe, the black man is the symbol of Evil.
One must move softly, I know, but it is not easy. The torturer is the black man, Satan is black, one talks of shadows, when one is dirty one is black--whether one is thinking of physical dirtiness or of moral dirtiness. It would be astonishing, if the trouble were taken to bring them all together, to see the vast number of expressions that make the black man the equivalent of sin. In Europe, whether concretely or symbolically, the black man stands for the bad side of the character. As long as one cannot understand this fact, one is doomed to talk in circles about the "black problem." Blackness, darkness, shadow, shades, night, the labyrinths of the earth, abysmal depths, blacken someone's reputation; and, on the other side, the bright look of innocence, the white dove of peace, magical, heavenly light. (1967: 188-189)

As Gilman observes, this is the projection of Western anxiety concerning the Other permitting the acute observation of the truism that skin color has mythic qualities. (1985:29) For Fanon, this constant admixture of myth and unconscious deformation of reality is the basis for stereotyping.

Myths about the Africans who were being captured in the Motherland and brought to the New World to be enslaved abounded. Chief among them were the claims that the Africans lacked character, integrity, intelligence, manners, and morals; thus in the eyes of God they deserved to be enslaved. This view was held by many during the beginning of the eighteenth century, but there was a group of German intellectuals who fought against these claims. And this group was able to point to one of its own, a young, gifted African, in a thorough refutation of these claims. How came this young, gifted African to be numbered among this group, and how came he to be a champion for the civil rights of blacks in Europe in eighteenth-century Germany? This, then, is his story.

The African scholar who is the subject of this humble study was born in Axim, an old African town situated on the "Gulf of Guines" in present-day southwest Ghana, not far from the Ivorian frontier. He signed himself in Latin Amo-Guines-After or Amo Guinea-Africanus (Amo the Guinean). His German name was Anton Wilhelm, a combination he received from his patron and his patron's son. In the first half

13. De Jure Maurorum in Europa

of the 1700s he was one of the leading intellectuals in the Enlightenment in Europe. Indeed, on April 17, 1734 young Amo made history by becoming the first African to be awarded the doctorate degree in philosophy and letters from a European university.

In the thirties and forties of the 1700s Dr. Amo was one of the outstanding professors at the Universities of Halle, Wittenberg, and Jena in present-day eastern Germany. This first great African scholar of the early modern age rose from student to master and ultimately professor/lecturer, the first of his race to be awarded a doctorate degree in philosophy and letters in Germany, and to teach the discipline at three European universities. Near the end of the first half of the eighteenth century, fate and the historical circumstances of racial prejudice joined forces in consigning his memory to oblivion until some scholars in the second half of the twentieth century, this writer included, have attempted to rescue the memory and accomplishments of this great African from oblivion.

The century in which Anton Wilhelm Amo lived and worked produced a philosophy and literature of the highest rank in Germany. By the 1800s Germany had become a leading intellectual power in Europe (Robertson, 1968). Leading figures responsible for Germany's intellectual growth were G. W. Leibnitz (1646-1716), the first of the great German thinkers of rationalism; Christian Thomasius (1655-1728), the founder of German rationalism who delivered the first lectures in German ever given at a German university; and, Christian von Wolff (1669-1745), through whom rationalism spread rapidly to all German universities. All had a profound influence on Amo's intellectual growth and development.

The year of Amo's arrival in Europe is unknown, and the circumstances of his being brought to Europe are unclear. One critic makes the contention that Amo was brought to Europe and educated, instead of being enslaved, because his owner shared the ideas of the Enlightenment (e.g., racial tolerance):

> Born in 1703 in Nkubeam near Asim, Ghana, he was brought to Amsterdam and later given to Duke Anton Ulrich of Brunswick-Wolfenbuettel of Saxony and his son, August Wilhelm. The affinity these aristocrats shared for the ideals of the Enlightenment may have been the reason they decided to have him educated instead of using him as a servant or plaything, a practice in vogue throughout Europe at that time. Perhaps they subscribed to the empiricist concept of the "tabula rasa" as interpreted by

John Locke et al., hence the inducement to experiment.(Fikes, 1980:215)

Unfortunately, this critic provides neither footnotes nor primary or secondary sources in his essay to support the many suppositions ("may," "perhaps," etc.) he employs. I find it difficult to pursue his reasoning. (Too, I would have liked a clarification of "the inducement to experiment" in the above passage. Alas, none is proffered.)

So there are three possible reasons for Dr. Amo's coming to Europe:

1. He was kidnapped by sea pirates who took him to Europe and sold him.

2. He was bought, enslaved and taken to Europe.

3. He was sent to Europe in order to train as a preacher in the Dutch Reformed Church.

(Hountondji,115)

On June 29, 1707, according to baptism records, a young black's name was entered into the church book in Brunschwik, Wolfenbuettel. This, then, is the first mention of the youth in Germany. Records indicate that the Dutch West Indies Society, one of the greatest slave-trading and exploitative organizations in Western Europe, sent to Duke Anton Ulrich von Wolfenbuettel a present (a usual practice in those days) of a young black by the name of Amo. This is the singular evidence that speaks for 1707 as the first mention of Amo in Western Europe (Brentjes, 1976).

But how came the Duke to have him baptized and educated? We take note here of the fact that, though he received the christian baptismal names "Anton" and "Wilhelm," he maintained his native "Amo" "as though he was afraid that his long European adventure might make him or his circle forget his African origins and ties" (Hountondji, 1983:113).

Was it a John Lockean experiment as has been suggested? I doubt it. Rather, I think that the answer lies in Petersburg, Russia. One year before Amo arrived in Europe, the Russian ambassador in Istanbul sent Czar Peter I a gift, a young African named Ibrahim Hannibal, who on being baptized was named Petrowitsch for his patron. At first he served the czar's daughter Elizabeth as a valet. When, however, he began to demonstrate great intelligence, Peter took him into his services as a private secretary. The czar determined that Petrowitsch should serve in the military, and the czar arranged a marriage for him. Thus Ibrahim Hannibal became the great-grandfather of Alexander Pushkin, who remembers him so affectionately in the story *The Moor of Peter the Great* (Killens, 1989).

The daughter of Czar Peter was the niece of Duke Anton Ulrich. When Ibrahim/Peter returned from artillery duty in France in 1723, he stopped on the way back to Russia to visit the Wolfenbuettel residence and the relatives of his patron. This living, breathing, young, gifted African, rather than some abstract "experiment," was the impetus to have young Amo educated. Thus, Amo did not suffer the fate of other blacks who, in the fashion of the times, were used as pages, servants, and living exotics. Paintings from this period often depict "Court Moors" in the background.

Receiving an excellent college preparatory education, Amo matriculated in the college of philosophy and liberal arts at the University of Halle in 1727. He most certainly came into contact with Thomasius, who helped to found the University of Halle, became professor of law there in 1694, and later was *Geheimrat* (privy counselor) and rector of the university. (As noted above, it was he who introduced the use of the German language in university teaching.) When Amo arrived, Thomasius, known for his liberalism and anti-clericalism, was still teaching at Halle and was to remain there until his death in 1728 (*Encyclopedia of Philosophy*,8:116-118).

Amo also most certainly came into contact with Christian Wolff, who had occupied the chair of mathematics there from 1706 to 1723. It was there that he composed his *Thoughts*, the first major philosophical work published in the German language. Wolff was expelled from Prussia by King Frederick William I because the Pietists were hostile to him, but with the accession of Frederick I in 1740, he was called back to the university as a professor of law, vice-chancellor of the university, and *Geheimrat*. In 1743 he became chancellor and in 1745 a baron of the Holy Roman Empire (EP,8:340-343).

After two years of intense study at the university, Amo produced his first disputation entitled *De Jure Maurorum in Europa* (*On the Rights of Blacks in Europe*). Amo's disputation revealed two things basically: it affirmed his link with Africa, his mother country, and it established his reputation at the art of disputation. In the disputation Amo addresses the social condition of blacks in Europe, and using law and history as references he shows

> how the kings of Africa had once been vassals of the Roman Emperor, enjoying an imperial franchise, which Justinian in particular had renewed. He also made a detailed examination of the question of how far the freedom or servitude of Africans living in Europe after being bought by Christians was in conformity with the laws commonly accepted at this time.

We have another clue to Amo's political preoccupations: the abbe' Gregoire mentions him in the long list of dedicatees of *La Litt'erature des Negres* as one of "all those courageous men who have pleaded the cause of the unhappy blacks and half-breeds, either through their writings or through their speeches in political assemblies, and to societies established for the abolition of the slave trade, and the relief and liberation of slaves." (Hountondji, 116-117)

Alas, the text of this disputation has not been preserved; it was probably never printed. That it indeed existed is attested to by the November 28, 1729 issue of the *Woechentliche Hallische Frage-und Anzeigungs-Nachrichten* published by the Enlightenment philosopher Johann Peter von Ludewig who took Amo under his wing when Amo matriculated at the University of Halle in 1729.

In 1730 Amo left Halle and traveled to the university city of Wittenberg, where he enrolled in the university's college of philosophy and liberal arts. Amo's reputation as a brilliant student and excellent orator had preceded. Once there, he pursued courses toward the doctorate degree in order to become a university professor. Finally, after four years of arduous and intense study (you may note that he entered the program on September 2, 1730), the time arrived for soon-to-be Dr. Amo to submit himself to the rigors of the defense of the doctoral thesis, written in the scholarly Latin of the day, of course. That historic event occurred, as noted elsewhere in this essay, on April 17, 1734. Young Dr. Amo subsequently served in the capacity of lecturer at the University of Wittenberg from 1734-1736 where he, in addition to teaching philosophy, numbered among his professional duties presiding over the defense of a doctoral dissertation. He taught philosophy at his alma mater, the University of Halle, from 1736 to 1739. There, too, he guided students through the doctoral program. During this period, in 1738 to be precise, he wrote one of his most important works entitled *Tractus de Arte Sobrie et Accurate Philosophandi* (*Treatise on the Art of Philosophizing Soberly and Accurately*). This work became the standard in its genre.

Moving in 1740 to another town, Dr. Amo continued to lecture on philosophy. He taught at the university there until 1747. But the tide of affairs had begun to change in Europe. The Enlightenment characteristic of racial tolerance, so evident in the earlier part of the century, was being replaced by racial hatred and jealousy (of course, they had always been there). Later, in the second half of the century, when theories declaring blacks to be racially inferior were being spread rapidly, Johann Friedrich Blumenbach in 1775 found it necessary to publish *On the Natural Variety of Mankind* in which he sought to prove that "the skulls of blacks and brains of blacks are the same as those of Europeans. Blumenbach's paper serves as a counter to the views of Voltaire, Hume, and Linne that blacks are akin to apes" (Ploski and Williams, 1983:5).

The mid-eighteenth century in Germany produced wars and with them turbulent times. And these bode ill for the gains of the early Enlightenment and of course for Dr. Amo, one of its most respected scholars and representatives and the champion for the civil rights of blacks in Europe. Satirical remarks, even put-down poems attacking this great man, began to appear in print in a few weekly journals.

One of the leitmotifs of this humble study has been to document the practice of stereotyping of blacks based on race and the perception of sexual fantasies in eighteenth-century Germany. These of course could be effectuated through the application of the principles of satire. Indeed it has been observed that were it not for the legal tolerance of innuendo, the eighteenth century could hardly have been known as the age of satire. In no other genre did the personal satirist enjoy so much scope and freedom to practice his malicious art. One of Dr. Amo's detractors in Germany got an opportunity to practice his malicious art, which contributed to Dr. Amo's decision to return to Africa.

The reference is two poems that have been preserved in the Cantonalbibliothek von Aarau. They were published in 1747 by one Leberecht Ehrenhold (it suffers from the translation, but it reads "Live Right Sweet Honor" as phony a pseudonym as you can get) under the bombastic title *Belustigende poetische Schaubühne, und auf derselben I. Ein possirlicher Student, Hanss Dümchen aus Norden, nebst zwölf seiner lustigen Cameraden. II. Die academische Scheinjungfer, als ein Muster aller cocketten. III. Herrn M. Amo, eines gelehrten Mohren, galanter Liebesantrag an eine schöne Bruenette, Madem. Astrine. IV. Der*

Mademoiselle Astrine, parodische Antwort...Zum Druck befördert von M. Leberecht Ehrenhold, Mitglied der deutschen Gesellschaft zu Leipzig. (Amusing poetic stage, and on the same I. A droll student, Johnny Simpleton from the North, with twelve of his comical comrades. II. The academic sham-virgin, as an exemplar of all coquettes. III. The gallant love-proferral of Mr. M. Amo to a beautiful brunette Miss Astrine. IV. Miss Astrine's parodic answer was published in Leipzig by Leberecht Ehrenhold, member of the German Academy.) This lampoon is attested to in a sales promotion in the "Wöchentliche Hallische Anzeigen" of October 23, 1747.

In the first poem (number III) a Mr. Amo, a learned black man, bares his soul and confesses his affections and love to a certain Mademoiselle Astrine.

Vorbericht.
Das Laubwerck dieses Briefs hat Amor ausgedacht,
Und wie er mir zugleich den Inhalt vordictiret,
Vorjetzo nur mit schwartz auf weiss darum gemacht,
Er hätte ihn mit Gold auf Purper ausgezieret,
Nachdem er, wie es sonst am besten sich
geschicket,
auf Atlas abgedrucket.
Allein, weil noch mein Herz in steter Trauer ist,
Es hat auch Herz und Brief die Trauer angeleget,
Du wirst was bessers sehn, wenn du mir güstig
bist,
Lass nur den Freuden Stern, der Leib und Seel
beweget,
Und stets Vergnügen strahlt, mir bald ohn
Untergehen,
Aus deiner Gunst
entstehen.

13. De Jure Maurorum in Europa

(Preface.
Love has devised the crocket of this letter,
And as it simultaneously dictated to me the content,
Provisionally done only in black and white,
He would have it decorated with gold on purple,
After he, as it is most fitting,
        printed it on Atlas.
But, because my heart is in constant sorrow,
For sorrow fills my heart and the letter,
You will see something better, if you favor me,
Let by your power the star of joy arise,
Transform the body and the soul, and let
Pleasure forever radiate and meet
        without setting.)

One quickly notes that the poem is full of references to color and to shadings: *schwarz und weiss* (black and white), *Trauer* (sorrow, grief), *strahlt* (radiates), *Untergehen* (setting [of sun]).

Mademoiselle Astrine's answer to him (IV) suggests to M. Amo that such offers of love would best be taken back to Africa and showered upon a female native there (I choose my words here carefully).

        Vorbericht.

Das Laubwerck deines Briefs ist ziemlich
        ausgedacht,
Und Amor hat dir wohl, Herr Amo, es dictiret;
Du hat auch Schwarz und Weiß mit Fleiß darum
        gemacht,
Weil jenes deine Haut, dies die Zähne zieret;
Werth wär es, daß man das, was du an mich
        geschicket,
        abgedrucket.
Leid ist mirs, das dein Herz in steter Trauer ist,
Wofür hat Herz und Brust die Trauer ist,
Wofür hat Herz und Brust die Trauer angeleget,
Du wirst was bessers thun, wenn du gelassen bist,
Weil mich der schönste Mohr zur Liebe nicht
        beweget;
Im Mohrenlande kan dein Stern ohne Untergehen
Dir noch vielleicht entstehen.

(Preface.
The crocket of your letter is rather devised,
And love has well dictated it to you, Mr. Amo,
You have also diligently depicted black and white,
Because the former adorns your skin, the latter
your teeth,
It would be better, if what you sent to me
were printed in copper.
It pains me that your heart constantly grieves,
Why are heart and breast in constant grief,
Why have heart and breast taken on grief,
Yu must look elsewhere, if you are to become tranquil
Because the most beautiful Moor could never
Move me to love; perhaps in the land of the Moors
Your star can arise
without setting.)

Here, too, there are references to color and to shadings. But the reference to color is explicitly to skin color. In the first poem M. Amo speaks of the foliage of the love letter as having been thought out by cupid and encased in black and white. In her response Mademoiselle Astrine tells M. Amo that he put the black and white around it, the black being the color of his skin and the white referring to the whiteness of his teeth (as in modern parlance "he was so black that you could only see the whiteness of his teeth").

In later stanzas of the poem Mademoiselle Astrine parodistically regrets that cupid has wrenched M. Amo's heart, but she assures him that cupid has not given it to her. She also advises him to control his sexual urges and not to speak to her of love. Finally she delivers the chilling blow: she tells him that no matter the high degree of his learning, he will have rough going continuing to try to live among Europeans.

Mein Herr Magister, sey ein Herrscher deiner
Triebe,
Und rede nicht von
Liebe,
Hat Venus selber dir der Musen Bild gemahlt.

13. De Jure Maurorum in Europa

> Wozu die Gratien die Farben eingemenget,
> Wenn gleich kein krauser Rand von Diamanten
> strahlt;
> Hat sie dir eine Schnur/wie du sprichst,
> angehänget;
> So bist du gleichwohl nur in derer Mohren-Orden
> Ihr bester Liebling
> worden.
> Bey Europärn wirst du schwerlich glücklich seyn.

> (My dear schoolmaster, control your urges,
> And do not speak of love,
> Even if Venus herself has painted you the
> Picture of the Muses.
> Why the Graces mixed the colors,
> If no irregular rim radiates from diamonds;
> If they, as you say, have hanged a rope
> Around your neck; Nevertheless you will
> Find your dearest love in the land of the Moors.
> Among Europeans you will hardly be happy.)

Dr. Amo had sought to win a young lady in Halle and his amorous overatures were rejected. He could conquer all else but not this.

Finally, when racial prejudice, intellectual backwardness, and nationalistic arrogance reared their ugly heads in the mid-1700s, Dr. Amo was forced to return to his native Africa. The Dutch colonial regime that oppressed his country, however, was hardly conducive to scholarly work there. The erudite man, highly respected by his people, was compelled to take up residence in a Dutch coastal fortress. Presumably the white slave dealers wanted to keep the author of the work *On the Rights of Blacks* under their thumb there. The available sources tell us nothing significant about his subsequent destiny. We do know, however, that he lies buried in his native Accra, Ghana.

Dr. Amo's inaugural dissertation (a prerequisite for admission to university teaching in Germany at that time) is entitled *De Hvmanae Mentis Apatheia* (*On the Absence of Sensation and the Faculty of Sense of the Human Mind*). It stands in the tradition of the great nominalist philosophy. In the work Amo seeks to substantiate that the human mind is not the seat of sensation and in itself cannot possess "the faculty of sensation." Here he shows himself to side with the mechanists against the vitalists.

At the conclusion of the defense of this work and because Dr. Amo's intellectual achievements had been so overwhelming, the rector of the University of Wittenberg was moved to say:

> The honor which he has won by his intellectual merits he has increased through his excellent reputation for probity, diligence and erudition which he has demonstrated by his public and private instruction. It was this demeanor that won him much favor among the best and most learned men and enabled him easily to outshine all the students of his age. Conscious of the honor and inspired by the enthusiasm that these latter showed him, he taught philosophy to a whole series of them privately. (Amo, 1724:116-117)

Throughout his life and through all of his efforts Dr. Amo championed the cause of civil rights for blacks in Europe. It remained his constant hope that prejudice against the natives of Africa on account of their color would disappear.

REFERENCES

Amo Afer. 1724 *Dissertation Inavgvralis Philosophica de HVMANAE MENTIS APATHEIA* (On the Absence of Sensation and the Faculty of Sense of the Human Mind.) Wittenbergae: Ex Officina Schlomachiana.

Brentjes, Burchard. (1976) "Ein Afrikaner in Halle vor 250 Jahren?" In Burchard Brentjes, ed. *Der Beitrag der Voelker Afrikas zur Weltkultur*, pp. 3-15. Halle-Wittenberg: Wissenschaftspublizistik der Martin-Luther-Universitaet.

Brentjes, Burchard. (1976) *Anton Wilhelm Amo.* Leipzig: Koehler and Amelang.

Fanon, Frantz. (1967) *Black Skin, White Masks.* New York: Grove Press.

Fikes, Robert. (1980) "Black Scholars in Europe During the Renaissance and the Enlightenment." *The Crisis*, vol. 87 no. 6 (June/July):212-216.

Gilman, Sander L. (1983) *Difference and Pathology.* Ithaca and London: Cornell University Press.

Grimm, Reinhold and Jost Hermand, eds. 1986 *Blacks and German Culture.* Madison: University of Wisconsin Press.

Killens, John Oliver. (1989) *Great Black Russian: A Novel of the Life and Times of Alexander Pushkin.* Detroit: Wayne State University Press.

Martini, Fritz. (1965) *Deutsche Literaturgeschichte*, 14th Edition. Stuttgart: Alfred Kroeher.

Ploski, Harry R. and James Williams, eds. (1983) *The Negro Almanac. A Reference Work on the Afro-American*, 4th ed. New York: John Wiley and Sons.

Robertson, J. G. (1968) *A History of German Literature*, 5th ed. Edinburg and London: William Blackwood and Sons.

V

Afterword

14

The African American Imagination in Language and Literature: An Afterword

Carol Aisha Blackshire-Belay

The preceding chapters have been devoted to theoretical aspects of African American language and literature. In this chapter I shall briefly comment on these discussions, and evaluate their contribution to redefining the dialogue and theoretical debates surrounding the maturing imagination of African American peoples.

In PART 1, "The Afrocentric Imagination: Theory and Analysis," four papers are presented. In Chapter One, the introductory chapter, the aim is to introduce the audience to the content of the volume. I have also sought to highlight some of the more relevant aspects contributing to the growing appreciation of African American literature. This chapter telegraphs the work to be done in literary analysis, theory development, and the influence of such factors as migration on the African American language community.

In Chapter Two, Molefi Asante in "Locating a Text: Implications of an Afrocentric Theory" discusses the need for an Afrocentric viewpoint on texts. In situating a text one must be aware of two important realities: location and dislocation of a text. Understanding both the Eurocentric and Afrocentric perspectives allows us to approach any and every form of discourse from an enlightened and multi-cultural point of view. In locating a text, there are several elements that help to assist the reader in his/her analysis: language, attitude, and direction. Based on these, Asante discusses the theoretical issues and moves into a personal examination of location in the works of Henry Dumas.

In Chapter Three, Frenzella Elaine De Lancey in "Refusing to Be Boxed In: Sonia Sanchez's Transformation of the Haiku Form" discusses Sonia Sachez's use of Afrocentric motifs to textualize the haiku. While she acknowledges that the haiku form is important for establishing discipline in novice poets, from her experienced position as a poet of twenty years, Sanchez alters the form dramatically. Using what is necessary to convey her themes and discarding that which is wholly useless to her art, she imposes her will upon the form. The most provocative result of this is the functionality demanded of poetry. Sanchez's haiku are unique in their terrible lyricism, beautiful in their profundity. According to De Lancey, Sanchez's work demands interaction from her readers. By acting upon the haiku in this manner, Sanchez forces the reader to become involved, to question what she is doing and why she is doing it.

In Chapter Four, Carolyn L. Holmes in "Reassessing African American Literature through an Afrocentric Paradigm" begins by discussing the impact of the Black Power Movement in the 1960s on African American writers. She pinpoints how the movement emphasized the necessity of black people to change the direction of time, to change the old symbols, songs, myths, legends, and history. She also emphasizes that as black people we have our art, our classical music too, that is, our culture, ethical survival, and spirit. Holmes's creative essay demonstrates the pervasiveness of our art forms in contemporary literature. She places a high value on the relationship of African American classics, music, art, and poetry on the general imagination of the writer.

In addition, this author analyzes the most pertinent works of Zora Neale Hurston and James Baldwin utilizing an Afrocentric paradigm. Each author is located within his/her own individual and collective African American historical and cultural aesthetic. To locate Hurston when she wrote *Their Eyes Were Watching God* in 1937, Holmes looks at her personal life in the rural South and her growing-up years and looked for that place in the sun. Hurston demonstrates the self-determination, pride, and sense of self-worth in a black woman. To locate James Baldwin, Holmes begins with his birth in Harlem, New York. His youth was a period of consciousness when he became aware of the cultural, social, and political realities of America.

PART 2, "Language Realities: Studies in Modern Societies," consists of three papers. In Chapter Five entitled "Cultural and Linguistic Transitions: The Comparative Case of African Americans and Ethnic Minorities in Germany," the author attempts to isolate the factors that have led to the present conditions in most of our major cities. In order to achieve this goal, Blackshire compares the African American situation to that of ethnic minorities in Europe. While there are differences between the various groups, there are striking similarities in the experiences of all

14. The African American Imagination in Language and Literature   199

the groups that have migrated from one place to another in search of a better standard of living and better education for their children.

The impact of migration on language and speech is well established in the literature. On the African American community, particularly in the movement from the South to the North, it was no less powerful than in other societies. A comparison with the ethnic communities of Germany demonstrates the salience of this position. The literary imagination of the African American is shown to possess many characteristics developed in the urban centers of the North.

In Chapter Six, Alamin Mazrui in "African Languages in the African American Experience" focuses on the concept of ethno-linguistics, which is the study of language in relation to ethnic types and behavior, especially with reference to the way social interaction proceeds. The ethno-linguistic identity of African Americans has been completely obliterated by centuries of European slavery and oppression in the United States. The phenomenon of language in all its manifestations, consequently became a factor in the struggles for equality in the Civil Rights movement of the 1960s. The "restricted genetic boundaries" of the English language as seen as the cause. But a new kind of consciousness among sections of the African American population gave it another dimension, not only the recognition of "Black English," "African American English," "Ebonics," "Palwh," but also a relinking with continental African languages. The author also discusses how racial circumstances among Americans of African descent have led to the emergence of a new African consciousness. African languages have come to play an important role because of the ability of African Americans to form a linguistic link to Africa. Mazrui provides an insightful examination from the standpoint of African linguistic connectedness in the Americas.

In Chapter Seven, Barbara J. Marshall in "Kitchen Table Talk: J. California Cooper's Use of *Nommo*--Female Bonding and Transcendence" focuses on the examination of the language and works of African American female writers and briefly looks at both theoretical and critical paradigms that have been used in providing critical viewpoints of their works. This author uses an Afrocentric paradigm in her analysis, focusing upon the themes of *Nommo*, female bonding, and transcendence in the short stories of J. California Cooper. She also discusses the issues of male-female relationships, mother-daughter relationships and other mother relationships. Finally the author explores the position of J.

California Cooper from an Afrocentric perspective. Marshall takes the position that although J. California Cooper writes about the black experience and uses black characters, she allows herself to become entrapped by the European definition of universality and at times seriously falls away from having an Afrocentric approach to writing.

In PART 3, "Literary Analysis: Style and Substance," three papers are presented. In Chapter Eight, Lonnell E. Johnson in "Dilemma of the Dutiful Servant: The Poetry of Jupiter Hammon" analyzes the work of Jupiter Hammon, the first known African American to publish a literary work. Johnson demonstrates that in order to fully understand Hammon and his development as a poet, it is important to be familiar with the socio-cultural background that gave rise to his literary works. In addition, one must also examine the environment in which his works evolved. Hammon's poetry is often described as awkward, rugged, with forced rhymes, and so forth, but despite this criticism, Hammon has set the tone for many of our fine poets today. Hammon was without a doubt African-centered and there are distinct patterns of learning in his writings that determine him to be one of the most prolific African American writers in the history of African peoples.

In Chapter Nine, Regina B. Jennings in "The Blue/Black Poetics of Sonia Sanchez" examines the works of this author and indirectly analyzes the Human Rights Movement and the Black Arts Movement that were catalysts for the aesthetics emerging from the 1960s. The Black Arts Movement marks the time when poets and activists in a sense married their conceptions for social change and together went forward to force American to live up to its democratic principles. Jennings emphasizes that in the poetry of Sonia Sanchez one finds that the inversion of symbols neutralizes the omnipotence of white power. For example, Sanchez's works assert that black is beautiful, not bad as it had been considered in the ideology of western culture. This author also examines the blues idiom and imagery that inform the poet's work. Since the blues is a significant concept from Black America, this blends with the theme of black consciousness that is so prevalent in the work of Sonia Sanchez. The theories of Kariamu Welsh and Houston Baker, Jr., are used to analyze the poet's corpus.

In Chapter Ten, Abu Shardow Abarry in "Afrocentric Aesthetics in Selected Harlem Renaissance Poetry" discusses literature by African and African American writers as a reflection of the necessity of all black people to be portrayed as subjects, no longer as objects of analyses. The need for an Afrocentric philosophy is both systematic and timely. Abarry emphasizes its impact and demonstrates Afrocentric theory as undoubtedly an important contribution to the understanding and expansion of critical Pan-African thought. Importantly, in this chapter Abarry discusses and analyzes some of the major African American works that appeared during the Harlem Renaissance period assessing the extent to which Afrocentric ideas are reflected in them.

PART 4, "Reflective Designs in Literary Works," consists of three papers. In Chapter Eleven, Kirkland C. Jones in "Folk Idiom in the Literary Expression of Two African American Authors: Rita Dove and Yusef Komunyakaa" examines the different types of language young poets have chosen as vehicles for their ideas. Using examples from the writings of Yusef Komunyakaa and Rita Dove, this author strives to demonstrate how these writers have adapted certain speech forms in the language of African Americans to exhibit vitality and humor in their literary works. Jones maintains that by reading these works in the language of black folk, we can also appreciate their "own" location in the texts in which they are writing.

In Chapter Twelve, Geta LeSeur in "From Nice Colored Girl to Womanist: An Exploration of Development in Ntozke Shange's Writings" explores the development of the female figure in Ntozake Shange's writings from a naive, nice colored girl's perspective to a mature black woman. Giving them a voice the author strives to provide a voice to our sisters. We are exposed to the issues facing black women as they grow into womanhood.

In Chapter 13 Reginald Bess in "De Jure Maurorum in Europa (On the Rights of Blacks in Europe): A Black Civil Rights Activist in Europe in the Eighteenth Century" investigates the tradition in Western Europe of creating stereotypes of the "Other." This chapter centers on the role of a black Civil Rights activist in Europe in the eighteenth century. This African scholar, Anton Wilhelm Amo, one of the leading intellectuals during the Enlightenment in Europe, became the first African to be awarded the doctorate degree in philosopy and letters from a European university. His efforts and constant hope was that prejudice against people of color would disappear.

Finally, the aim of this book was to present the context, contours, and character of the African American imagination in language and literature through the eyes of several scholars who have studied African American culture. Thus, we have examined the literary and linguistic aspects of black culture from the standpoint of rhetorical, linguistic, and comparative foci. Including writers from literature, philosophy, linguistics, communication, and Africology, this volume has attempted to combine a broad outline of the issues within the centered structure of the emerging themes in literature and language in the African American community. It is decidedly an Afrocentric project in the sense that it devotes considerable space to theoretical ideas and concepts that explore African Americans as subjects of historical experiences rather than as subsets of other worldviews or perspectives. In essence, the volume presents critical and theoretical essays that seek to interpret the African American language and literary imagination from aesthetic and philosophical principles embedded in the culture itself.

Index

A

Abarry, Abu Shardow, 9
Adler, Mortimer, 10, 13
aesthetics, 133, 134
Africa-centeredness, 133
African aesthetic, 125, 164
African American heritage, 19
African American
  imagination, 201
African American language, 16
African American worldview, 43
African centered perspective, 19
African centered worldview, 91
African deities, 128
African enslavement, 122
African Methodist Episcopal
  Church, 152
African names, 17
Afrocentric aesthetic ideal, 144
Afrocentric aesthetics, 134, 144
Afrocentric approach, 99
Afrocentric artist, 125
Afrocentric center, 98
Afrocentric consciousness, 136
Afrocentric content, 22
Afrocentric critic, 13, 15
Afrocentric discourse, 31
Afrocentric images, 27
Afrocentric literacy, 9
Afrocentric location, 18
Afrocentric motifs, 21, 23, 197
Afrocentric paradigm, 50, 91
Afrocentric perspectives, 197
Afrocentric philosophy, 201
Afrocentric space, 16
Afrocentric structure, 36
Afrocentric theory, 10
Afrocentric vision, 34, 36
Afrocentric womanist
  philosophy, 22
Afrocentric writers, 18, 19
Afrocentricity, 133
Agassiz, Louis, 12
Al Dar, 70
Amo, Anton Wilhelm, 182, 183
Ancient Kemet (Egypt), 38
Arbeiterwohlfahrt, 70
Asante, Molefi, 38, 50, 79, 84
attitude, 13, 15
Ausländer Anwerbestopp, 59

B

Baçim, 70
Baker, Houston Jr., 5, 9, 44,
  120, 125, 127
Baldwin, James, 5, 6, 13, 14, 38,
  40, 46, 47, 49

Bambara, Toni Cade, 5
Baraka, Imamu Amiri, 22, 78, 119, 121
Barksdale, Richard, 129
Bernal, Martin, 11
Black academy, 150
Black art, 144
Black Arts Movement, 37, 135
black culture, 201
Black English vernacular 63
Black English, 63, 77, 78, 79
Black Power Movement, 37, 119
black speech, 154
black woman poem, 125
blackness, 180
Blackshire, Carol Aisha, 9, 50
blue/black motif, 120
Blyden, Edward, 13
Bontemps, Arna, 136
Brooks, Gwendolyn, 24, 156
Brown, John, 34, 35
Burundi Watusi, 22

C

Caritas, 70
Carmichael, Stokely, 37
center of experience, 19
Chancellor Williams, 11
Christian, Barbara, 4, 91
circular motif, 46
Cooper, J. California, 6, 91, 92, 98, 100, 101

Cullen, Countee, 123, 136, 144
Culler, Jonathan, 126

D

Davis, Ossie, 77
decapitated text, 13, 14
deconstruction, 91
Diakonishes Werk, 70
Dillard, J. L., 78
Diop, Cheikh Anta, 11, 12
direction, 13, 16
Douglass, Frederick, 13, 48
Dove, Rita, 149, 150, 152, 157, 163
DuBois, W. E. B., 13, 135
Dumas, Henry, 10, 16, 17, 19, 197
Dunbar, Paul Laurence, 4, 178

E

Eagleton, Terry, 87
Ebonics, 16, 19, 63, 78, 134, 167
Ellison, Ralph, 5, 13
Enlightenment, 183
ethnic identity, 63
ethnic linguistic variety, 63
ethnicity, 63
ethno-linguistic identity, 79
ethno-linguistics, 199
Eurocentric idea, 13
Eurocentrism, 123
Eurocentricity, 87
European aesthetic, 136

Index

European slave trade, 12

F
Fanon, Frantz, 182
Fanset, Arthur, 139
female bonding, 91
Fitch, Nancy, 4
foreign workers' German, 63
Frazier, E. Franklin, 55
Frisch, Max, 58
Frost, Robert, 156
Fuller, Charles, 10

G
Garvey, Marcus, 135
Gastarbeiter, 58, 59
Gates, Henry Louis, Jr., 5, 9
Giddings, Paula, 4
Gould, Stephen Jay, 12
Great Enslavement, 12
Great Migration, 73
Griechische Gemeinden, 72
Griffin, John Howard, 59
Gullah, 4

H
haiku master Basho, 22
haiku, 21, 22, 23, 24, 30
Hammon, Jupiter, 5, 105, 200
Hannibal, Ibrahim, 184
Hansberry, Leo, 11
Harlem Renaissance, 134, 139, 201

Harris, Trudier, 9
Harris, William, 121
Harrison, Paul Carter, 5
Hausa, 76, 88
Hegel, Georg Wilhelm Friedrich, 12
Henderson, Stephen, 35
Herskovits, Melvill, 55
Hilliard, Asa, 50
Hughes, Langston, 6, 13, 97, 129, 135, 136, 140, 149, 156
Hume, David, 12
Hurston, Zora Neale, 5, 6, 7, 13, 38, 50, 95, 139, 149

I
illiteracy, 62
imbuing the haiku form, 23

J
James, C.L.R., 135
James, George, 11
Japanese haiku, 27
Jefferson, Thomas, 12
Johnson, Charles S., 135
Johnson, James Weldon, 135, 136, 144
Joyce, Joyce Ann, 4

K
Karenga, Maulana, 50, 86
Kawaida, 86

Kennedy, X. J., 27, 31
Kent, George, 28
Killens, John A., 14
King, Martin Luther, Jr., 13, 119
Komunyakaa, Yusef, 149, 150, 157, 163
Kwanza, 86, 88

L
LaBelle, Patti, 125
language, 13, 15
laying on of hands, 97
Leibnitz, G. W., 183
Leibowitz, Herbert, 32
Lewis, Claude, 47
liberation, 93, 98
Lingala, 88
lingua franca, 76
linguistic Africanisms, 78
location, 15, 19
Locke, Alain, 135
Lorde, Audre, 91
lynched text, 13, 14

M
Ma'atic principles, 134
Mademoiselle Astrine, 190
Malcolm X, 62, 119, 122, 126
Marshall, Paula, 5
Marxism, 91
McDowell, Deborah, 4
McKay, Claude, 123, 136, 144

medium of communication, 82
Melhem, D. H., 121
migration experience, 3, 55
Miller, David, 125
Moore, Robert, 77
Morrison, Toni, 5, 13, 14
mother wit, 96
motif of transcendence, 94
Mutoro, Juma, 80

N
narratology, 91
National Alliance of Black School Educators (NABSE), 38
Naylor, Gloria, 5
Neal, Larry, 5, 37, 41, 48, 121, 128
Nile Valley, 41
Nommo, 5, 91, 94, 95
Nubia, 11
Nyerere, Julius, 76

O
Obenga, Theophile, 11
other mothers, 97, 101

P
Painter, Nell, 4
Palwh, 78
Pan-African, 133, 201
Pan-Africanism, 82
Parks, Rosa, 46

Petrowitsch, Peter I., 184
principle of expression, 13
Purity of the bloodline, 75
Pushkin, Alexander, 185

R

racism, 167
Redmond, Eugene, 17
revolution, 84
rhythm, 44
Richards, Dona, 125
ritual motif, 97
Robeson, Paul, 34
Rodgers, Carolyn, 28, 29

S

Sanchez, Sonia, 6, 21, 27, 119, 130, 200
self awareness, 176
sexism, 167
Shange, Ntozake, 167
Simon, Paul, 125
sisterly bonding, 94
speech patterns, 149
spirituals, 139, 140
stereotypes, 201
Student Nonviolent Coordinating Committee (SNCC), 37
Swahili, 76, 79, 82, 83, 88

T

tanka, 23, 26

techniques of language, 15
textualizing haiku, 28
Thomasius, Christian, 183, 185
To Spiti, 70
Toomer, Jean, 136, 144
Toure, Kwame, 85
Toynbee, Arnold, 12
traditional African culture, 119
Traditional haiku
  conventions, 25
transcendence, 91, 93, 98
Traylor, Eleanor, 4
true universalism, 20
Turner, Lorenzo, 78
Turner, Nat, 34
Tuthmosis IV, 11

U

Ujamaa, 82

V

varieties of language, 63
von Ludewig, Johann Peter, 186
von Wolfenbuettel, Duke Anton Ulrich, 184
von Wolff, Christian, 183

W

Walker, Alice, 5, 13
Wallraff, Günter, 59
Wheatley, Phillis, 5, 35, 115
Wideman, John Edgar, 14

Williams, John A., 5
Wohlfahrtsverbände, 70
Wolof, 88
Woodson, Carter G., 135
Wright, Richard, 5, 13, 14, 46
writers of English haiku, 26

Y
Yerby, Frank, 14

Z
Zulu, 88

About the Contributors

ABU SHARDOW ABARRY is associate professor and associate chair in the Department of African American Studies at Temple University. Dr. Abarry has published numerous articles on African and African American literatures. He has also authored a number of monographs on reading and writing.

MOLEFI KETE ASANTE is professor and chair of the Department of African American Studies at Temple University. Professor Asante is the author of the three ground-breaking works on Afrocentric theory: *Afrocentricity*; *The Afrocentric Idea*; and *Kemet, Afrocentricity and Knowledge*.

REGINALD BESS is professor and fellow of the Louisiana Scholars' College at Northwestern State University. Professor Bess holds the B.S. in German and Spanish Education from West Virginia State College; both the M.A. in German Literature and Philology and the Ph.D. in Medieval German Studies from The Ohio State University.

CAROL AISHA BLACKSHIRE-BELAY is director of the International Afro-German Network and teaches German/Germanic linguistics and cultures at The Ohio State University. Widely recognized as one of the leading experts on minorities in contemporary German society, Blackshire-Belay's publications have appeared in the *Journal of Black Studies*, *University of Pennsylvania Review of Linguistics*, *OSU Foreign Language Publications*, and *ERIC Resources in Education*. Included among her books are *The Image of Africa in German Society, Language Contact: Verb Morphology in German of Foreign Workers*, and *Foreign Workers' German: A Concise Glossary of Verbal Phrases*. Her major interests are cultural and linguistic diversity in society, in particular on the issues confronting *Afro-Deutsche* in Germany as well as on the continent of Africa, and the enormous impact of African culture on language and society.

FRENZELLA ELAINE DE LANCEY is an assistant professor of humanities at Drexel University. She is the editor of the *Sonia Sanchez Newsletter*, and is faculty advisor for the Ida B. Wells Club, a student organization she founded at Drexel University.

CAROLYN L. HOLMES is a curriculum specialist in African and African American studies and coordinator of Philadelphia's School District's multi-disciplinary program. She earned her B.A. at the University of Connecticut, a masters degree in African American Studies at Atlanta University, and is currently a Ph.D. candidate in the Department of African American Studies at Temple University.

REGINA B. JENNINGS teaches African American literature and creative writing at Franklin and Marshall College in Lancaster, Pennsylvania. She is a doctoral candidate in Africalogy at Temple University. A published poet, essayist, and fiction writer, her latest projects include a film script entitled *Vanguard Girls*, two novellas entitled *In Back of God's Eye* and *When the Shadows Whisper and the Wind Swings By*, and a manuscript of poetry entitled *Panthers, a Sister Remembers*.

LONNELL E. JOHNSON is assistant professor of English at Fayetteville State University. Dr. Johnson has published poetry and biblical research articles in a series of scholarly journals and is author of *Ears Near to the Lips of God*, a collection of poetry published in 1984.

KIRKLAND C. JONES, a professor at Lamar University, has published a series of articles and reviews in scholarly journals and has co-edited the book *The English Language Arts in Wisconsin*, a curriculum guide, K-12. He also has authored two works on the African American presence in the Presbyterian Church.

GETA LESEUR is assistant professor of English and women studies at the University of Missouri at Columbia. Dr. LeSeur has published a series of essays and articles on black literature in particular on black female writers.

BARBARA J. MARSHALL is a doctoral candidate in African American studies at Temple University in Philadelphia, Pennsylvania. She is also a teacher consultant for the Philadelphia and Pennsylvania writing projects. She has also published several pieces of fiction.

ALAMIN MAZRUI is associate professor of African studies and coordinator of the African languages program in the Department of Black Studies at The Ohio State University. Dr. Mazrui holds a Ph.D. in linguistics from Stanford University and has taught in both Kenya and Nigeria. Dr. Mazrui also does some creative writing in Swahili.

SAINT JOSEPH'S COLLEGE, INDIANA

3 2302 01030 3438

DATE DUE

JUN 27 1995

DEMCO, INC. 38-2931